GCSE Business Studies

J Pratten and NN Proctor

TUDOR

To Lesley, Anthony and Felicity,
Amanda, Zoë and Gregory

First published in Great Britain in 1997 by Tudor Business Publishing Ltd.

© 1997 NN Proctor and J Pratten

The right of the authors of this work has been asserted by them in accordance with the Copyright, Designs and Patents Act, 1988.

All rights reserved. No part of this publication may be reproduced or transmitted in any form or by any means, electronically or mechanically, including photocopying, recording or any information storage or retrieval system, without prior permission in writing from
Tudor Business Publishing Ltd at Stanton House, Eastham Village Road, Eastham, Wirral, Merseyside L62 8AD.

British Library Cataloguing in Publication Data
A catalogue record for this book is available from the British Library

ISBN 1-872807-12-7

1 2 3 4 5 97 98 99

Typeset in Novarese by GreenGate Publishing Services, Tonbridge, Kent
Printed in Great Britain by Thanet Press Ltd., Margate,

Contents

Introduction	iv
List of Figures	v

1 The Business Environment — 1
Scarcity and choice — 1
Types of economy — 8
The role of business — 12
The location of business — 17

2 Business Aims and Organisation — 23
Business structures — 23
Internal organisation — 26
Business aims and measures of success — 31
The growth of firms — 36

3 Human Resources — 43
Communication — 43
Motivation — 48
Recruitment, training and the management of change — 55

4 Business Finance — 60
Sources of business finance — 60
Costs and revenues — 63
Financial records — 67
Financial controls — 71

5 External Influences on Business — 77
Central and local government — 77
The European Union — 82
Trade unions, employers' associations and other pressure groups — 86
Training, support and advisory services — 92
Protective legislation — 94

6 Business Behaviour — 100
Market research — 100
Product development — 106
Marketing and the marketing mix — 110
The product life cycle — 117
Production methods — 121

7 Business Studies Coursework — 127
Coursework titles — 127
Presentation, evaluation and analysis of data — 130
Coursework sources and general guidelines — 134

8 The Business Studies Examination — 138
The examination paper — 138
Sample specimen material — 140
Sample examination with outline answers — 146

Index — 149

Introduction

This book has deliberately been written to meet all of the needs of students following the 1996 GCSE Business Studies syllabus. It should also be an ideal introduction to the subject for those not following an examination course.

Throughout the book we have integrated coursework and case study material. As experienced examiners and moderators we feel that too many students fail to achieve their full potential in the coursework and examination situation due to a lack of guidance. To this end we have also deliberately added chapters on 'Coursework' and 'The Examination'. Knowledge of these areas is as important as the knowledge of business itself.

All of the case study material is based upon a fictional company, 'Restoration Builders'. This company has been developed to experience all of the business situations a student needs to cover. We hope that this makes learning more enjoyable and that students will want to follow the progress of Restoration Builders.

We decided, along with the publishers, to set the case study questions at three different levels rather than the two prescribed by SCAA. The intention is to provide questions for the less able and A* candidates, many of whom are neglected.

The varying degree of difficulty should provide testing questions for every student.

John Pratten and Nigel Proctor

ACKNOWLEDGEMENTS

The authors thank the following for granting permission to reproduce photographs in the book:

Universal Pictorial Press and Agency Ltd page 4
Liverpool Daily Post and Echo pages 13 and 61
Philip Michey page 14
County News Service, Wigan page 20
Unilever page 24
Cliché CCE page 83
Health & Safety Executive page 96
Vauxhall Motors Limited page 108
Lever Brothers Limited page 108

Every effort has been made to obtain necessary permission with reference to copyright material. The publishers apologise if inadvertently any sources remain unacknowledged and will be glad to make the necessary arrangements at the earliest opportunity.

List of Figures

Chapter 1

1.1	What are people's basic needs	1
1.2	The economic problem	2
1.3	Economic choices	3
1.4	The planning process	7
1.5	The forces of supply and demand	8
1.6	Consumer sovereignty	8
1.7	Types of economic system	9
1.8	The factors of production	12
1.9	Opportunity cost	14
1.10	The forces of location	17

Chapter 2

2.1	The size of businesses in the UK in 1989	24
2.2	Directors reporting to the managing director	27
2.3	Staff reporting to the production director	28
2.4	Spans of control	28
2.5	Profit and sales revenue of a firm	31
2.6	Economies of scale	37
2.7	The principle of multiples	37
2.8	Methods of growth	38
2.9	Types of merger	40
2.10	Diseconomies of scale	41

Chapter 3

3.1	Types of communication	44
3.2	Communicating with body language	45
3.3	Different aspects of non-verbal communication	45
3.4	Financial motivators	50
3.5	Non-financial motivators	51
3.6	Formulating a training plan	56

Chapter 4

4.1	Calculations to find profit per unit	65
4.2	Chart showing profit per unit	65
4.3	Marginal revenues and marginal costs	65
4.4	Figures necessary for the calculation of minimum sales required	66
4.5	Diagram to show the analysis of break-even point	66
4.6	A simple cash book layout	68
4.7	A simple sales ledger layout	69
4.8	The trading account	72
4.9	The profit and loss account	72
4.10	The balance sheet	72
4.11	The balance sheet: capital account	72
4.12	Cash-flow forecast for Munchers restaurant	75

Chapter 5

5.1	UK government expenditure	80
5.2	Local government expenditure	82
5.3	Number of working days lost through strikes per 1,000 employees	89
5.4	Number of trade unions 1950–1995	89
5.5	Membership of trade unions 1950–1995	89

Chapter 6

6.1	Sources of information	103
6.2	Sources of secondary information	104
6.3	Product development stages	110
6.4	The marketing environment	114
6.5	The marketing process	114
6.6	The factors affecting price – the price of petrol	115
6.7	The distribution process	117
6.8	The marketing mix	117
6.9	The product life cycle	120
6.10	The product portfolio	121
6.11	How to produce?	124
6.12	Division of labour	125

Chapter 7

7.1	Important advice on coursework	131
7.2	Know about your examination	132
7.3	Advice on choosing a coursework topic	132
7.4	An example of breaking down a topic: pricing policy	132
7.5	An example of breaking down a topic: factors affecting demand	133
7.6	Advice on choosing a coursework title	134
7.7	Presenting your work	135
7.8	Coursework guidelines to follow	135
7.9	One method of organising your work	136
7.10	Student price survey	137
7.11	General guidelines for your report	140

Chapter 8

8.1	Sample examination paper instructions	143
8.2	Allocation of marks on an examination paper	144
8.3	Calculating the time available for each question	144

1

The Business Environment

The situation which gives rise to the need for businesses and their role within this environment

1.1 SCARCITY AND CHOICE • 1.2 TYPES OF ECONOMY
1.3 THE ROLE OF BUSINESS • 1.4 THE LOCATION OF BUSINESS

This section should enable students to:
- understand the concepts of scarcity and choice – how these forces create demand and a need for firms
- understand the concepts of opportunity cost and exchange
- identify the role of business within the different types of economy
- understand the forces of industrial location.

1.1 SCARCITY AND CHOICE

Wants and needs

People all over the world have different wants and needs. All countries have basic needs for items such as food and water. In Less Developed Countries (LDCs) these basic needs are often in very short supply. In the more advanced countries the basic needs are usually ample and are replaced with a desire for other things. These items are not really necessary for survival: they are what people **want** rather than what they **need**.

As the basic needs are satisfied people turn to new items that they think they need. People are never satisfied with what they have and this is true of the rich as well as the poor. If your rent a house you want to buy your own. If you own your own house you want a bigger one and then one with bigger grounds and a double garage, maybe even a swimming pool.

It is possible for everyone to produce a list of what they want. If these wants are satisfied it would be a simple task to produce another list and then another. This happens because even with simple needs such as food and shelter there is a big difference between a basic need and what is actually wanted. Stale bread is food but so is caviar; a wooden hut is shelter but so is Buckingham Palace.

A family of six will need a larger house than a single person; could they therefore say that a four bedroomed detached house is a basic need? It is clearly difficult to show the difference between people's wants and needs.

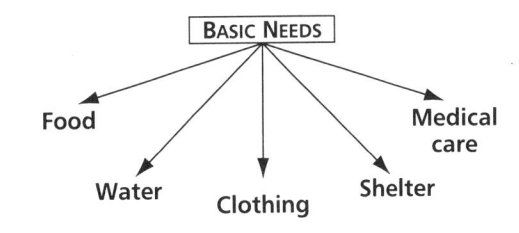

```
                    BASIC NEEDS
          ↙       ↙    ↓    ↘       ↘
       Food                          Medical
                                      care
            ↓         ↓         ↓
          Water   Clothing   Shelter
```

Figure 1.1 What are people's basic needs?

The confusion between what human beings need and what they think they want creates a desire for more and more. This desire can be described as ambition, trying to improve ones lifestyle, or greed. However it is described the presence of this desire

2 GCSE BUSINESS STUDIES

in people produces a never ending **demand** for goods and services. This is increased by the fact that goods are used up or wear out and need replacing, or are replaced by better versions. The end result is that the human race possesses an **unlimited demand** for goods and services.

If everyone's wants and needs are to be satisfied a constant supply of goods and services must be produced. This is only possible if there are enough resources, an unlimited supply of resources, to produce everything that is demanded. In other words, unlimited demand should be matched by unlimited supply.

The problem is that the resources needed for production, raw materials, workers, machinery and buildings, are **limited in supply**.

ACTIVITY 1

Produce a list of ten items that you would like. Imagine that these have been given to you. Can you produce a list of ten more? How many lists do you think you could make?

Using your first two lists can you say how many items you want and how many items you really need?

Scarce resources

The resources, known as the factors of production, are described as the factors land, labour, capital and enterprise. The factor land is all of the raw materials beneath the ground and in the seas and rivers, as well as on the surface of the land and grown on the earth's surface.

Labour is human effort, work performed by the work force. The workforce includes all of those willing and able to work, even the unemployed.

Capital is the machinery, factories and buildings used to help and increase output.

Enterprise is the organising factor, the person who makes the decisions and takes the risks, the 'boss'.

All of these factors are limited in supply. There is not an infinite supply of labour or oil or land on which to build.

ACTIVITY 2

List as many raw materials as possible. How many of these can be found in the UK?

Try to find how many years supply of oil and coal the UK has.

Using official statistics try to calculate the size of the UK workforce in one, five and ten years time.

If the factors of production are limited or **scarce** then the supply of goods and services will be limited and the unlimited demand cannot be satisfied. This creates a problem, the **economic problem**: how can people's unlimited demand be satisfied?

Unlimited consumer wants	Limited or scarce resources
Large house Fast car Villa in Spain Yacht Personal computer Camcorder Compact disc player	Raw materials **(Land)** Workers **(Labour)** Machinery Tools Buildings **(Capital)** Organisational skills **(Enterprise)**
↓	↓
Unlimited demand	Limited supply

Demand is greater than supply

THE ECONOMIC PROBLEM

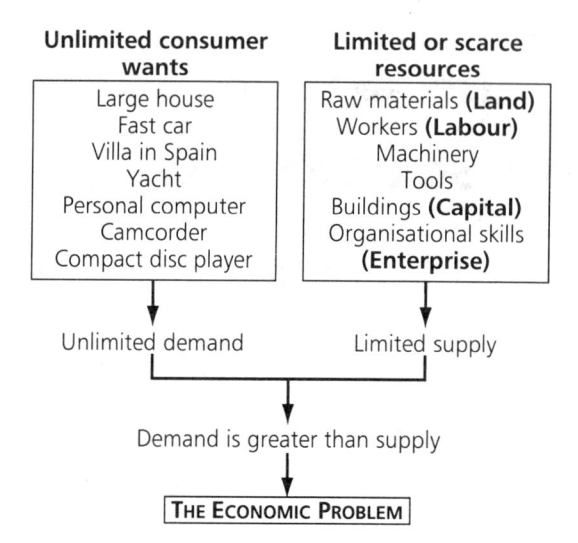

Figure 1.2 The economic problem

Choices

The economic problem is faced by every country and community. Everywhere resources are limited or scarce and demand is unlimited, but in some countries the problem is more obvious than in others. A commodity that is scarce in one country, or in one community, is not necessarily scarce in another. For example, food is scarce in many African countries but in the UK it is plentiful.

If resources are scarce and all of the people's wants and needs cannot be satisfied, what is needed is organisation, a way of producing as much as possible with the resources available to satisfy as many of the wants and needs as possible. This form of organisation is called an **economy**.

Different economies around the world exist because there are many different solutions to the economic problem. Economic decisions are made by different groups or in different ways and this produces entirely different types of economic system.

If it is impossible to produce everything that people want and need then some decisions have to be made.

The first decision is **what to produce**? The second decision is **how to produce**? and the final decision is **to whom to distribute** (how to share out the goods and services produced).

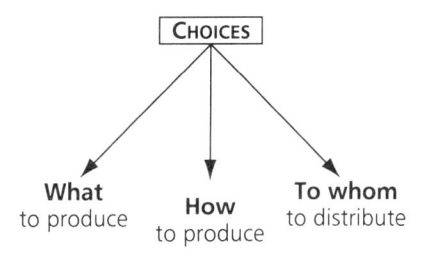

Figure 1.3 Economic choices

What to produce?

When a community or society sets out to decide what it is going to produce with its scarce resources there are basically three options.

Firstly, the ruling body which may be a government or a dictator, could decide what should be produced. This would be based upon what they thought the people needed rather than what they wanted. There would be little or no choice for the people and no way in which they could register their likes and dislikes. This option assumes that the ruling body knows better than the people.

The second option is to let the people, the consumers, make the decision through their demand for goods and services. This allows the consumer to dominate the system, giving **consumer sovereignty**, producing exactly what the consumer wants. This produces a freedom of choice with no intervention by the Government.

The third option is a combination of the previous two, decisions about what to produce being taken both by consumers and the government. Those goods and services considered to be basic needs could be provided by the government and the consumers would then determine what else is to be produced through their demand for goods and services.

How to produce?

Once the decision of what to produce has been made the next step is to decide 'how to produce?'. This is usually decided by the type of good or service to be produced and the amount of labour and capital available.

Production can be **capital intensive**, using more machinery than labour, or **labour intensive**, using more labour than capital. If the community has a large supply of labour and very little capital, or a poor level of technology, then a labour intensive method of production would be sensible. However, if the level of technology in the country was very advanced with a small highly-skilled workforce available then capital intensive production would be better.

In some cases the choice of production method is determined by the good or service itself. Delivering letters or cutting people's hair cannot be done by using capital intensive methods. Handmade furniture needs skilled craftsmen, not machines. If only small quantities of a good are required again capital intensive methods would not be suitable.

The decision 'how to produce' is not influenced by the type of economy nor does it determine, or influence, the type of economy.

Distribution

The final decision that has to be made is 'to whom to distribute' the goods and services produced.

One solution is to share the goods and services according to tradition: the elder comes first, the worker comes first or the religious leader, and so on.

Modern example of scarcity: effects of the Ethiopian famine

A second solution would be for everything to be shared out according to people's ability to pay. Those that can afford the goods and services can have them, those that cannot go without.

ACTIVITY 3

List 15 jobs and then put them into two columns under the headings labour intensive and capital intensive.

Using the two columns, try to find:

a) any similarities between the jobs in each column

b) any differences between the jobs in the different columns.

Imagine you are going to start up your own business. List those factors that would influence:

a) what you decide to produce

b) how you are going to produce it.

A third solution would be for everyone to have an equal share of everything produced. This would need the state to own the factors of production and individuals to have total equality.

A final alternative is that some goods such as health and education should be shared equally, and other goods, consumer durables, according to people's ability to pay. This would ensure that every person has a fundamental right to the basic needs of survival but must compete for goods and services that they want.

Review terms

Wants; needs; demand; unlimited demand; limited supply; scarce; economic problem; economy; what to produce; how to produce; to whom to distribute; consumer sovereignty; capital intensive; labour intensive.

Fred is offered redundancy

As a boy, Fred Norman wondered what he would do later. He wanted to work with his hands, and to spend part of his time outdoors. One of his father's friends told him that there would always be a demand for houses, so if he could build them, he would always have a job. Fred was impressed and decided to be a bricklayer.

In November 1975 he was 28 and worked at Scallies Builders, Ltd. He was always used on the most difficult of jobs, where his speed and attention to detail meant that work would both be completed on time and be of high quality.

He had married in 1973. His wife, Jennie, was then a secretary at a firm of accountants. In 1974 they allowed her to go to the local college on day release, and she gained several qualifications, including an HNC in Business and Finance. By 1975 she no longer acted as a secretary, but prepared trading accounts for small businesses. Fred and Jennie's joint incomes meant that they had enough money to satisfy their wants and needs.

Scallies Builders Ltd.

The Yard
Mill Street
Thornton

27.11.75

Dear Fred

You will already have read about the problems we are facing at the moment. We are not at all sure that we will be able to remain in business. There are three resources needed to produce anything - capital, which we do not have, land, which we need as a base, and labour, which we cannot afford - so we are going to have to reduce our workforce.

If you would like to leave now, we are prepared to offer you a redundancy deal that is above the state minimum. If you decide to remain with us, we may not be able to do this in the future. The decision is entirely yours.

You have been with us 12 years, and for 10 of these, you have been over the age of 18. We can offer you £500 for every year of service over the age of 18, and £250 for every year of service under the age of 18.

This offer must be accepted within the next seven days, or it will be withdrawn.

Yours sincerely,

A. Browning
Company Secretary

Fred becomes self employed

THE THORNTON GUARDIAN

Scallies in difficulties – many redundancies

(26 November 1975)

The British economy has experienced a building boom in recent years, and until recently it appeared that there was an unlimited demand for the services of building firms.

However, there are problems in the building industry, centring around the payment for work done. The large local builders Scallies have suffered from serious financial difficulties as a result of cash-flow problems. Scallies are still owed almost £500,000 by Superior Homes, who went bankrupt at the start of the year, and it appears unlikely that any of this will be paid. This loss is at the root of the problems faced by Scallies, who hope that a reduction in the workforce will allow them to continue trading.

A representative of Scallies said, 'We are suffering from the classical economic problem – we have plenty of work but because we have not been paid for work that we have done we are short of money. There will be redundancies, but if we concentrate on the jobs that allow us to make use of the machines that we have, and our wage bills are low, we can survive'.

Fred and Jennie had little time in which to make a decision. Fred could stay at Scallies, and hope that things would improve, or he could accept the offer of redundancy. However, he needed to work and jobs were scarce. Of course, there was the possibility that he could work for himself.

Like most people in the building trade, he had sometimes done jobs for friends and neighbours at the weekends, but he had never wanted to work for himself because he did not want the worry of looking for, and then pricing, jobs and asking to be paid. He liked the security of being in employment.

Now, however, he had to review his position. Fred thought that he should be able to obtain small building jobs which would keep him going for several months – all he had to do was let everyone know that he would be available.

The sort of work that he would do was not capital intensive, so he would not have to lay out much money – he already had his tools and a cement mixer – so he had everything that he needed, and was ready to become self-employed.

Data Questions

Foundation level

1 Explain the meaning of the following terms:

(a) demand
(b) needs
(c) wants
(d) economy
(e) scarcity.

2 In the newspaper article, the representative from Scallies outlined the factors of production. Outline them for yourself, and explain how they are connected.

Intermediate level

1 Explain the meaning of the following terms:

(a) unlimited demand
(b) needs and wants
(c) capital intensive
(d) economy
(e) scarcity.

2 The spokesman for Scallies in the newspaper article refers to 'the economic problem'. How does his description compare with what you have been taught?

Higher level

1 Explain the meaning of the following terms:

(a) unlimited demand
(b) needs and wants
(c) capital intensive
(d) the economic problem
(e) scarcity and choice.

2 How does an economy work?

Coursework Suggestions

Idea

Different people have different wants. Why is this? Think of a variety of items that people can buy, such as:

- designer clothes and a car or a house
- a multi-media computer or a music system
- a mountain bike or a television set.

Find out why they have made their choice, and ask other information about them, so as to see if different age groups, occupations, marital status, age or anything else helps to shape their choices. Analyse your answers, and draw conclusions. What implications will this have for businesses? Will it affect what they sell or how they sell their products?

Idea

What would people do if they had more money? How would this affect different businesses? Would different people spend it in different ways; in other words, are there different markets?

Suppose that you were given £1,000 or £10,000:

- How would you spend it?
- How would other people spend it?
- Would different people make different choices and if so why?

Interview as many different types of people as possible and ask them what they would do with the money. Make sure you interview distinct groups of people. For instance, you could ask ten people who are single and in their 20s, ten young married couples, and ten pensioners. Or you could ask ten people with well paid jobs, ten people who have moderately paid jobs and ten who are unemployed. Or you could ask ten people who work in a large city, ten people who work in a small town or village, and ten people who work from home.

Analyse their responses: are there any patterns in their demand? What implications might this have for different businesses or businesses in different locations?

1.2 TYPES OF ECONOMY

The economic problem of scarcity and choice exists in every society and community, no matter how large or small or how wealthy.

As discussed in section 1.1, there are various solutions to the three decisions that have to be made: what to produce, how to produce and to whom to distribute. It is the solutions to 'what to produce' and 'how to distribute' that have created different types of economy. These have tended to fall into one of four categories:

- traditional economies
- planned, or command, economies
- market economies
- mixed economies.

The traditional economy

In a traditional economy the decision of what to produce and how to share out the goods and services is based upon tradition, custom and habit. What happened previously is repeated. It could be that the elders, religious leader or the most productive workers receive the greatest share of output, but whatever has happened before will be repeated year after year. Nothing ever changes, the same crops are planted and so on.

This is a very primitive agricultural type of society reinforced by religion and superstition. Any change in the pattern of things could upset the 'gods' or bring bad luck. This type of economy has virtually disappeared except in very remote tribes.

Planned economy

This method of solving the economic problem has a long history and until recently was the method used by the countries of Eastern Europe and the USSR. The best example now is possibly China, although this is not a perfect example.

In this type of economy all the decisions are made by some all powerful authority – a government, dictator or ruling group, often described as the 'state'. The 'state' decides what to produce, how it should be produced, and how it is to be shared out.

In this type of economy all of the factors of production, with the exception of labour, are owned by the state. No individual is allowed to own their own house, shop or factory. This creates equality of income, wealth and opportunity. Hence no one can influence output through their personal economic power.

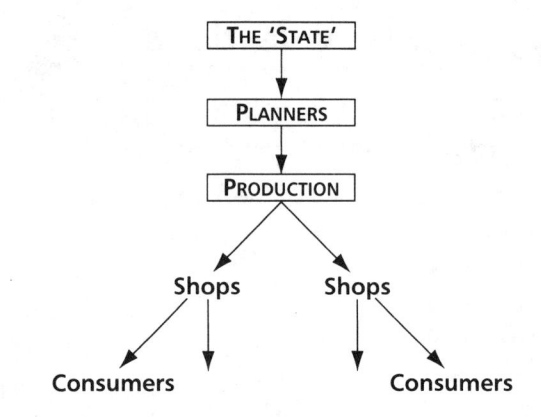

Figure 1.4 The planning process

The state, because it has control over all of the factors of production can plan exactly what is to be produced and how. It is the state that decides the broad policy of what is to be produced. These ideas are then passed to 'planners' who put them into practice, deciding upon quantities, methods of production, materials to be used and so on.

The detailed plans are put into practice in state-owned factories. Goods are produced for need and so choice is never really a priority. Clothes are functional and food is basic. In the shops the consumer accepts what is provided and has no choice. There are no means by which the consumers can actually inform the planners of their likes or dislikes. The only information that reaches the planners is the news that queues are forming for particular goods due to shortages.

Goods are distributed and not sold using prices. Each consumer has an entitlement to a quantity of products. This is done via a voucher system, which rations the goods available.

Basic freedoms over what you buy, what you own and who you work for do not exist.

The market economy

The market economy, also known as the free market or Capitalist system, is the complete opposite of the planned economy. All of the economic decisions are left entirely to the market forces of **demand** and **supply**. There is no role for the state

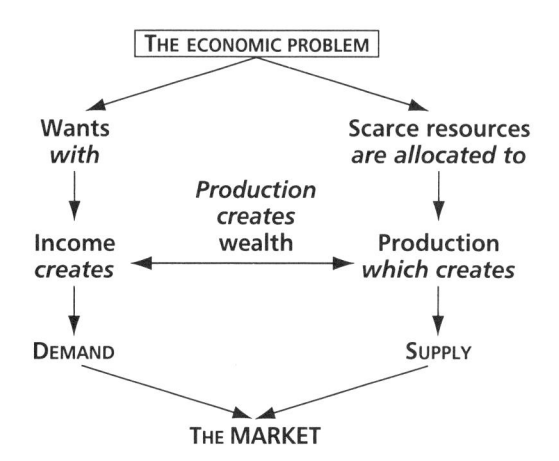

```
                THE ECONOMIC PROBLEM
               ↙                    ↘
          Wants                   Scarce resources
          with                    are allocated to
            ↓         Production        ↓
          Income      creates       Production
          creates  ←  wealth  →     which creates
            ↓                           ↓
          DEMAND                     SUPPLY
               ↘                    ↙
                    THE MARKET
```

Figure 1.5 The forces of supply and demand

or government, except as a figurehead. Taxation and the provision of goods and services by government would not exist.

The essential features of a pure market economy are as follows.

- **Private ownership** of the factors of production, the exception being labour. It is the services of labour that are purchased.
- Total **freedom of choice and enterprise**, within the framework of the law.
- **Self interest** as the dominating motive. Consumers are interested in satisfying their needs and wants and producers wish to make as much profit as possible.
- **Competition**. This is price competition, one of the most essential features. The level of competition should be such that no single firm or individual has the power to influence prices or output. This is known as perfect competition.
- **Prices and markets**. A market exists for every product and the price mechanism is used to allocate every good or service. If a good or service is not demanded, or no firm is prepared to supply it, a market will not exist.

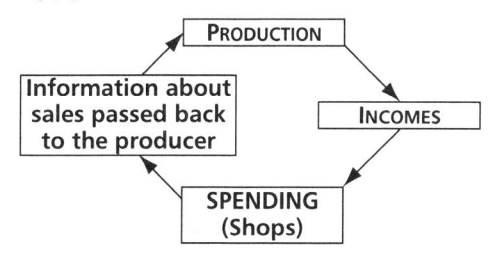

```
                    PRODUCTION
                  ↗            ↘
    Information about
    sales passed back         INCOMES
    to the producer
                  ↖            ↙
                    SPENDING
                    (Shops)
```

Figure 1.6 Consumer sovereignty

The consumer dominates this system because the best way for a firm to make a profit is to sell what the consumer wants, and to sell as many as possible. Therefore whatever the consumer wants will be produced if the firms can make a profit. The term used for this is **consumer sovereignty**.

The best example of this type of economy is the USA, although this is not a perfect example as the USA does have a tax system, some state benefits, and an army, navy and airforce.

ACTIVITY

Think about your week: what goods and services have you purchased or enjoyed? Make a list of these goods and services.

Place these goods and services into two columns, column 1 for those purchased from or provided by the government, column 2 for those not purchased from or provided by the government.

Take column 1 and split this into two further lists: (a) those goods and services only produced or provided by the government and (b) those goods and services produced and provided by the government and private enterprises.

The mixed economy

The mixed economy is the most common type of economic system in the world today. It is a mixture of market forces: the **private sector**, and state intervention, the **public sector**. Every economy is really a mixed economy, even the USA, due to government or state intervention, but the best examples are to be found in Western Europe.

The reason for the popularity of the mixed system is the problems that exist with both the planned and market economies.

The planned economy does not allow any economic freedom and this has to be enforced by a very strict method or control, either through a strong police force or a military system. The actual planning of output and so on is very, very complicated and plans often go wrong. In a democratic society neither of these features are acceptable.

In a market economy a number of features also exist that are thought of as being unacceptable. To begin with, a pure market economy is very unstable. It moves from periods of great prosperity and expansion, boom periods, to times of great hardship and depression, a slump period or a recession. The need for firms to make profits leads towards monopolies. The way to gain greater profits is to produce more and become larger and larger; this produces a monopoly. When a monopoly occurs consumer sovereignty disappears and the market fails to operate freely.

A further feature of a market economy is **inequalities**. The ability to own the factors of production creates excessive market power which in turn creates inequalities in income, wealth and opportunity. The market system only takes into account private costs and benefits; this includes the private production costs of the firm and the private benefits of the individual. Market price does not include the benefits and costs to society as a whole, the **social costs and benefits**. The market ignores factors such as pollution and noise and does not consider benefits unless a profit can be made. Finally the market economy does not provide pure **public goods**. These goods would not be produced by the market because it is impossible to charge for them due to their unique qualities. Such goods include defence and law and order.

The mixture of the two types of economy tries to overcome these problems. The market allows freedom of choice for most goods and services. Government or state intervention creates greater stability, ensures a more equal distribution of income and wealth through the taxation and benefits system and produces public goods such as defence. Strict control over monopolies and other restrictive practices helps to prevent consumers from being exploited, whilst government taxes and subsidies attempts to take account of social costs and benefits by changing market prices.

ACTIVITY 5

List the countries of the European Union (EU)

Draw a horizontal line of 20 centimetres. Mark the left-hand-side planned economies, the right-hand-side free market economies and the centre mixed economies.

Place the countries of the European Union on the line according to the type of economy they have.

See if you can add any countries outside of the EU.

Review terms

Traditional economies; planned economies; market economies; mixed economies; demand; supply; private ownership; freedom of choice and enterprise; self interest; competition; prices and markets; consumer sovereignty; private sector; public sector; inequalities; social costs and benefits; public goods.

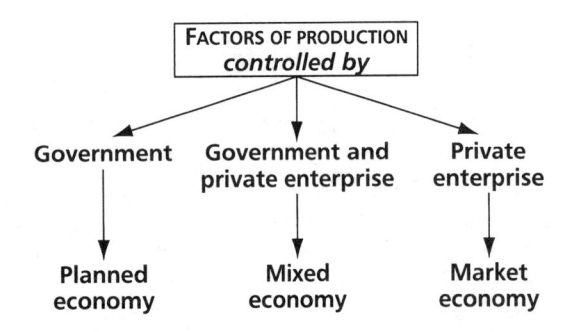

Figure 1.7 Types of economic system

FACTORS OF PRODUCTION *controlled by*
- Government → Planned economy
- Government and private enterprise → Mixed economy
- Private enterprise → Market economy

The European Union annoys Fred

At first, the work kept arriving. It was nothing big, but labour intensive, such as repairing a garden wall, bricking up a fireplace or repointing the side of a house, and Fred was happy. He enjoyed working for himself as life seemed easy. There was a natural routine to his life. He looked at a job and gave a price. The householder had probably asked other people for prices and would select the most suitable. If his price was accepted, Fred ordered the materials, did the work, received his money and moved on.

He knew the correct expressions to describe this sort of a routine, as his wife had used them when she was at college. In fact, it gave Fred satisfaction to know that he was part of the private enterprise system. He worked in competition with other builders to obtain work from the consumer, who had freedom of choice. He smiled to himself as he remembered these terms, but his pleasure changed to anger as he looked at the notice on the wall of the builders' merchant who supplied him with materials.

Fred had not been taught metric measures at school, and he found the conversions difficult. More than that, however, he liked the British measures. They made Britain different, so he disliked the changes. He had been content in the belief that he lived in a society where market forces prevailed, but things like this made him wonder how the country would end up. Every piece of legislation led the country away from a market economy towards a planned one. Of course, Fred accepted that there had to be rules and regulations, laws and legislation, just to make sure that everyone behaved properly, but some things did not seem to be necessary. As he calmed down, he asked himself if his response had been one of self interest. Young people understood the metric system, so he would have to adapt, and, working in the private sector, of course he would oppose anything that the government did if it made his life more difficult.

Important notice to customers

Metrication

As part of Britain's membership of the European Union the metrification policy now forbids the sale of sand, gravel, or concrete by the yard. It must now be ordered by the metre.

Data Questions

Foundation level

1 Explain the meaning of the following terms:

  (a) labour intensive
  (b) supplier
  (c) competition
  (d) private enterprise
  (e) planned economy.

2 Outline the main features of a mixed economy.

3 Explain the difference between the private and the public goods.

Intermediate level

1 Explain the meaning of the following terms:

  (a) consumer choice
  (b) supplier
  (c) market forces
  (d) private enterprise
  (e) planned economy.

2 How would you expect a mixed economy to be organised?

3 What are social costs and benefits?

Higher level

1 Explain the meaning of the following terms:
   (a) freedom of choice
   (b) self interest
   (c) market economy
   (d) private sector
   (e) planned economy.

2 Which features of a planned economy and a market economy are you most likely to find in a mixed economy?

3 What factors limit the sovereignty of the consumer?

Coursework Suggestions

This is not an easy nor an obvious topic area for business studies coursework. Whatever you do could too easily become an economic study rather than a business one. If you wish to investigate this area ask the advice of your teacher before you begin.

Idea

Why are some goods and services provided by the government or local authority and others by private firms?

- Investigate the possibility that goods and services by the local authority or central government could be provided by private firms. What would be the problems, what might be the advantages?
- In some cases this has already happened: investigate why. Are the private firms producing a better service than the local or central government? If so why? If not why not?
- What if the government, central or local, decided to produce those goods and services produced by private firms at present. Would this be possible? What problems might be encountered?

Idea

There has been a considerable amount of change in local and central government. Many of the goods and services provided by the government are now supplied by private firms.

- Investigate the ways in which these changes have affected the services provided: are they now more efficient?
- How did these changes affect the running of the service/business and the people involved?
- Why were these changes thought to be necessary, and how have they worked?

1.3 THE ROLE OF BUSINESS

It is shown clearly in section 1.2 that the private sector has no role to play in the planned economy. However, it is central to the workings of the market economy and very important in the mixed economy.

The UK, as a mixed economy, has a large private sector that provides everything from entertainment and food to healthcare.

The private sector, **private enterprise**, is a collection of businesses owned wholly by individuals, and without any government involvement, which have been set up for the main purpose of making a profit for their owners.

Individuals, **entrepreneurs**, see the opportunity to make a profit by producing goods and services that people want. They purchase capital and raw materials, hire labour and organise the factors to produce the items required. If they are successful the business will make a profit, their reward for organising the production and taking the risks. If they are not successful the business will make a loss and stop trading.

Markets

The role of the private firm in the market and mixed economy is vital. Individuals have wants and needs (see section 1.1) and it is the role of the economy to satisfy as many of these as possible. In the UK some of this responsibility lies with private firms.

A market for a product does not exist without both demand and supply. Demand is created by individuals, who have wants and needs and the ability to purchase the product. It is the role of the entrepreneur to decide if the resources are available to produce the goods and services to fulfil those wants and needs.

The entrepreneur will find the best raw materials, in sufficient quantities and of the right quality for production. Labour with the right skills has to be found, again in sufficient quantities. Finally capital, machinery, buildings and so on are needed if production is to take place. These factors have to be organised in order to produce the right good in the right quantities. Each factor also needs a reward for taking part in the production process, including the entrepreneur who wants a profit. When all of these different aspects are put together the firm can supply the market. Differing amounts of goods will of course cost different amounts of money to produce due to influences such as **economies of scale**. This means that the firm will wish to sell its goods at different prices according to the quantity provided.

The result of all of this work by the firm is supply:

the quantity of a good or service that the firm wishes, and is able, to sell at a given price.

Once a supply exists to match demand then a market is formed.

The firm has taken note of the wants and needs of individuals, assessed the availability of the factors

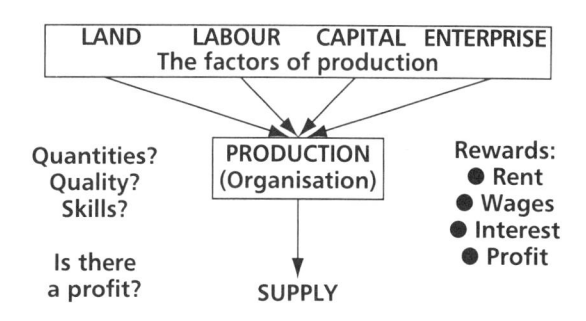

Figure 1.8 The factors of production

of production, land, labour, capital and enterprise, organised these factors, rewarded them and produced the goods and services that the people want or need.

The exception to this would be where the resources were not available, or not of the right quality and the firm decided that it would not make a profit. In this case supply would not exist and a market would not be formed. In this situation wants and needs would remain as dreams and desires.

Efficiency

A further role for firms in the mixed and market economies is to use those resources that exist in the most efficient way. If resources are not used efficiently then they may wear out or disappear totally. This would leave the firm unable to produce any further.

A typical retail fruit and vegetable market

A typical supermarket shelf

Another aspect of efficiency is that the firm that is more efficient, makes the best use of its resources, will be able to produce more goods and services for each item of capital, or from each worker, therefore producing more goods or services in total and earning more profit.

Firms are constantly looking for ways to improve their use of resources. This ranges from more energy efficient machines to synthetic materials to replace natural raw materials and so prolong the life of the natural product.

A major efficiency gain is to encourage labour to produce more. Labour is the most valuable of all of the resources and also the most adaptable. Firms are constantly trying to increase **labour productivity**, that is output per person per period of time. If labour is able to produce more, with extra rewards, without working longer hours then more wants and needs can be satisfied.

Efficiency is also using the right resources for the job. Nobody would be happy having an operation if they knew that the person performing the operation was a gardener and not a surgeon. Using the wrong raw materials or labour with slightly different skills is equally wrong and inefficient. It is the role of the firm to select the right workers for the job, the correct raw materials and the best machinery.

Business sectors

Not every business performs the same function. Some businesses produce goods, some provide services and other produce goods and services for businesses rather than the consumer. An example of a firm that produces goods for other businesses would be a mining firm that extracts raw materials from beneath the earth's surface. This raw material would then be used by another firm to produce goods.

It is because of the many activities of businesses that they are classified into three distinct groups according to their function.

- *The primary sector.* This includes those firms involved in the extraction and production of raw materials. It includes mining, quarrying and agricultural firms.
- *The secondary sector.* This includes all of those firms that convert raw materials into finished goods. It includes the production of cars, household goods and clothing.
- *The tertiary sector.* This includes those firms that provide services, including the distribution and sale of goods. It is often known as the service sector and includes retailers, banks, insurance companies and firms providing entertainment.

In the UK there has been a growth in the tertiary sector and a decline in the primary and secondary sectors during the last 15 years. The UK now produces less of its own goods and relies upon the services it provides around the world.

ACTIVITY 6

Produce two examples for each of the business sectors from the firms that you know.

Take a road in your local city or town and list all the businesses that you can see. Place your list into three columns, primary, secondary and tertiary.

Select three different businesses, preferably reasonably small ones. Try to find out why they decided to provide their service or produce the goods that they do.

Opportunity cost

The need for firms to produce as efficiently as possible involves the decision of how to produce (see section 1.1). The method of production, capital intensive or labour intensive, is very important.

Whatever choices firms make in terms of what they produce and how they produce, a cost is involved. For every good or service produced something has to be given up, a sacrifice has to be made. This cost is described as the **opportunity cost**. The opportunity cost of any item is:

the next best alternative that has to be given up.

If an individual has two spare hours and decides to watch the television instead of completing their homework, the opportunity cost of watching the television is the homework that has not been finished.

Opportunity cost is a part of everyone's life. All economic goods have an opportunity cost. Every day everyone makes choices in their life, or for their business: what to buy, what to eat and how to spend their time. All of these involve an opportunity cost.

Firms have to make the choice of what to produce and how to produce. If they employ a worker and ask him to sweep the floor he cannot be producing goods. If they use their raw materials, labour and capital to build houses they cannot build a factory or offices with the same resources; this is the opportunity cost.

One of the biggest decisions that has to be made in any economy is whether to produce consumer goods and services or capital goods. Capital goods, such as factories and machines increase output in the future giving everybody more to enjoy. The cost, the opportunity cost, of increasing output in the future is a decrease in the output of consumer goods and services now. Consumer goods and capital goods cannot both be produced using the same resources; a choice has to be made.

Figure 1.9 shows how the concept of opportunity cost actually works. If a country has a set amount of the factors of production then it can either produce all consumer goods (point A) or it can produce all capital goods (point B). It cannot produce at point A and B.

Between points A and B are a number of different combinations of consumer goods and capital goods than can be produced with a set amount of the factors of production. These combinations are shown by joining points A and B together, known as the **production possibility frontier**.

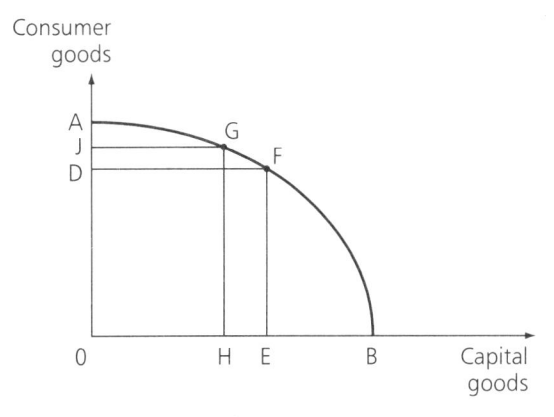

Figure 1.9 Opportunity cost

If this country decides to produce at point F they can produce O–D units of consumer goods and O–E units of capital goods. If they then move to point B increasing consumer goods and decreasing capital goods an opportunity cost is involved. The opportunity cost of increasing consumer goods by D–J units is H–E units of capital that are lost.

Firms will be faced with a very similar situation, although on a smaller scale. They have set resources, including their labour force, and cannot produce everything they wish to. Whatever they decide, an opportunity cost is involved.

ACTIVITY

Produce a list of all of the things that you could do instead of reading Chapter 1. What is the opportunity cost of reading?

It is often said that there is no such thing as a 'free meal'. If this is true what is the cost of a 'free school meal'? Try to calculate the cost.

Some goods really are 'free'. Try to list as many as possible. Other goods have a zero price and are thought of as free. What are these goods and services and what is their true cost?

Fred is offered help

> ### The Private Enterprise Help Agency
> 17 Adam Smith Square
> Kronar
>
> Tel: 0134-763521
>
> To all entrepreneurs:
>
> **Do you want to make larger profits?**
> *You need to have greater business efficiency.*
>
> We can assess your business so as to make production cheaper by economies of scale.
>
> We can look at your labour force and make suggestions to improve labour efficiency.
>
> Tick the box to indicate the sector you are in:
>
> ❏ Primary   ❏ Secondary   ❏ Tertiary
>
> Indicate the number of employees:
>
> ❏ 0–5   ❏ 6–20   ❏ 21–50   ❏ 51–100   ❏ 101–1000   ❏ 1001+
>
> Now return this form for further information.

Fred's correspondence regularly contained letters such as this one. Everyone seemed to want to help him to do better. He wondered how anyone could make him more efficient. He was a builder working on his own, and did not understand the relevance of the advice offered to his own situation, so he consigned the letter to the bin. His worry was whether to book a holiday for himself and his wife or spend the money on another van to carry his tools and materials.

Review terms

Private enterprise; entrepreneurs; economies of scale; labour productivity; primary sector; secondary sector; tertiary sector; opportunity cost; production possibility frontier.

Data Questions

Foundation level

1 Explain the meaning of the following terms:
   (a) profit
   (b) private enterprise
   (c) primary sector
   (d) secondary sector
   (e) tertiary sector.

2 Fred is faced with a decision that is known as an opportunity cost. Define this term, and give three examples that have happened to you.

3 How can a firm benefit from economies of scale? Can expansion cause any problems?

Intermediate level

1 Explain the meaning of the following terms:

(a) profit
(b) private enterprise
(c) entrepreneur
(d) labour efficiency
(e) business sectors.

2 Identify the opportunity cost faced by Fred. Carefully define the term and give an example from your own experience.

3 How can a building firm benefit from economies of scale? What problems might be encountered?

Higher level

1 Explain the meaning of the following terms:

(a) business efficiency
(b) private enterprise
(c) entrepreneur
(d) labour efficiency
(e) business sectors.

2 What economic quandary is faced by Fred? Explain the term and give other examples of similar situations faced by Fred so far.

3 How, if at all, could The Private Enterprise Help Agency help a small business such as Fred's?

Coursework Suggestions

This is not a particularly easy area on which to base your coursework. Think carefully before you proceed and discuss your ideas with your teacher. The ideas given below could prove to be quite difficult to follow, requiring information that might not be easily obtained.

Idea

Are there any new businesses in your area? What sector are they in? Why did they decide to set up their particular type of business? Did they consider other types, if so which ones, if not why not?

Idea

Choose a couple of retail stores. What is the country of origin of most of the goods? Has this changed recently, or in the last ten years? If the country of origin has changed, why?

- What does this tell you about UK industry?
- Are there any patterns regarding UK industry?
- Who could help with these questions?
- Is there any evidence produced by the UK government that might help, such as Central Statistical Office materials?

1.4 THE LOCATION OF BUSINESS

A very important business decision that has to be made is where should a company locate its factories, plants and offices. A bad decision can cause many problems such as poor sales, increased costs, the failure to make a profit or a shortage of the right sort of labour.

There are many factors that influence where a business might locate its premises, ranging from those that affect the small corner shop to those that relate to the large national company.

The factors that influence location have changed over time; some that were very important are no longer vital. However there are now factors that have become very important that were not considered previously.

Power

The existence of a **source of power** was at one time the most important influence on the location of businesses. The main industry that existed in the UK was heavy manufacturing industry and the main source of power was coal. It was therefore obvious that all major heavy industries should be situated near to coalfields.

The situation now is very different. Heavy industry does not dominate the UK economy; services and technologically advanced light industry are the major parts of the economy. Their demands for power are not as great and at the same time alternative sources of energy now exist.

The UK has a national grid for gas and electricity and both are clean and efficient. The UK has its

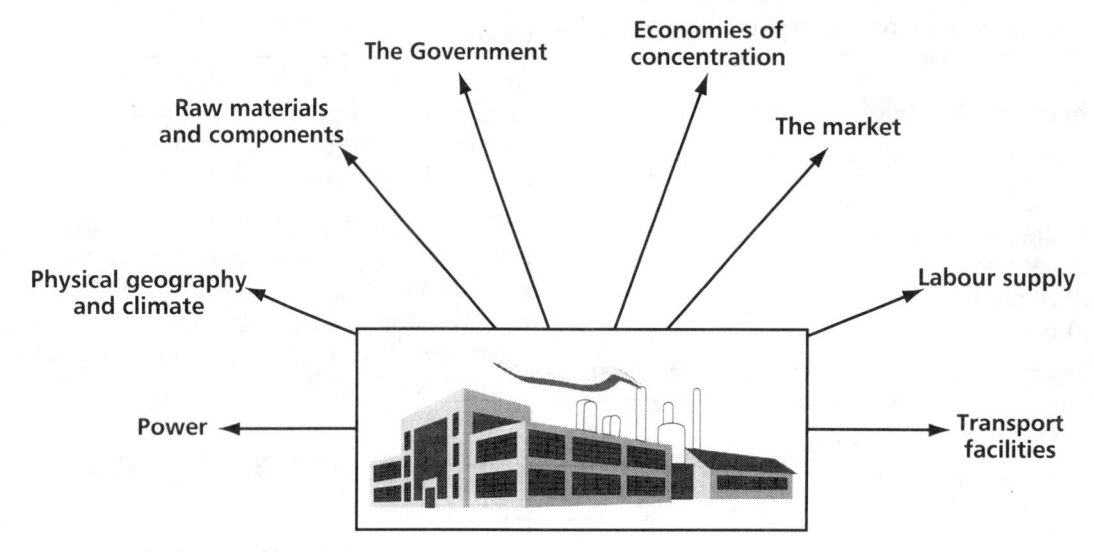

Figure 1.10 The forces of location

own source of oil, the North Sea, and this oil can be transported using the motorway network.

The result is that power is no longer a major influence when firms are deciding where to locate their factories.

Raw materials and components

Access to **raw materials** was once a strong influence on the location of industry. The cotton and steel industries had to be close to ports for the import of raw materials. Again over time this influence has declined, synthetic materials have replaced natural products and the improved transport system has meant that other influences are now more important. For those industries still dependent upon imported raw materials, the ports are still a major attraction but many more firms now use components produced by other smaller firms and so their location is a factor to consider.

The product

The nature of the product is still important. Some products are **weight-losing**, an example being steel. In this case the finished product is lighter than the raw materials and so it makes sense to produce near the source of the raw materials. However, some products are **weight-gaining**, an example being beer. The finished product is heavier than the essential ingredients because water is added. Water can be obtained anywhere, therefore it is better to produce near to the market so that the heavy product has a short distance to travel.

Transport

Transport facilities have always been important and still remain so. What has changed is the nature of the transport. At one time rail transport was the most important but this has gradually been overtaken by road transport and an increasing influence is the nearness of airports rather than seaports.

For the modern firm it is the **infrastructure**, the existence of a varied transport system, that is important so that whatever the situation, or the nature of their product, they can deliver efficiently at the least cost.

Physical geography and climate

The **physical geography** and **climate** of an area are important for certain industries. Agriculture must take account of the contours of the land and the soil, coal mining must be over coal seams, shipbuilding must be near to the water and factories cannot be built on the side of a mountain.

Climate influences the type of crops that can be grown and industries such as tourism.

Labour supply

The **supply of labour** has always been a consideration when firms have been deciding where to locate. Labour is a very valuable yet scarce resource. There are many classic examples of firms, and even whole industries, locating in certain areas because of the supply of labour that exists. For example, the car industry located initially in the West Midlands because there existed a supply of labour in the motorcycle industry that had similar skills. The textile industry located in Lancashire because of an abundant supply of cheap female labour, among other things.

A more modern influence has seen firms locate in areas where the labour supply has a good reputation for labour relations or where a large supply of unemployed labour exists. This has been shown by the siting of new Japanese car firms in Washington, Tyne and Wear and Burnastone in Derby.

The market

The market has also become a very important influence in the location of modern industries. As the UK has moved closer to becoming a tertiary based economy, producing services, then the consumers have become the most important factor influencing firms. There is little point siting a bank away from the people, so they are found in the middle of densely populated areas. Many firms that produce perishable foods, such as bread, have to be close to the market because the product does not travel well. It is a feature of many modern towns that bakeries and market gardens are located on the outskirts. All retail establishments need to be close to the market, as do any items that are bulky to transport. Goods that are for export are often found close to a port or airport.

The building of the Channel Tunnel will see more firms locate to the south of London to take advantage of the easy access to France and the rest of Europe. The rail links to the Channel Tunnel will also attract firms exporting to Europe.

Economies of concentration

When an industry is concentrated in an area certain advantages are enjoyed by the firms who are situated there. These advantages are called **economies of concentration**, or **external economies of scale**. These external advantages decrease a firm's costs in the same way that internal economies of scale decrease costs (see section 2.4).

To begin with, if an industry is concentrated in an area then the labour force tends to acquire the skills that are needed and local educational institutions provide relevant courses. For example, all the colleges along the coast have always provided courses on tourism and catering. It is only now that other colleges have begun to provide the same courses. In Northampton, once the centre of the shoe industry, there are many courses on shoe manufacture and technology as well as leather technology. This effectively means that those firms situated within the area of concentration have a ready-trained supply of labour. This decreases costs because training is virtually complete and the workers can produce almost immediately.

A further advantage is that the many support services that are needed, such as banking, insurance, repairs and so on, gain a specialist knowledge of the industry because the majority of their customers will be in that industry. For the firms, access to specialist knowledge means a better and more efficient service for the same cost.

The concentration of an industry provides many opportunities for enterprising businesses. For example, the waste leather from one shoe factory might not be of much use but if it is from 20 factories then the waste could be useful. Shoe firms who had to pay to have their waste removed might now be able to charge someone for it. This will turn cost into a revenue. Service specialists and information services will move to this area, all helping to decrease costs. If the firms are close together they might even collaborate on **research and development**, again reducing their individual costs.

Finally, the concentration of an industry in an area often leads to that area gaining a reputation. The Potteries is known for china and Sheffield for cutlery. Firms can gain from this reputation with increased sales and preferential treatment from banks and other financial institutions.

The government

The government can have a very powerful influence on the location of industry. In many areas planning permission is required before factories can be built.

Derelict land for sale

The government or the local council can prevent building in areas that are already overcrowded.

On the other hand the government does try to encourage industries to move to areas of high unemployment. They can do this by offering financial help, in the form of grants and subsidies, or by improving the infrastructure.

The government has designated certain areas around the country that are in need of help and industrial development. These have been designated as **development areas** and **intermediate areas**. Inner city areas with special problems have been designated as **enterprise zones**. Packages of financial help exist for these areas and this naturally attracts many industries.

The European Union has a social fund which is used to help depressed areas within any member state. The UK receives money from the social fund to help set up industries in depressed areas and provide employment amongst other things.

Review terms

Source of power; raw materials; components; weight-losing; weight-gaining; transport; infrastructure; physical geography; climate; supply of labour; the market; economies of concentration; external economies of scale; research and development; development areas; intermediate areas; enterprise zones.

ACTIVITY 8

Choose five products, or services, and list the most important factors affecting the location of the firms producing these products. Put these in order of priority.

Using a modern motorway map, plot the major growth industries in the UK. Do you notice any patterns, if so, why?

Using a map of your local area, plot any major firms or industries. What do you think influenced their location decision?

The DTI visits Fred

One morning, just as he was about to leave his house, he received a visit from an official working for the Department of Trade and Industry. He was conducting a survey into small businesses and he wanted Fred to fill in a survey form (see below).

Fred looked at the form with confusion. It was explained to him that a firm's head office was the address used for postal purposes, and was where the administration of the firm was to be found.

Product and market orientation were meaningless to him, and the official explained that it related to firms where there was a weight-loss or a weight-gain in the production process.

Department of Trade and Industry
Small Business Survey

(Please take the time to fill in this form.)

Name:
Type of business:
Head office:

1 Why have you chosen this site as your Head Office?

Please answer yes or no, and give details if appropriate

   a) You are product orientated
   b) You are market orientated
   c) Geographical reasons
   d) Transport links
   e) Near supply of workers
   f) To gain economies of concentration
   g) Government grants
   h) Other (please specify)

2 Which types of power supply does your firm use?

3 Specify which (if any) raw materials your firm uses.

4 Name the components that your firm uses.

5 How much money and time do you devote to research and development?

(Thank you for your cooperation.)

Data Questions

Foundation level

1 Explain the meaning of the following terms:
   (a) transport links
   (b) supply of workers
   (c) economies of concentration
   (d) weight-gain
   (e) weight-loss.

2 Imagine that you are Fred: answer the survey.

3 Where do you think most small businesses choose to locate, and why?

4 What could the government do with the information it has collected about the location of industry?

Intermediate level

1 Explain the meaning of the following terms:
   (a) transport links
   (b) supply of workers
   (c) economies of concentration
   (d) weight-gain
   (e) weight-loss.

2 Assume the role of Fred, and respond to the survey.

3 Outline and explain the usual location of small businesses.

4 What could the government do with the information it has collected?

Higher level

1 Explain the meaning of the following terms:
   (a) raw materials and components
   (b) supply of workers
   (c) economies of concentration
   (d) research and development
   (e) product orientation
   (f) market orientation.

2 Assume the role of Fred, and respond to the survey.

3 What are the main differences between the location decisions of large and small firms?

4 How could the information collected be effectively used?

Coursework Suggestions

Idea

Years ago, the reasons for the location of industry were more obvious than today. However, many firms are still able to explain their locations. Why are firms where they are?

- Go to a firm that will help you, and ask the reasons for its location.
- Compare the reasons with those that you have been taught.
- Would the firm be better to move to another location?

Idea

Is there a new industrial area near to your school, college or where you live?

- Why has the new industrial area been set up?
- Is there any money from the government, local council or the EU, available? If so, what is being offered?
- How successful have these incentives been?

2

Business Aims and Organisation

The structure, organisation and control of the main forms of business

2.1 BUSINESS STRUCTURES • 2.2 INTERNAL ORGANISATION
2.3 BUSINESS AIMS AND MEASURES OF SUCCESS
2.4 THE GROWTH OF FIRMS

This section should enable students to:
- appreciate the various types of business organisation
- understand the different tasks that are necessary for a business to operate
- identify the aims and objectives of a business and how success is measured
- understand how and why firms grow.

2.1 BUSINESS STRUCTURES

There are many types of business organisation, ranging from the sole trader working without any employees to very large nationally recognised firms and to state owned industries. Together, they make up the business structure of the country.

The public sector
Nationalisation

Some industries have attracted particular attention from government. These include coal, gas, electricity, water, the railways, the post and telephones. These industries are vital to the public, and so governments have tried to make sure that they do not act against the national interest.

There are two ways of ensuring such an end – by strict rules on the way they behave or by the state actually owning and running the industries. This is known as nationalisation, which became a policy of the UK Government in the period 1945–50. Before 1945, civil aviation, the post, telephones and the BBC were state owned. To these were added coal, gas, electricity, the railways and road transport.

Nationalised industries are called public corporations, and are run in the same way as any other business, but are responsible to specific Cabinet ministers for their activities.

Privatisation

Mrs Thatcher became Prime Minister in 1979, and her Government and subsequent Conservative Governments decided that many of the nationalised industries should be returned to the public sector, where they could be owned and controlled by shareholders rather than the state. Thus, the public were offered the opportunity to purchase shares in a variety of these industries, which are now Public Limited Companies (PLCs). This also helped to raise money which the government could use as an alternative to increasing taxation.
Until 1980, the nationalised industries employed about 8% of the workforce. By 1992, as a result of **privatisation**, this had fallen to 3%.

The private sector

The main types of business organisation in the private sector are:

- sole traders
- partnerships
- limited companies
- cooperatives.

The sole trader

The **sole trader** owns his own business. This does not mean that the owner needs to be the only person who does the work. He can employ as many people as he wants, and pays them wages. The profits that remain belong to the owner.

The size of the firm is likely to be determined by the amount of money that the owner can raise.

The owner has unlimited liability or responsibility for all of the debts of the firm.

It is very easy to set up as a sole trader. In the UK, four out of every ten businesses are sole traders, but they only represent 3% of the total turnover of business.

Partnerships

Instead of working on your own as a sole trader, you could form a **partnership** with other people. For instance, a bricklayer and a plasterer may form a partnership so as to offer a wider service to customers.

The partners will each provide a share of the money needed to start the business, and each will take a share of the profits.

Like the sole trader, the partners can employ workers if they wish.

The partners are responsible for the debts of the business, including those incurred by the partners. This is known as unlimited liability.

About a quarter of all businesses are partnerships.

Limited companies

The main difference between **limited companies** and sole traders and partnerships is that the financial liability of the owners is limited to the amount of capital that each has contributed. All such companies must include the word 'Limited' in their names, so that everyone is aware of their position.

The head office of Unilever PLC

The companies are legally separated from their owners. The company can sue and be sued; it can enter into contracts, and can incur debts which are not those of its owners.

There are two types of Limited company: private and public.

Private Limited companies are distinguished by the fact that they have the term 'Limited' or 'Ltd' after their names. They cannot offer shares for sale to the general public.

Most Limited companies fall into this category. There are about half a million in the UK, but only about 3 per cent are large enough to be **Public Limited Companies (PLCs)**, whose shares can be openly traded on the Stock Exchange.

In order to protect other businesses, the public, and those who want to buy shares, a series of Companies Acts has been passed. These require the publication of details regarding the financial position of the firm and its management.

Limited companies are owned by the **shareholders**, who, each year, can attend a meeting at which they elect a **board of directors** who are responsible for the running of the company.

Number of employees	Number of businesses	Total employment
1–99	134,797	1,201,000
100–199	2,471	342,000
200–499	1,495	460,000
500–999	520	366,000
1,000+	587	2,506,000

Source: *Annual Abstract of Statistics*

Figure 2.1 The size of businesses in the UK in 1989

Cooperatives

In a **cooperative**, the business is controlled either by the workers themselves, or by the consumers of their products.

The first consumer cooperative began in Rochdale in 1844, and rapidly spread to other parts of the UK. The customers paid a small amount of money to buy a share in the business, and the shareholders elected a committee which decided how the business would be run and appointed staff to do the work and ensure that their wishes were carried out. Goods were sold at normal retail prices and the profits returned to the shareholders in the form of a dividend, which varied according to how much each had spent.

Some societies continue to operate in this way, while others have reduced the actual price of the goods, so as to attract customers into their shops.

The number of consumer cooperatives has declined in recent years as a result of competition from supermarkets. In 1950, they had about one eighth of retail turnover, but by the beginning of the 1990s this had fallen to one twentieth.

Much of the produce sold by the consumer societies is bought from the Cooperative Wholesale Society, which manufactures and imports on their behalf.

Employee cooperatives also began in the nineteenth century. In these, the workers themselves share the profits. They declined throughout the twentieth century, but revived in the 1980s as workers continued to run the firms after management decided to close them.

ACTIVITY

Find five industries that have been privatised. What were they called before and after privatisation? What are the advantages to the consumers of nationalisation? Why did Mrs Thatcher's Government support privatisation?

In the area around where you live, list five sole traders, five partnerships, five private and five Public Limited Companies.

Where is your nearest cooperative?

Review terms

Nationalised industries; privatisation; sole trader; partnership; unlimited liability; Limited company; Public Limited Company; shareholder; board of directors; cooperative.

Fred and Harry become partners

Fred began to consider his position as a sole trader. He was being asked if he could undertake jobs that required more skills than just bricklaying, but he turned them down, as he did not feel that he was competent to undertake them.

At this point he bumped into Harry Adams, who had been a plasterer at Scallies. He was a good tradesman who had also been made redundant and was also trying to work for himself. He had bought a lock-up garage to store his tools and materials, and was using the family car to go to his jobs.

Harry, too, was finding that there was less work than when he started, and, strangely, he was receiving requests for more complicated work.

Fred and Harry liked and trusted each other, and each respected the other's ability to work. They talked about working together, and finally decided to form a partnership. Fred brought his van and equipment into the partnership, and Harry offered his lock-up garage, which had cost almost £4,000. Both were happy that an equal partnership had been created.

They discussed the possibility of becoming a Limited company, but decided to remain with unlimited liability after talking to Jennie and some of the accountants in the practice where she worked.

Data questions

Foundation level

1 Explain the meaning of the following terms:
   (a) sole trader
   (b) partnership
   (c) limited company
   (d) unlimited liability.

2 Outline the main advantages and disadvantages of limited and unlimited liability.

Intermediate level

1 Explain the meaning of the following terms:
   (a) sole trader
   (b) partnership
   (c) limited company
   (d) unlimited liability.

2 Why might a small business want to have unlimited liability? What disadvantages might a limited company experience?

Higher level

1 Explain the meaning of the following terms:
   (a) sole trader
   (b) equal partnership
   (c) limited company
   (d) unlimited liability

2 What advice would you give to Fred and Harry on the question of limited and unlimited liability?

Coursework Suggestions

Many books suggest that firms do better when they become limited companies.

Test that idea.

- Find a sole trader who is unlimited, and ask why he is unlimited.
- Find a small business that is limited, and ask why.
- Pose questions about the ease of obtaining credit, to see if being limited makes any difference.
- Find out how the owners feel about the type of business organisation that they have chosen.

  See if they are happy with their choice.

- Ask some wholesalers if they treat limited and unlimited companies any differently, especially over credit.
- Approach a bank, and see what the attitude is there.
- Ask a few ordinary people if they know the difference between limited and unlimited companies, and see if the status of a firm affects their use of it.

You will have started your coursework by posing a question. You will have collected evidence and analysed it. Now draw a conclusion.

Idea

There are several types of business organisation. How much do the general public know about them? Does it influence buying habits?

Draw up a questionnaire to find out, and interview a range of people.

Analyse the results and draw a conclusion.

2.2 INTERNAL ORGANISATION

No matter how large or small a business is, there are a variety of widely different tasks that have to be undertaken, such as book-keeping, selling and purchasing, as well as actually making the good or offering the service.

As a company grows, its success may depend on the establishment of a system which ensures that these **specialist tasks** are undertaken effectively. This means the appointment of suitable staff and a system which ensures cooperation between the staff in order to achieve the aims of the company as a whole.

Different firms have different needs, but most need to consider the following areas.

Research and development

This department designs and tests new products, and improves existing products. It has to work closely with the production department to develop and construct new products, to ensure that they satisfy legal and safety standards and to make sure that the company has the equipment to make a product.

The production department

These are the people who actually make what the company sells. They need to reduce waste to a minimum and maintain the quality of the product. The work can be boring and repetitive, but without production there would be no product, and so the company would not exist.

The marketing department

This section discovers what people want to buy, and at what price. It also looks to the development of new products and the updating of existing products, coordinating with the research and development department.

It needs to communicate with the production department, as there is no point in deciding that a new product must be made if the production department does not have the equipment or the skills to make the product.

The accounts department

This department is responsible for all the financial aspects of the Company. It records and monitors sales and purchases. It calculates the profits of the company and provides information on all areas which involve the receipt and expenditure of money.

The personnel department

This department tries to ensure that the company has the staff to do the various jobs that the company requires. It is usually responsible for staff training and for welfare. Many personnel departments are responsible for discipline within the company. Other personnel departments are seen to have a responsibility for morale within the company, and may organise social events in order to keep up the spirits of the members.

The administration department

This department provides a service for other departments in coordinating their activities. It will, for example, ensure that materials are ordered and delivered in time for their production, and will know when goods have to be ready for sale. If there is no administration department the tasks involved remain, so someone needs to be responsible for such coordination.

This is a very important area, as there are often rivalries between the departments. Each department tends to see its own work as the most important, and problems are blamed on other sections. In addition, people tend to identify with their own particular task, and ignore the company as a whole. Someone needs to know exactly who is responsible for what, so that no matter what problem arises, the person who can deal with it most effectively can be contacted at once. That is why the role of coordination is crucial to the success of the company.

The maintenance department

This department exists to make sure that the business is properly maintained – floors are washed, offices vacuumed, toilets cleaned and so on.

Managing director

The managing director is the head of the firm, with authority over all the staff. Very often, this is the person who will fulfil the role of coordination.

Organisation charts

The structure and organisation of a firm is often depicted as an organisation chart, which can also show the internal hierarchy.

Figure 2.2 shows a traditional type of chart. Companies use these charts to spot communication problems. They show the communication chain and so any communication problems can be traced. Organisation charts also show firms where they may need specialist help and provide the workers, including the managers, with a picture of how they fit into the organisation. Who is responsible for what, and who is in charge of each sector or group of workers can be clearly shown.

28 GCSE BUSINESS STUDIES

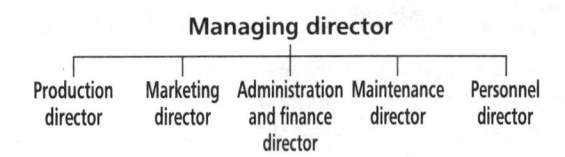

Figure 2.2 Directors reporting to the managing director

A chart on its own is of little use to a company. It is the way that it is used that is important. Figure 2.2 shows clearly that the production and marketing directors are at the same level in the firm but have different responsibilities. Figure 2.3 shows that the production director is responsible for the factory manager and the research and development manager.

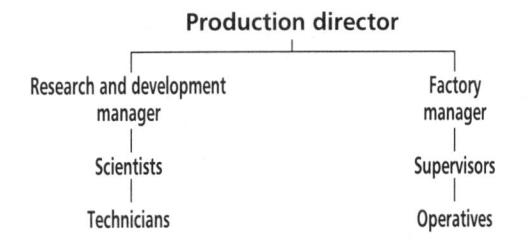

Figure 2.3 Staff reporting to the production director

ACTIVITY 2

What is the structure of your school or college?

Identify the main departments and who is responsible for each.

Draw up an organisation chart for your school or college.

Span of control and chain of command

When a company decides upon its organisational structure it has to take into account two important factors, the **span of control** and the **chain of command**.

An organisation chart shows the **hierarchy** of a business, this is the different levels of management from the highest, usually the managing director, to the lowest, the shop-floor worker. This is the chain of command within the company. It is the way in which orders or instructions are passed down. Using Figures 2.2 and 2.3 together, the chain of command would extend from the managing director, through the production director, the factory manager, supervisors and finally down to the operatives. A long chain of command through which information is passed can create communication difficulties (see section 3.1).

The span of control is the number of people that one manager or supervisor is responsible for. In Figure 2.2 the managing director has a span of control of five, the production director in Figure 2.3 only has a span of control of two. A narrow span of control has the advantage of allowing close supervision and greater coordination; it also improves communication. A wide span of control can improve decision-making and motivation, and may decrease the costs of supervision.

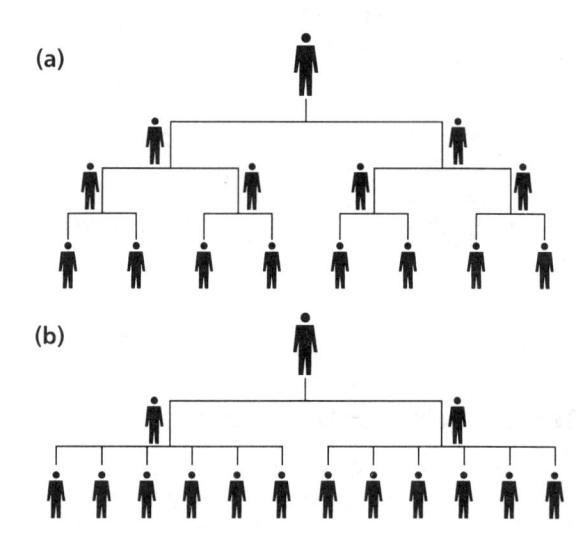

Figure 2.4 Spans of control

ACTIVITY 3

Using the organisation chart you produced in Activity 2, find the span of control for your principal or headteacher.

Which department in your college or school has the greatest span of control? What is the chain of command in your college or school?

Authority, responsibility and delegation

It is often thought that these three terms mean the same thing; they do not.

Managers often delegate tasks to people who work under them. **Delegation** is the act of asking or giving someone else a task or job to complete. For example, the managing director of a firm is responsible for everything that the firm produces. He or she delegates that responsibility to the production director who in turn delegates the responsibility to the supervisors and operatives. The managing director does not supervise the operative, nor does he or she produce the items: the job has been delegated.

Authority is the power or ability to carry out a task. For example, it is likely that the finance director will have the authority to sign company cheques but is unlikely that the marketing director will have the same authority. Authority is often seen as power.

Authority can be delegated. The finance director may delegate the signing of cheques up to a certain limit to the chief cashier. The finance director would still be responsible for all the cheques signed but would have delegated some of his power.

Responsibility is the duty of an individual to make sure that a job or task is completed properly. If it is not, then it is the fault of the person with the responsibility. If the chief cashier makes a mistake with one of the cheques then it is ultimately the fault of the finance director who delegates the authority, and not the chief cashier.

Authority can be delegated but responsibility cannot.

Organisational structures

There are a number of factors that can decide the structure of a company. Size is very important. As a company increases in size the chain of command tends to increase.

Changes in technology can change the structure of the business. In recent years, for instance, the use of information technology has decreased the size and role of the finance and administration departments in many firms.

The state of the economy has a great deal of influence on the structure of a company. During a recession many companies need to cut their costs and often layers of management are removed, shortening the chain of command. The opposite is true in periods of economic growth: firms expand and need more workers and supervisors, increasing the chain of command and often the span of control.

Situations such as mergers, takeovers and overseas expansion create very great changes in the structure of a company. All of these situations increase the span of control as well as the chain of command.

Review terms

Specialist tasks; research and development; production; marketing; accounts; personnel; administration; maintenance; managing director; organisation chart; span of control; chain of command; hierarchy; delegation; authority; responsibility.

The partnership expands

The partners were able to extend their work considerably. Fred laid the bricks while Harry mixed the cement for him and then Harry plastered while Fred mixed. The types of work available also increased. Internal and external walls could be built or altered, ceilings hung, damp proof courses inserted, and so on.

They gained a reputation for alterations and restorations to old houses, and they both enjoyed this type of job so they worked together well. On many occasions, they were asked to remove old stoves or fireplaces and these they stored in their lock-up, along with old bricks, tiles and slates from other jobs. They found that they could use all these items elsewhere and that this helped to enhance their name for the type of work they did.

It was at this stage that their success began to cause problems. They needed a new van and larger premises, so they obtained a loan from their bank to allow them to expand and provide extra working capital. They were able to employ a labourer to fetch and carry while they concentrated on their specialist tasks. As a result, the partnership continued to prosper.

Jennie agreed to work part-time with the accountant and part-time for the partners; she answered the phone, dealt with visitors and helped more with the administration. Her presence and persuasive techniques led to many more requests for quotations. Fred undertook this task. His knowledge of the trade, his ability to handle people and his salesmanship meant that he inspired confidence and was more likely than Harry to gain a job.

Further expansion was possible, so the partners approached a business efficiency firm and asked them to prepare a report.

Summary of the proposals made by the business efficiency firm

1. Fred Norman should concentrate on visiting potential customers, pricing jobs, ordering materials, inspecting work in progress and discussing the progress of projects with customers.
2. Harry Adams should act as the supervisor of work in progress.
3. Jennie Norman should be employed as full-time secretary and book-keeper.
4. A bricklayer, a plasterer, a joiner and a general labourer should be employed full-time and a local architect part-time. The latter would be used to draw up plans, help secure planning permission and liaise with Fred on the progress of work.
5. The sale of materials collected from the sites should be increased, as there is a real demand for the stoves, bricks and so on that have been collected.

Data questions

Foundation level

1 Explain the meaning of the following terms:
   (a) specialist
   (b) part-time work
   (c) full-time work
   (d) book-keeper.

2 Draw an organisation chart to show the specialist tasks undertaken by everyone involved in the business at the beginning of the period described above.

3 Draw another chart to show the structure if the proposals were accepted at the end of the period.

Intermediate level

1 Explain the meaning of the following terms:
   (a) specialist
   (b) part- and full-time work
   (c) salesmanship
   (d) work-in-progress.

2 Draw an organisation chart at the beginning of the period described above.

3 Draw another chart to show the structure if the proposals were accepted at the end of the period.

Higher level

1 Explain the meaning of the following terms:

  (a) specialist
  (b) business efficiency
  (c) salesmanship
  (d) working capital.

2 Draw an organisation chart at the beginning of the period described above and another to contrast the changes that would be made if the proposals were accepted.

Coursework Suggestions

Idea

Use the organisation chart for your school or college that you produced in Activity 2.

Identify everyone in the organisation

Work out the span of control and the chain of command in each faculty, section and department within the school or college.

- Is the structure effective?
- Could the structure be changed?
- How could the structure be changed to make the operation more effective?

Idea

Choose a local firm, maybe one that you know or one that employs your parents. Maybe you have a part-time job and can use that company.

Produce an organisational chart for your firm.

Now consider all of the points in the idea above, together with span of control, chain of command, effectiveness, efficiency etc.

Could the structure be changed to make it more efficient and if so, how?

2.3 BUSINESS AIMS AND MEASURES OF SUCCESS

All businesses have aims, or objectives. These are the purposes the company was originally set up to serve. The aims and structures are decided by the people who set up the company in the first place, or by those that lead and control it.

It is thought that the group of people dominating a business will determine its objectives. If the owners are in control then profit will probably be the major objective, but there are other factors that influence a company's aims. The size and age of the business are important, as are the state of the economy and the firm's public image.

Profit maximisation

Profit maximisation is usually thought to be the only aim of every company in the private sector, but this is not true. Profit is the major aim of a majority of the companies in the private sector. Profit is earned when the total revenue received from the sales of goods or services is greater than the total costs of producing those goods or services (see section 4.2). When the difference between total revenue and total costs is at its greatest then maximum profit will be earned.

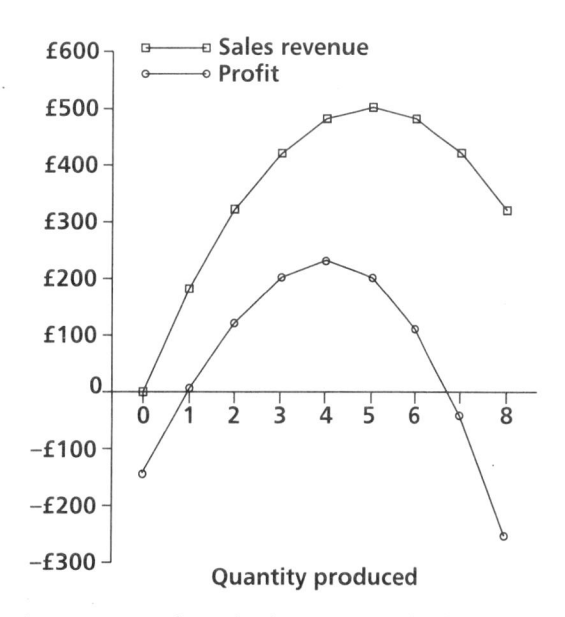

Figure 2.5 Profit and sales revenue of a firm

Profit is seen as a reward for the owner of the business and is often used to expand or improve the company. Some companies save their profits to protect themselves against times when they make a loss.

Sales maximisation

A popular objective amongst firms is to maximise their sales revenue. Quite simply, it involves selling that quantity of goods that gives the highest income from sales. This is not necessarily the same as making maximum profit.

The aim of **sales maximisation** might exist where managers and sales staff are paid according to the number of goods that they sell. This would be a performance-related pay, which increases as sales increase, rather than a profit-related pay.

In Figure 2.5 the sales revenue and the profits of the company are clearly shown. If the company was profit maximising it would sell four units but if was maximising sales revenue then they would sell five units.

> ### ACTIVITY
> Use Figure 4.4 in section 4.2.
> Plot the sales revenue and the profit either as a bar chart or a line graph (you will need to calculate the profit).
>
> Calculate the output if the firm is profit maximising.
>
> Calculate the output if the firm is maximising sales revenue.

Survival

At some stage in the life of a company its aims may be simply to survive. Most companies start on a small scale and find the first few months very difficult due to lack of customers and the competition they face. In this case the sole aim of such a company will be to survive the early months, gain as many customers as possible and hope to compete in the future.

Survival is often a major aim of firms when the economy is going through a recession. Demand will fall and interest rates may rise, reducing a firm's revenue and increasing its costs. If a firm can survive until the economy improves it will see demand increase again and interest rates fall. Then it will begin to make a profit once more. In this situation survival could be a major aim for large as well as medium and small companies.

Expansion

Many businesses have **growth** or **expansion** as their aim (see section 2.4). Expansion, that is growing larger, helps a company to survive and may make it more competitive. The larger a firm is the more it can dominate the market; it may even have some **monopoly power**. If a firm is large enough it may benefit from **economies of scale**, reducing its cost per unit of output and therefore making more profit.

Large firms are able to **diversify** into several markets and so reduce the risks if demand should fall in one market. The larger a firm the more important are its directors and managers, and the more powerful they feel. Thus the aim of expansion is often to satisfy the aim of the management for greater status.

Behavioural theories

Behavioural theories are based on the idea that the aims of a business are not always determined by the owners and managers of that firm. Other outside groups and bodies often affect the company's aims. These outside groups include the government, trade unions, consumer groups and bodies such as Greenpeace and Friends of the Earth.

Environmental groups have had a considerable effect upon businesses aims in the past ten years and many firms have changed their aims to satisfy these groups. For example, firms may still wish to maximise their profit but they aim to do so without damaging the environment, for instance by using recycled materials and minimising the use of harmful chemicals.

The UK government has an effect because companies have to pay tax. Government also introduces laws that may help companies, such as the trade union laws, or may make their operation more complicated, such as health and safety laws. In the case of tax laws companies may respond by aiming to minimise the amount of tax paid.

Quite often the aims of a business are a compromise. A firm may wish to maximise profits, satisfy the environmental groups and pay the minimum tax. The aim of maximising profits would then be a compromise: this firm would earn the maximum profit possible before tax is paid and in a way that is environmentally friendly.

Small firms

Small firms often have very different aims because of their size. Many small firms are set up by individuals who have a skill and wish to work for themselves. They do not wish to expand or earn enormous profits. The sole aim of setting up the business is so that the individual can work for themselves and not for someone else. Their firm gives them independence. Any change would bring extra responsibility and a more complicated life.

Many small firms aim to avoid registering and paying VAT.

The aim of yet more small firm owners is to earn a comfortable living doing what they like, when they like.

Measures of success

There are many ways to measure how successful a company is. The most obvious method is to look at the amount of profit made. A company that makes a large profit, such as British Gas or British Telecom, is thought to be successful. This is a good measurement if profit is the aim of the company. If, however, it has other aims and objectives then size of profit may not be such a good measurement of success.

If the aim of the company is to maximise its sales then **turnover** (annual sales) is the best method of measurement. A comparison of the turnover achieved over a number of years will show the growth in sales and any trends that may exist.

The **image** of a company and its standing in the business world and the wider community can often be a measure of success. If a company has a good image and reputation then they will be well liked. This would mean that the consumer and interest groups like Friends of the Earth see them as doing their best for the consumer and society; it would be seen as being **socially responsible**.

To some companies image is very important because their image sells their goods for them.

The size of a company can also be seen as a measure of its success; the bigger a company is the more successful it is thought to be. This is not necessarily so but to expand the company must have made large profits or borrowed huge sums from a bank. Banks do not lend money to unsuccessful companies. So a large company must have been successful in some way in the past in order to grow.

If the major aim of a company is to survive then just doing that means that it has been successful. For a small firm providing the owner with an occupation and a regular income is a success.

One of the most widely accepted measures of success is a company's **share price**. If the company is a PLC, a Public Limited Company, then its shares are quoted on the Stock Exchange. If investors believe that the company is successful they will buy its shares; this increases demand for the shares and the price increases. An increasing share price therefore indicates a successful company.

The judgement upon which the shares are purchased does not tend to be based on profits alone. The company is looked at in terms of its **efficiency**. Is the company making the best use of the capital it has? Could it be expected to sell more or make more profit than it is at present? It is the answer to these questions that determine whether the company is successful and whether people will wish to buy the shares.

ACTIVITY 5

Choose five large companies, quoted on the Stock Exchange, that you think are successful. Put them in order, the most successful at the top.

Look at the share price page in a national newspaper. Write down the share price of each company you have chosen and put them in order, the highest price at the top. Now put them in order of size (capital value). Is your last list the same as the first two?

Think of three local firms which you feel are successful. Write down why you think they are successful. Are any of your reasons the same as those given in this chapter?

A typical small business

> **Review terms**
>
> Profit maximisation; sales maximisation; survival; growth; expansion; monopoly power; economies of scale; diversify; turnover; image; socially responsible; share price; efficiency.

Fred and Harry plan a new venture

Fred and Harry sat a table in their local pub one night, talking about how the business was progressing. They had conversations of this type quite regularly. The current management jargon for what they were doing would be 'brainstorming', but it really was not quite like that at all.

They had a chat about how they felt, and sorted out any problems that they might have. They regarded these meetings as an essential way of ensuring that they knew each other's minds.

Fred explained that, after his redundancy at Scallies and he became self-employed, his turnover was low and his business aims had really centred around survival. Now, with the partnership and their expansion, his attitude was changing. They were efficient, because everyone was happy with their work, they were earning reasonable profits – more than the wages they had received when they were employed – and there was a real satisfaction in being self-employed. It was the ability to take their own decisions, they concluded. Fred had noticed something else. When he worked for an employer, people would describe him as 'the brickie from Scallies', but now he worked for himself was 'the builder'. This alteration in the respect accorded to him was important. It made him feel that his image had changed.

Harry was just about to consider this view when someone came to their table. It was a student from the local university, trying to interest them in conversation. Neither Fred nor Harry were rude men, and they both recognised that the young man was serious, so they allowed him to express his views.

Perhaps it was fortunate that they did, for his words eventually had an effect on their lives. He condemned the waste of modern society – the bottles that are used and destroyed, the cans that are thrown away, the packaging that is burnt. He suggested that we are destroying resources by throwing away such items because they could be re-cycled. He then mentioned building materials. Houses are demolished, and the bricks, the tiles, the slates are ignored when they could be used again. Furniture and fixtures and fittings are simply put on a bonfire, when, with a little effort, they could be re-used.

Fred and Harry listened to this, first politely and then with greater and greater interest. The young man knew a little about the types of building equipment used at different times, and a long conversation took place.

At the end of it, Fred and Harry had become very interested in the renovation of building materials. They may not have been convinced about the social responsibility of such actions, but they did understand the financial common sense that was involved. They worked for money, and this was an idea that could make them money.

Data Questions

Foundation level

1 Explain the meaning of the following terms:

(a) profits
(b) redundancy
(c) turnover
(d) business survival
(e) re-cycling.

2 What do you think are the main business aims of Fred and Harry?

3 How do Fred and Harry judge their success?

Intermediate level

1 Explain the meaning of the following terms:

(a) image
(b) business aims
(c) turnover
(d) business survival
(e) re-cycling.

2 Identify and comment on the business aims of Fred and Harry.

3 What criteria have Fred and Harry adopted to measure their success?

Higher level

1 Explain the meaning of the following terms:

(a) image
(b) business aims
(c) brainstorming
(d) business survival
(e) social responsibility.

2 To what extent are the main business aims of Fred and Harry typical of small business?

3 Analyse the criteria Fred and Harry use to measure their success and suggest suitable realistic alternative measures.

Coursework Suggestions

Idea

Find a firm that is willing to assist you.

- Describe the business – what it does, when it was founded, how many work there, its organisation, etc.
- Prepare a series of questions to ask the owner about his business aims and to what extent he has achieved these aims.
- Prepare a slightly different series of questions for his employees, but find out what they think his business aims are, and to what extent he has realised his aims.

You now have two different views of the same firm. Compare the two views. Explain why you think there are differences of opinion and perception.

2.4 THE GROWTH OF FIRMS

In the UK there are hundreds of thousands of firms, all of different sizes and structures. They range from companies like Procter & Gamble down to the local shopkeeper. All businesses start as small enterprises (for example Marks & Spencer started as a street trader) and then grow. Some firms prefer to remain small (see section 2.3) but the majority do not.

The size of a firm can be determined by its turnover. According to the Companies Act 1985 the following categories apply:

- small firm – turnover of less than £1.4m
- medium firm – turnover of between £1.4m and £5.75m
- large firm – turnover of over £5.75m.

The size of a firm can also be determined by the number of employees:

- small firm – under 50 employees
- medium firm – between 50 and 250 employees
- large firm – over 250 employees.

These two methods can be very misleading; a firm can have a large turnover and yet a small number of employees. If profit is used as a measure this further complicates the situation.

Reasons for growth

Most firms grow but they do so for different reasons.

A popular reason for the growth of a company is to increase their profits. By increasing in size a company will hope to sell or trade more and increase their turnover. An increase in turnover should produce an increase in profits.

Survival is important for many firms and an increase in size can protect a firm against takeover or help to decrease their costs through **economies of scale** (see below).

A number of firms grow to gain the cost advantages of economies of scale which in turn make them more **competitive**. This competitive edge may help them to increase their **market share** and give them more power in the market in which they operate.

Finally many firms increase in size so that they can **diversify** into different markets. This helps them to reduce the **risk** of trading. If they sell in more than one market, any change in one of those markets will have less effect upon the business.

Economies of scale

For a company to ensure that it makes a profit it must organise itself so that its costs are as low as possible and it can sell as many goods and services as possible. A method of achieving both of these objectives is to produce goods on a large scale. Large scale production not only increases output but at the same time ensures certain cost advantages. This means that the company can produce more while the cost per unit, the average cost, can actually decrease. These cost advantages are known as **economies of scale**.

Economies of scale can be both internal and external. Internal economies of scale are obtained when the individual firm expands. External economies of scale are gained by all firms in an industry when that industry is concentrated in a certain location. The most important are usually the internal economies of scale which are under the control of the company itself, unlike external factors. All six categories lead to decreased production costs for a large firm.

Technical economies allow the firm to use a division of labour and unit of capital that would not be practical on a small scale.

The rule of increased dimensions explains why supertankers and container lorries are used for transport. In the following example, if the dimensions of a tanker are doubled, then the capacity increases by a factor of eight, not two.

- A tanker 300 m × 200 m × 100 m = 6,000,000 cubic metres.

if this is doubled:

- A tanker 600 m × 400 m × 200 m = 48,000,000 cubic metres.

Thus carrying capacity has increased by a factor of eight:

- 48 million = 8 × 6 million.

A tanker twice the size would not need eight times the number of staff and even if twice as many staff

Figure 2.6 Economies of scale

Internal Economies of Scale

- **Technical**
  - Industrial capital
  - Increased specialisation
  - Increased dimensions
  - Principal or multiples
- **Financial**
  - Better sources of finance
  - Lower rates of interest
  - Share issues
- **Managerial**
  - Employ specialists
  - Spread management costs
- **Commercial**
  - Bulk buying leads to lower administration and packing costs
  - Specialist buyers and sellers
- **Risk bearing**
  - Product variety
  - Market diversity
  - Better market information
- **Research and development**
  - Only large firms can justify
  - New product development leads to expansion and increased competitiveness

were needed the cost per unit of oil carried would still decrease.

A further technical economy is the principle of multiples (see Figure 2.7). Machines often work together, performing part of a task. This often means that production is limited to the least efficient machine. Small firms can often only afford one of each machine type but larger firms are able to employ a number of machines for each process, that is, multiples. These machines can be arranged in such a way that the maximum for each one is gained. Using each machine to its maximum reduces waste and costs.

In the small company machines A and C will only be running at 40% capacity which is a waste of resources and will increase costs. The large firm can afford to buy quantities of each machine. If they buy two of machine A, five of B and two of C

Small company

	Machine A	Machine B	Machine C	Final output
Flow	50/h →	20/h →	20/h →	
Maximum output:	50/h	20/h	50/h	20/h

Large company

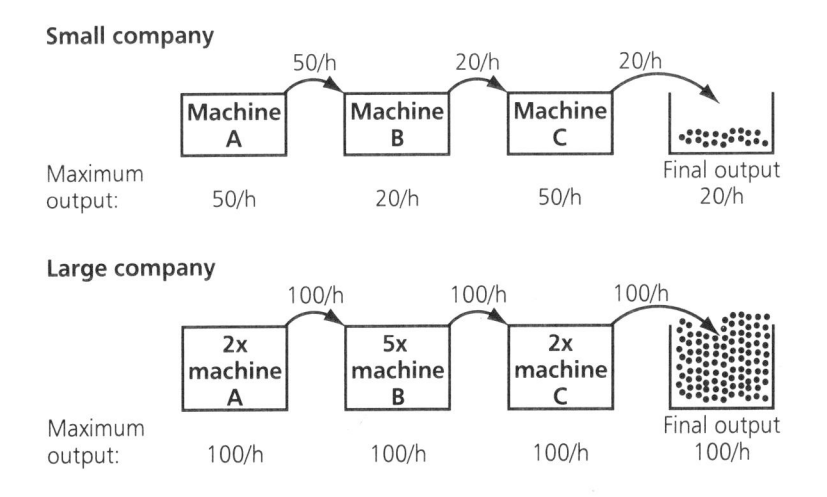

	2x machine A	5x machine B	2x machine C	Final output
Flow	100/h →	100/h →	100/h →	
Maximum output:	100/h	100/h	100/h	100/h

Figure 2.7 The principle of multiples

all machines will work at their maximum capacity. Output will increase by 400% whilst the cost for A and C will increase by only 100%, although they will increase by 400% for B.

Financially, large companies have many advantages. Not only do they have access to more sources of finance but usually they are offered lower rates of interest than small companies. It is only practical for large companies to raise finance through shares and debentures (see section 4.1) so again large companies gain through **financial economies**.

If output is increased, more workers are needed but the number of supervisors and managers need not necessarily increase in proportion. Specialists can also be employed making further cost savings, hence **management economies** can be made.

Commercial economies exist when firms are able to buy in bulk at cheaper rates and only large companies can afford to buy in such quantities. Packaging and administration costs also decrease per unit as the quantity of goods increases.

A large company has better market information and is therefore aware of changes in the market before the small company. In this way the large company can avoid potential problems and has the resources to diversify into different products and markets. They can also buy from a variety of suppliers. All of these factors are **risk bearing economies** which avoid potential problems and reduce costs.

Finally **research and development** (R and D) is only practical for large companies. Its benefit is that it can produce more competitive products or new production processes, all helping to cut costs.

ACTIVITY 6

Find out the rate of interest charged for (a) mortgages of £40,000, £75,000 and £100,000; (b) overdrafts of £40,000, £75,000 and £100,000.

Visit either (a) a cash and carry or (b) a large butcher's. Compare the prices charged for large and small quantities of the same good. Why are the two activities examples of economies of scale?

Methods of growth

There are three ways in which a firm can grow.

A firm may expand by selling more of its goods and earning more profit. This is known as **internal** or **organic growth**. The problem with this method is that it can often take a long time for a firm to grow to any significant size.

An alternative is **external growth**. External growth involves other firms. A company grows by taking over another company, a **takeover**, or it joins with another company to form an even bigger company, a **merger**.

Mergers and takeovers are popular ways for a business to expand because they are often quick and easy. They are certainly quicker than internal growth. If a retailer with four shops wished to open another four shops it would take a long time through internal growth, but if the retailer merged with another that already had four shops the aim would be achieved immediately.

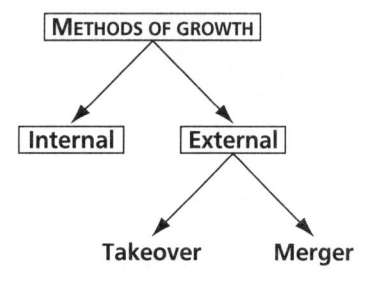

Figure 2.8 Methods of growth

Mergers and takeovers are often cheaper than organic growth and allows the new company to gain from economies of scale. If a company has surplus cash it could buy another company, a takeover, and expand very quickly instead of slowly building up the business over many years.

Sometimes firms merge to protect themselves from the even larger competitors they suspect might try and take them over. A merger may also enable them to compete in a large market. The Single European Market has seen many firms merge and others taken over to produce big firms that are equipped to compete in this international marketplace.

Takeovers

Takeovers take place between public limited companies. If one company can buy 51% of the shares of another company then it can control that company and effectively owns it. In reality a company can gain control over another with much less than 51% of its shares. Once a company has a controlling interest in another company it usually offers to buy the remaining shares.

If any company has 5% or more of the shares of another company it must, by law, declare this to the Stock Exchange. This is so that shareholders can be made aware of the situation.

If the takeover is likely to result in a larger company that has a monopoly position then the Department of Trade and Industry (DTI) usually asks the **Monopolies and Mergers Commission (MMC)** to investigate. The MMC will decide if the new company is in the public interest.

Takeovers can be friendly or hostile but usually the company being taken over loses its identity. For instance, company B takes over company A, the new company is company B and company A no longer exists. The directors and shareholders of the company being taken over might be offered a role or shares in the new company but it is not usual for this to happen.

Mergers

A merger exists when two companies agree to join together to form a new company. Usually the two companies have an equal share in the new company, with the directors and shareholders all being treated equally. It is usual for the merger to create a new third company: company A and B merge to form company C. It has also been a trend for the newly formed company to contain the names of the two old companies merging, for instance Cadbury Schweppes.

Mergers can be classed in a number of ways. The term frequently used is integration. The classifications are:

- horizontal integration/horizontal merger
- vertical integration/vertical merger
- lateral integration/lateral merger
- conglomerate or diversifying merger.

A horizontal merger occurs when two companies at the same stage of production decide to join together. This could be two retailers or two producers. In the UK it has been common for car producers to merge to try to gain from economies of scale and therefore make themselves more competitive.

Lucky strikes deal with Gold

Lucky Leisure, the central London fitness group, and London-based Gold Gyms have decided to join forces.

By combining the three fitness clubs at Lucky with the six Gold health and wellness sites, the new company, Lucky Gold, has gained an increased share of the profitable after work workout market. Lucky Gold now has an estimated 15 to 20 per cent of the total market.

Each of the nine sites comes complete with extensive weightlifting, exercise machine and swimming pool facilities. Full membership will be honoured at any of the nine sites.

Toddler in merger deal

Toddler Toys, the multi-national plastics giant and toy retailer, has just completed a merger with North-east Seats, the Boston-based manufacturers of train and aeroplane seating.

"This is a new departure for both of us," said Ned Bennett, Chairman of Toddler Toy Holdings, the ultimate parent company. "But it is in line with our aim to diversify and extend our operations and consistent with the aim of North-east to cushion the effects of an increasingly erratic transportation market."

The combined strength of the new company is upwards of £3 billion in net sales.

The news of a merger breaks in the newspapers

A vertical merger can be a forward vertical merger or a backward vertical merger.

A vertical merger takes place when two companies merge who are at different stages in the production process. A forward merger would be between one company, and another at the next stage of production. For example, a clothing manufacturer and a retailer merging would be forward vertical. Brewery firms owning public houses or car firms owning car showrooms would be other examples.

If the merger is with a company at a previous stage, then it is a backward vertical merger. A car firm merging with a producer of car parts would be an example of a backward vertical merger.

Vertical mergers exist to secure raw materials and parts for a producer or to ensure that there is an outlet for a company's goods. In the UK vertical mergers are rare.

A lateral merger (lateral integration) takes place between companies with similar, related products. The goods of the two companies do not compete directly but may use the same type of production process or raw materials. It might even be that the two goods are sold in the same retail outlets. The classic example of lateral merger is Cadbury-Schweppes: the separate companies used similar raw materials and the same retail outlets.

Many firms merge in order to protect themselves and decrease the risk of failure. In this situation a diversifying or conglomerate merger sees a firm with two totally unrelated products, as in Figure 2.9 If one market should fail or suffer due to external influences the other market exists to protect the firm. It is thought unlikely that both markets would fail at the same time. A conglomerate is known as a holding company.

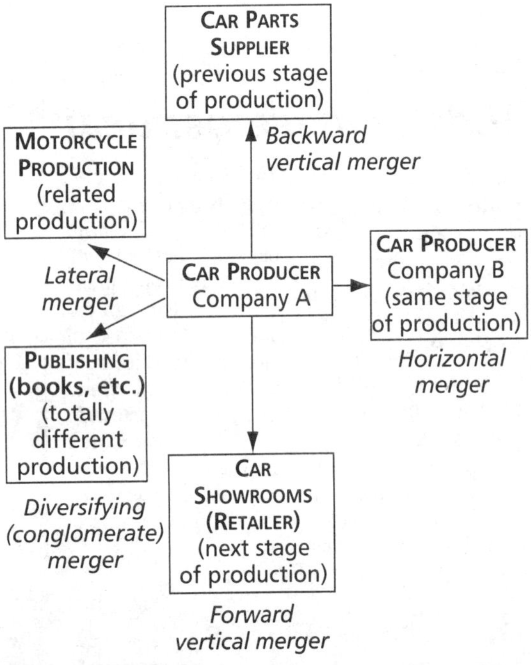

ACTIVITY 6

Try to find one example of a takeover and one example of a merger that has taken place in the last five years. Ask your parents, teacher or librarian if they can help.

Try to analyse why the merger or the takeover that you have listed actually took place.

If Marks & Spencer, J. Sainsbury and Tesco decided to merge, what would be the benefits? Can you see any problems and costs involved?

Diseconomies of scale

The growth of a firm is not always a good thing. With growth comes certain problems. Firms initially increase their size to gain the cost advantages, but once a firm begins to grow and goes public it becomes difficult to stop the growth. At this point **diseconomies of scale** can set in. These are the disadvantages of being too large. A large firm is difficult to coordinate and therefore control becomes a problem. The management do not know the workers and the workers feel as if they are unimportant. This lowers morale and decreases output. Customers are faced with a large bureaucratic structure and also feel as if they are only a number. These problems lead to increased costs and a breakdown in the smooth running of the company.

Figure 2.9 Types of merger

DISECONOMIES OF SCALE

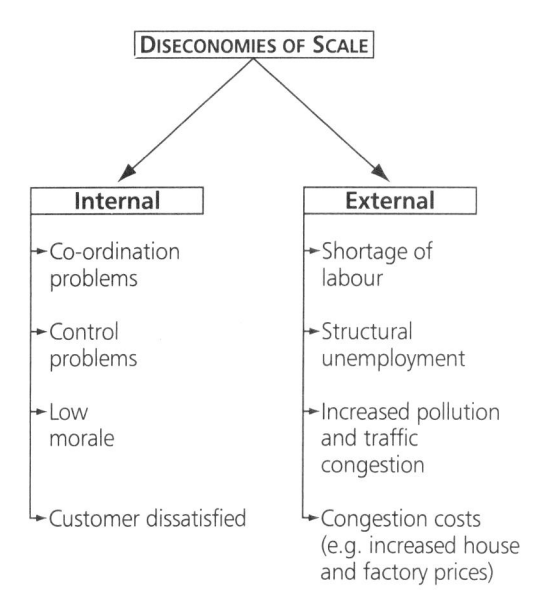

Internal:
- Co-ordination problems
- Control problems
- Low morale
- Customer dissatisfied

External:
- Shortage of labour
- Structural unemployment
- Increased pollution and traffic congestion
- Congestion costs (e.g. increased house and factory prices)

Figure 2.10 Diseconomies of scale

> ### Review terms
> Profits; survival; competitive; market share; diversify; risk; economies of scale; technical economies; financial economies; management economies; commercial economies; risk bearing economies; internal, organic growth; external growth; takeover; merger; monopoly; monopolies and mergers commission; horizontal merger; forward vertical merger; backward vertical merger; lateral merger; conglomerate/diversifying merger; holding company; diseconomies of scale; external diseconomies of scale.

There are external diseconomies of scale and these occur when an industry becomes too concentrated in an area. An example of this is in the City of London. When an over-concentration occurs overcrowding creates a shortage of labour, higher house prices, congestion and pollution which all increase costs. The initial advantages all disappear because the demand for the factors becomes greater than the supply thus increasing the price.

Fred and Harry to be taken over?

Fred and Harry had started up a business on their own, had formed a partnership and had expanded twice as a deliberate policy. They were pleased with their business growth and hoped that all their efforts would continue to bring a reasonable financial reward.

It was at this time that Harry took a telephone call from a representative of Shoeman-Ironline, a fast growing regional firm of builders.

Harry left the phone in a state of excitement, explaining that Shoeman-Ironline wanted to merge with them. Fred was rather more calm. He did not believe that a merger could have been proposed, and suggested that a takeover could have been mentioned.

Harry was not sure – in fact, he probably did not know the difference – and said that a representative would be calling to discuss the matter. Needless to say, it was not a merger or an amalgamation that was being proposed, but a simple takeover, which would leave Fred and Harry in charge of the local operation.

The reasons for the offer were clear. Shoeman-Ironline would gain a foothold in the area, and they would offer economies of scale: immediately in the commercial areas of purchasing, marketing and administration and later in the other internal sectors.

Fred and Harry were tempted, as the financial package they were offered was quite generous, but they decided that they had worked for themselves for too long. They enjoyed taking decisions and being in charge, so they declined the offer.

Data questions

Foundation level

1 Explain the meaning of the following terms:

   (a) business growth
   (b) merger
   (c) amalgamation
   (d) takeover
   (e) economies of scale.

2 What differences might Fred and Harry have found if they had been offered a merger rather than a takeover?

3 Explain how economies of scale would have resulted from the takeover of Fred and Harry.

Intermediate level

1 Explain the meaning of the following terms:

   (a) financial reward
   (b) merger
   (c) amalgamation
   (d) takeover
   (e) economies of scale.

2 Describe the differences the owners and employees would experience in a merger rather than a takeover.

3 Outline the economies of scale that would have resulted from the takeover of Fred and Harry.

Higher level

1 Explain the meaning of the following terms:

   (a) financial package
   (b) merger
   (c) amalgamation
   (d) takeover
   (e) internal economies of scale.

2 Analyse the likely impact of a merger and a takeover, outlining the similarities and the differences.

3 Outline the various economies of scale which would result from the takeover. Explain how they would result, and try to indicate a time scale for each to take effect.

Coursework Suggestions

Idea

Expand upon Activity 6. Is there a merger or takeover taking place now that you know of?

Collect newspaper cuttings, listen to the radio and watch the television, make notes on what is said.

- Why are they merging, or why is the takeover taking place?
- Who will benefit?
- If there are any losers, how will they lose out?

Check the share prices of the companies involved and plot their movements. Can you explain why they are changing?

- What are the main arguments for and against the merger/takeover?
- Do you think it is a good idea? Why?

Idea

This is not as good as the idea above but you could imagine a takeover/merger was taking place as in Activity 6. You must be careful with this approach because it could become very descriptive; this is not what you want to happen.

You could then look at the reasons for a merger/takeover, the benefits to everyone – customer, shareholders, management and other competitors. You could also analyse the potential problems: who would suffer and why?

Idea

Choose a local firm that you know, preferably a small firm, and see if you can investigate its possible growth.

- Can it grow? If so, how? If not, why not?
- Does it wish to grow? If so, why? If not, why not?
- How would the firm benefit from growth?
- What problems might it encounter?
- Has it considered growth? Has it tried?

You should then be able to draw some conclusions about the growth of small firms.

3

Human Resources

> The ways in which individuals within a business work and cooperate in a changing environment
>
> 3.1 COMMUNICATION • 3.2 MOTIVATION • 3.3 RECRUITMENT, TRAINING AND THE MANAGEMENT OF CHANGE
>
> This section should enable students to:
> - understand the importance of communication within a business and the options available
> - appreciate the need to motivate the workforce and the methods available
> - understand the role and functions of training and retraining, including the role of government
> - appreciate the burden upon the workforce and business of constant change.

3.1 COMMUNICATION

The internal organisation of any business is extremely important (see section 2.2). It provides the structure for decision making and the chain of command. The organisation of a company also produces a network through which the different decision makers can communicate their decisions and receive feedback.

Communication is as important as anything within a business. A company cannot hope to be successful without a good communication system.

What is communication?

Communication is defined as:

> the imparting or exchange of information, ideas and emotions by means of messages, signs and behaviour.

Simply stated, it is any method that we can use to pass a particular message to someone else, or a group.

Communication is a two-way process: one person has an idea or makes a decision and the other person responds. This is known as **feedback**. Effective communication within a business can only work if feedback is provided. Communication in one direction is not good communication.

The method of communication is equally important. What one person believes to be good communication can be seen by others as poor and inappropriate communication. Often the wrong word or gesture can give the wrong message or one that is not intended.

Communication in a business involves not only communicating with the workforce and between the managers but also communicating with the company's customers, suppliers and any other outside agency with which it has contact.

Types of communication

There are a variety of methods of communication. These include **written communication**, **oral communication**, **visual communication** and **IT methods**.

Written communication can take the form of:

- **a letter**
- **a memorandum**
- **a report**
- **minutes**
- **a notice**.

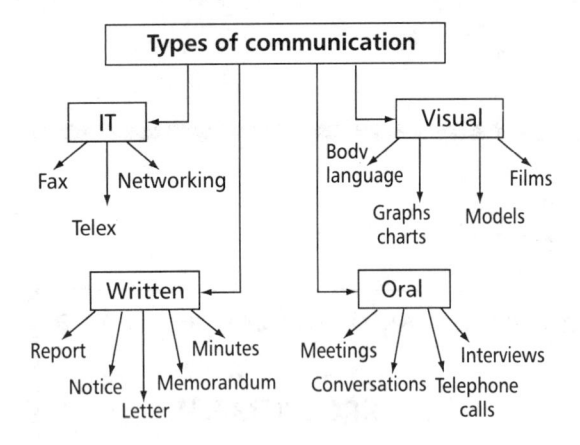

Figure 3.1 Types of communication

Types of communication
- IT: Fax, Networking, Telex
- Visual: Body language, Films, Graphs charts, Models
- Written: Report, Notice, Letter, Minutes, Memorandum
- Oral: Meetings, Conversations, Interviews, Telephone calls

These forms of communication have the advantage for a business of providing a permanent record of what was said or done. They can contain all forms of information and decisions, and can be the basis of a contract. The problem is that they take time to produce, and are very formal, which can offend the receiver. The wording may not be fully understood, which could lead to problems or disputes.

Oral communication includes:

- **conversations**
- **interviews**
- **meetings**
- **telephone calls**.

Oral communication has the advantage of allowing for immediate discussion and clarification. The tone of a manager's voice may also convey an urgency that is difficult to stress in a written form. Equally, many workers, and indeed some managers, are better able to express themselves orally than they are in writing.

The major disadvantage of oral communication, for a business, is that there is no record of what has been discussed and agreed. This frequently causes problems. Decisions may also be hurried because there is a lack of time to think out answers and solutions.

Oral communication relies not only on a person who can give the message properly but also upon the listener, someone who will concentrate upon what is being said in order to understand the message given.

ACTIVITY 1

Write a list of your friends, locally and in other parts of the country. Now put beside each name the way in which you communicate with each person. What is the most popular method of communication you use and why?

Take a small extract from a book or an article in a newspaper and read it to a few of your friends. Leave a gap of one or two days and then ask them to write down what the article was about and as many details as possible. Compare these with the original. What does this prove about oral communication?

Try to find an article about the same incident in two or more newspapers; do they differ in any way? What does this prove about written communication?

Visual communication includes:

- **body language: expressions and gestures**
- **films and videos**
- **graphs and charts**
- **models**.

Many messages can be given both as a listener and as someone speaking to others by using the correct body language. Body language is the term used to describe an extremely effective way of communicating with other people and can be used to support or challenge a verbal message that has been given. However, if a person is not aware of their body language they can accidentally give the wrong messages.

Facial expressions can be used to show agreement, pleasure and understanding or dislike, annoyance and bewilderment. Frowning or smiling are the most common ways of giving these messages.

These are important factors for a manager within a business to consider. Facial expressions could provide messages to the worker but also the expression of a worker could provide a manager with important feedback.

| Smiling to show agreement and understanding | 'I don't understand' | 'I'm not happy about that' | 'I agree' |

Figure 3.2 Body language is an extremely effective way of communicating

As well as facial expressions the way a person sits or stands, their posture, can give certain messages. A manager who stands with folded arms signifies a person who is closed to ideas, who does not understand.

Another form of visual communication is films and videos. These are particularly useful to train workers. Situations can be acted out and then the workers can discuss possible solutions.

Graphs and charts are favourite ways to look at sales figures and financial information and models can be used by a research department to show how a product might look when it is finally produced.

Information technology has greatly changed the way in which many firms communicate. The fax machine has gradually replaced the telex and the Internet and e-mail are quickly becoming standard for many firms.

All these are written means of communication and so carry all of the problems discussed before. The great benefit is the speed of communication and the distance that can be covered.

Barriers to communication

A barrier to communication is anything that prevents the clear transmission of a message from the sender to the receiver. In a business this is crucial because it delays a decision or action or worse still it may change or distort a decision or instruction.

The length of the **line of communication** can be an important barrier. A business that has many tiers of management often suffers from messages

Gestures	Physical contact	Facial expressions
Pointing is rude	Too close is threatening	Smiling shows agreement or pleasure

NON-VERBAL COMMUNICATIONS

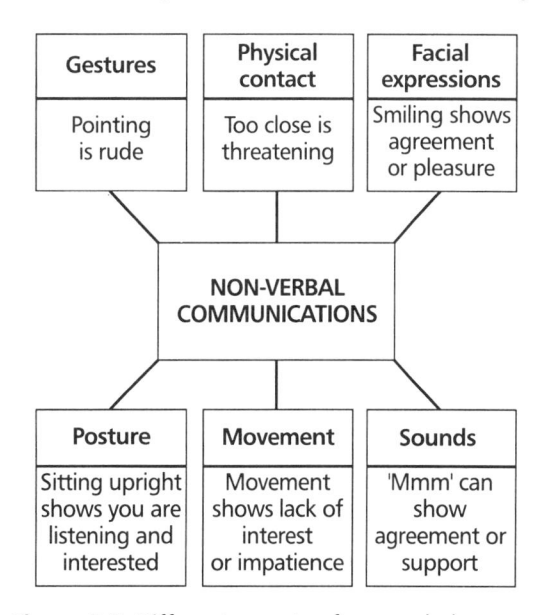

Posture	Movement	Sounds
Sitting upright shows you are listening and interested	Movement shows lack of interest or impatience	'Mmm' can show agreement or support

Figure 3.3 Different aspects of non-verbal communication

being distorted or lost. The game of 'chinese whispers' begins to operate in a large organisation with many levels of hierarchy.

A **lack of expertise** on behalf of the sender or the receiver may cause problems. If the person giving the message cannot do so clearly and precisely, or if the person receiving the message does not concentrate and listen properly, communication may break down.

It is often within a business that different departments have their own **specialist terms** or **jargon**. Production, finance and marketing departments are good examples of this. People within the company who do not have this specialist knowledge or do not understand the jargon are missed out of the communication chain.

Information overload is often a major barrier to communication with a business. If the amount of information given is too great for the other person to receive it effectively then the message may be lost or ignored.

Prejudice can cause problems. If the two people trying to communicate do not like one another because of their sex, colour, class or nationality, then the message may not be received.

Finally **physical conditions** act as a barrier to communication. Distance is less of a problem with modern methods such as fax and e-mail but if the fax machine breaks down or the computer crashes then the message will not get through.

Good communication

There are a number of principles that must be followed if good communication is to take place. These principles, or stages, are as follows:

- decide what is to be communicated
- make sure the right person gets the message
- decide on the method or medium to be used
- identify any possible barriers to communication
- be ready to become a receiver
- decide whether to provide feedback.

Channels of communication

Channels of communication are the lines through which messages within a business are sent. Channels from a manager to someone below are known as **downward**, and from a worker to a manager above as **upward**. Channels between people of equal status within an organisation are known as **horizontal**.

Downward (vertical) communication, between a boss or manager and the workforce, is used to:

- issue instructions
- explain job roles and company rules
- encourage or discipline the workforce and
- motivate the workforce.

Upward (vertical) communication, between the workforce and the managers, provides valuable feedback in the management of the business. Subordinates are often worried about giving their bosses too much information, especially about things that have gone wrong.

This pattern of communication is often in the form of a written or oral report.

Horizontal communication is between people in the same position within an organisation. It is used to:

- provide support by sharing problems and solutions
- encourage cooperation between different departments with the company.

A final channel of communication is the **grapevine**. This is an informal network of contacts with no particular structure. It is often based upon social links within the business rather than the organisation's hierarchy; however, because it is informal it can be very dangerous. The grapevine often spreads inaccurate or half-truth information. It can be a destructive force within a company.

Information technology

IT has greatly improved the speed of communication and the distance over which it can take place, as discussed earlier. Developments such as the Internet have also increased the amount of information available.

In many organisations IT has led to changes in the companies' structures, with fewer middle managers. However, it does depend upon well-trained operators and can lead to all of a company's information being stored in one central location. This may even hinder the communication process.

IT may remove barriers such as prejudice, distance and lack of expertise but it is still liable to breakdown.

ACTIVITY

Consider how information is spread within your school or college. What channel is used? Does a grapevine exist? Is it accurate?

Make a list of all of the methods used by your teachers to communicate to you. Which are the most effective and why?

Which of the subjects that you study to you find the most difficult? Look at the list of barriers to communication; are any of these the reason why you have difficulties? How might you overcome these problems?

Review terms

Feedback; written, oral, visual communication; IT methods; letter; memorandum; report; minutes; notice; conversations; interviews; meetings; telephone calls; body language; films & videos; graphs and charts; models; information technology; line of communication; lack of expertise; jargon; information overload; prejudice; physical conditions; downward, upward and horizontal channels of communication; grapevine.

Fred and Harry discover problems with expansion

Fred and Harry thought that expansion of their business would make their lives so much easier, but their expectations were not met by reality.

Taking on employees meant that more work had to be undertaken. This meant dealing with more telephone requests for quotations and coping with the need for more site meetings with potential clients and the need to produce reports outlining the work to be done and the prices. This in turn led to more letters to the business asking for further details.

Jennie decided that a typewriter was now insufficient for her needs. She was used to using modern information technology, and wanted a wordprocessor and a good printer so that her written communications looked as neat and professional as the firm she represented.

She also argued that a telephone answering machine was essential to cover for the times that she was not working as any lack of oral communication made the firm appear inefficient.

Fred was finding that he was being visited more often by representatives of suppliers, who were using graphs, charts and models that he found hard to comprehend as he lacked that type of mathematical expertise.

Moreover, the actual work was more complicated. When Fred and Harry had worked together they knew what had to be done and could discuss the problems easily. With even just a few employees, this was far more difficult. Employees need to be told exactly what to do, and sometimes there was a breakdown in communications. When Jennie suggested that they should have a mobile phone, so that men on site could take to Fred or Harry, their first reaction was to demonstrate a level of prejudice by laughing and saying that such toys were suitable for bankers and businessmen, but not builders.

However, Fred and Harry were sensible and so they took advice on how to improve their lines of communication.

Data Questions

Foundation level

1 Explain the meaning of the following terms:

(a) written communication
(b) oral communication
(c) information technology
(d) graphs and charts.

2 Identify five different types of communication in the article above and explain how each is used.

3 What would you suggest should be done to improve communications in this firm?

Intermediate level

1 Explain the meaning of the following terms:

(a) written and oral communication
(b) lines of communication
(c) information technology
(d) models.

2 Explain the similarities and differences between five types of communication outlined in the article above.

3 Offer advice on communication to the firm.

Higher level

1 Explain the meaning of the following terms:

(a) written and oral communication
(b) lines of communication
(c) prejudice
(d) models.

2 Assess the relative effectiveness of five different types of communication mentioned in the article above.

3 Write a report to the firm suggesting how their system of communication could be improved.

Coursework Suggestions

Idea

If you are able to get the cooperation of a firm, preferably a small firm, you could investigate their system of communication.

- How do they communicate?
- Interview the workers. Are they happy with the present system of communication?
- Is Information Technology used? Is it used effectively?
- How could their communication be improved?

Idea

Instead of a small firm you could use your own school or college. Make sure that you ask the permission of your teacher or your Principal or Headteacher before you start your research.

The same points from the idea above could be used.

You could also add your own view.

- How do you and your parents receive information?
- Is it effective?
- Could it be improved?
- How could your school or college communicate effectively at a lower cost?

You could interview staff, other students and parents.

Make sure that you ask the permission of your teacher/headteacher before you start your research.

3.2 MOTIVATION

The most valuable resource that a company has is its workforce. They are central to the production of all goods and services.

For a business to be successful it must get the best out of its workers. This includes the managers as well as those on the shop floor. To perform well the workers within a business must enjoy their work and feel as if they are valued by the owners of the business. This is the theory of motivation.

People are motivated by a number of different factors. Not everyone in the same situation is motivated in the same way.

A **motivated** worker will be efficient and effective. This is done by using **motivators** which are rewards, incentives or circumstances that **motivate** people.

Motivators fall into two groups, financial motivators and non-financial motivators.

Financial motivators

Profit is seen as a measure of success for a business and similarly individuals see a high wage or salary as a measure of their success. A low wage can indicate that a person is not valued; a high wage can mean the opposite. Many workers look to other groups doing similar jobs and demand relative pay.

Frederick Taylor (see page 51) believed that a worker could only be motivated by money, especially if their job was routine and boring.

There are a number of ways in which workers can be rewarded financially.

Time rate

The time rate system of payment is based upon the time that individuals work. It does not take into account the amount of work a person does or the quality of the work. It is cheap and easy to administer and a good way to reward workers whose jobs are difficult to measure or do not have an end production, such as office work.

The problem is that it does not encourage workers to produce their maximum output.

Piece rate

The piece rate system of payment is based upon an amount per unit produced or job completed. It rewards those workers who produce more and is best used where mass production takes place. Again it does not measure quality and so extra quality checks are often needed. Health and safety also becomes more of a problem as workers may rush and take risks and so this method is more expensive to administer.

It can provide very high wages but is very insecure. Illness and supply problems within a firm can drastically reduce a worker's wage. In this case piece rate can **demotivate** a worker.

Most businesses use a combination of time and piece rate payments. Employees are paid a basic time rate to cover any time lost through late supplies or machine failures, and then after an agreed number of items or jobs completed the piece rate system is put into action. This provides security but keeps the incentives for increased output.

Bonus payments

Bonus payments can be used for a variety of reasons, for instance good time keeping or for producing above an agreed level of output. It can be paid to an individual or a group of workers. Bonus payments are simple to work out and usually understood by the workforce. They must be seen to be fair otherwise they can cause resentment among other workers. A further problem is that they can come to be seen as a standard part of the pay and then they no longer have an incentive effect.

Productivity deals are very popular amongst firms. These encourage output by using a combination of piece rate and bonus payments.

Share ownership

In recent years **share ownership** has been seen as an ideal way of motivating employees. If employees own shares in the company in which they work, they will benefit if the company is successful. This is the motivation they need to work as hard and as efficiently as possible. A successful company will make large profits and the shareholders will gain a part of that profit.

The government has helped this idea with tax concessions for employee share schemes. There are usually a limited number of shares for employees and these are usually shared out according to length of service.

Profit related pay (PRP)

Profit related pay can be a simple bonus which shares the profits of the company according to the time an employee has worked for the firm; it is usually paid at a time such as Christmas, or by system where part of the employee's wage or salary is directly linked to the profits of the company. If the company is successful salaries can be large but if it is not employees can be demotivated, especially if they feel that the failure of the company is the fault of the management or market conditions.

Other money incentives

Businesses offer a wide variety of other money payments to compensate workers in different situations. Extra pay is given for night shift working, unsocial hours and dangerous jobs.

Benefits in kind

This is an extremely popular way for businesses to reward workers. **Benefits in kind**, or **fringe benefits**, have a money value for the employee but this is paid in the form of a good or service.

For management these benefits may include health insurance, the membership of clubs, free or subsidised travel, discounts on the company's products and so on. For the general staff these benefits can include subsidised meals, recreational facilities for the whole family, low interest loans, discounts on the companies products and so on.

A favourite benefit in kind is the company car that can also be used for private reasons.

The benefits are popular because unlike money they are difficult to tax and so the employee gets the full value. However the UK Government taxes company car usage as well as most other benefits in kind.

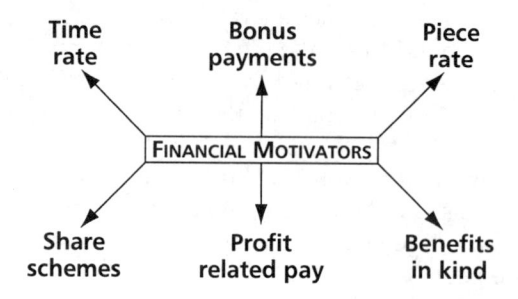

Figure 3.4 Financial motivators

(Time rate, Bonus payments, Piece rate, Share schemes, Profit related pay, Benefits in kind — FINANCIAL MOTIVATORS)

Production Manager

Challenging post with advancement opportunities
£25–30K + bonuses + car – Surrey

Based in Godalming, Caravaggio Yachts is one of the UK's leading manufacturers of top quality, luxury yachts. Our yachts have become an industry standard through the application of the most up-to-date technology and the delicate balancing of valuable resources.

We get it right the first time. And we need to appoint a first-rate manager who can play a central role in taking this £15m business forward by maximising operational efficiency.

Reporting to the Managing Director, you will take immediate responsibility for all aspects of manufacturing, including production engineering, and you will meet or exceed your bi-monthly cost forecasts. Also, we are keen to bring on board someone who can not only motivate and encourage our workforce, but lead us into further exponential growth.

You will have an impressive track record in manufacturing, assembly operations and engineering management along with the charisma needed to build on the essentially stunning successes of our hard-working team.

To the right candidate we are prepared to offer an excellent package of salary by negotiation, as well as bonuses linked to performance and the future success of the business. A company car will be provided and re-location expenses are available if required.

Please write in strict confidence providing comprehensive career details including current salary, quoting reference Prodman 1 to our recruitment consultant: Mr Turner, River Recruitment, Light House Lane, Kingston Upon Thames, Surrey xxx xxxx. Tel: (xxxx) xxxxxxx. Fax: (xxxx) xxxxxxx.

An advertisement for a job, listing both payment and benefits in kind

ACTIVITY 3

Enquire amongst your family and friends how they are paid for the jobs that they do. Try to ask at least ten people. What is the most popular method of payment?

Take the most popular method and ask those same people if this makes them work harder, has no influence or makes them work more slowly?

Do any of these people receive benefits in kind? What effect would it have on their work if these benefits were taken away?

Non-financial motivators

Not everyone is motivated by money. Many need to feel respected, enjoy their job, enjoy the company of those they work with, have status and feel that they have prospects for promotion in the future.

All these factors affect the morale of the business. If these conditions do not exist then it is likely that the workers and the management will be divided, a 'them and us' division. There are a number of ways that job design and a share in the decision-making process can achieve this objective.

Job enlargement

Job enlargement involves increasing the variety of tasks within a job. It involves re-designing a job so there is less repetition and so that the worker has more control over their working day and what they do.

Jobs can be rotated to produce the same effect. A worker can spend some time on one operation or task and then move to another. **Job rotation** requires a team of workers to cooperate but, like job enlargement, it can be a major motivator, relieving boredom.

Job enrichment

Job enrichment is the process of increasing the amount of responsibility a worker has for their own job. This can include the way in which they organise their work, responsibility for allocating tasks to their team and quality control. Job enrichment needs to be supported by a training programme to help the workers adjust to the increased responsibility.

Worker participation

This involves members of the shop floor taking part in management meetings, or even Board meetings, to decide company policy. It is thought that workers will feel better about any decision made if they are part of the decision making process. There is a great deal of evidence to support the view that **worker participation** is a very effective motivator.

Quality control circles

Quality control circles are a new development in UK industries. A small group of workers meet regularly to discuss any problems that they might be having with their jobs. They try, as a group, to find solutions to these problems.

The workers must be allowed to put their solutions into operation or the motivation will be lost. Therefore this process needs the support of the management and any necessary resources.

Non-Financial Motivators
- Job enlargement
- Job enrichment
- Job rotation
- Worker participation
- Quality control circles

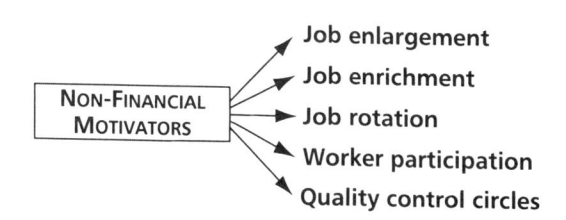

Figure 3.5 Non-financial motivators

Motivation theories

Theories of motivation were virtually non-existent before the beginning of the century. Since then the value of a willing and efficient workforce has been realised and many theories developed.

Frederick Taylor saw people motivated by money. He believed that work did not offer satisfaction for all of a person's needs but a high money wage would allow them to satisfy those needs outside the work place.

Elton Mayo believed, after much research, that the way in which people behaved at work was influenced by the people they were in contact with during the day. If they were happy and felt valued they would be productive.

Abraham Maslow developed his '**hierarchy of needs**'. He argued that everyone had needs, but at different levels. Once the lower level needs had been satisfied, the earning of money, their security and social needs would then become important. Jobs should allow workers to achieve these levels of needs.

Douglas McGregor developed his '**X theory**' and his '**Y theory**'. Simply stated these looked at the ideas that workers needed constant supervision and direction by management (theory X) and that it was the responsibility of the management to motivate workers. Every worker can be motivated if the right method is chosen (theory Y).

Frederick Herzberg saw the motivation of workers in two categories, **maintenance factors** and **motivators**. Maintenance factors are identified as good eating, pay and social facilities and motivators as promotion prospects, job satisfaction and job enrichment. He believed that both were a necessary part of every job.

ACTIVITY 4

Think about your own situation. Why are you at school (ignore the legal aspect)? Why did you choose to do Business Studies?

Do you work hard? If you do, why do you? If you do not work hard, why not? What would make you work harder?

Which lessons do you enjoy the most? Why do you enjoy these lessons? Can you link your reasons to any of the motivators given in this section? Do any of your reasons fit any of the theories briefly outlined? (You could investigate one of these theories further.)

✓ Review terms

Motivated; motivators; time rate; piece rate; demotivate; bonus payments; productivity deals; share ownership; profit related pay; benefits in kind; fringe benefits; job enlargement; job rotation; job enrichment; worker participation; quality control circles; Frederick Taylor; Elton Mayo; Abraham Maslow; Douglas McGregor; Frederick Herzberg; hierarchy of needs; X theory; Y theory; maintenance factors.

Fred and Harry learn about motivation

Having taken professional advice, Fred and Harry found that their system of communications improved greatly. All enquiries were dealt with promptly and accurately; appropriate IT equipment had been installed, and Fred had attended a short course which gave him an adequate understanding of graphs and charts. He could use a spreadsheet, and was delighted with his new skills.

However, this did not mean that the firm was able to flourish with no further problems. Fred and Harry were partners and they shared the profits, so they would work the hours needed in order to complete a job on time.

They had forgotten that employees were not always so motivated. Workers in the building trade are paid by the hour – on a time rate as it is known technically. Sometimes, there might be piece rates – for instance, payment per number of bricks laid – and occasionally there are bonus payments, usually as a result of completing a job ahead of schedule, or some similar reward for productivity.

If someone is paid to start work at 8 a.m., then they have no incentive to start earlier, and if they are expected to stop for lunch at 12 noon, then that is when they will stop, even if it leaves unused cement, which will harden and be useless later. Fred and Harry would start when they arrived at the site, and they would not think of taking a break at an unsuitable time.

At first, this difference between the employer and employee annoyed Fred and Harry, until, one day, they saw an article in The Builders' Journal. Fred and Harry read the article and determined to alter their approach to man management.

THE BUILDER'S JOURNAL

Job enrichment in the building trades

Quality control circles originated in Japan, and they remain foreign to building trades, but some firms have found improvements in productivity and greater job satisfaction by involving the employees in some of the decision making.

Ask yourselves – do you make sure that your employees know what the contract is and when it should be finished? Do you ever ask them their opinions about the best approach to a job? This is a simple piece of worker participation. If you do, then you are likely to have a happier workforce.

Have you explained the waste that can result from taking breaks to the minute? Have your offered some sort of bonus for the elimination of such waste? This could be more money or a benefit in kind such as use of a company car for holidays.

You can save money, and have a happier and harder working work force, just by treating them with more respect.

Data Questions

Foundation level

1 Explain the meaning of the following terms:

   (a) spreadsheet
   (b) motivated workers
   (c) time rate
   (d) piece rate
   (e) bonus payment
   (f) productivity.

2 What could Fred and Harry do to improve the productivity of their workers?

3 Write a sentence to explain what each of the following people would have thought about the article from The Builders' Journal:

   (a) Frederick Taylor
   (b) Elton Mayo
   (c) Abraham Maslow
   (d) Douglas McGregor
   (e) Frederick Herzberg.

Intermediate level

1 Explain the meaning of the following terms:

   (a) spreadsheet
   (b) motivated workers
   (c) time rate and piece rate
   (d) job enrichment
   (e) benefit in kind
   (f) productivity.

2 What possible actions could Fred and Harry take to improve the efficiency of their workers?

3 Rewrite the article from The Builders' Journal, as though it had been produced by each of the following people:

   (a) Frederick Taylor
   (b) Elton Mayo
   (c) Abraham Maslow
   (d) Douglas McGregor
   (e) Frederick Herzberg.

Higher level

1 Explain the meaning of the following terms:

   (a) motivated and motivator
   (b) worker participation
   (c) time rate and piece rate
   (d) job enrichment
   (e) fringe benefits
   (f) quality control circles.

2 Examine the options open to Fred and Harry to improve efficiency and productivity.

3 What advice would each of the most famous motivation theorists have given to Fred and Harry so that they could have a more willing and efficient workforce?

Coursework Suggestions

Idea

Think about Activity 3. Could this be the basis for a good piece of coursework?

- Is money the major motivator for all workers?
- Are higher wages the only way for a firm to increase or improve its output?

Expand your sample to 20 or 25 people, ask the same questions.

- What job do they do?
- Does the method of reward depend upon their job?
- Can you link certain types of reward with certain types of job or occupation?

Ask your teachers how they are paid. How would you feel if they were paid by results, or by a bonus scheme? Would they like a company car instead of a proportion of the money?

Idea

This is a little more difficult and requires you to ask the help of a company. Ask a company, preferably a small one, how they pay their workers. Ask the workers, via a questionnaire, how they feel about this.

- How does the company's reward system fit in wit the theory?
- Does it work?
- How might it be improved?

Suggest alternatives to the workers and the management!

How can you tell if the reward system actually works?

Remember to be discreet: you might gain answers or comments that the management or the workers would not like anyone else to know!

3.3 RECRUITMENT, TRAINING AND THE MANAGEMENT OF CHANGE

Every business is constantly facing changes. These changes are many and varied, some are large and immediate and others slow and quite small.

The business environment can be changed in a number of ways and by a number of different forces (see Chapter 5). Examples include:

- decisions of the UK courts
- decisions of the European courts
- the intervention of new technology
- changes in consumer tastes
- changes in consumer incomes
- increased competition
- new government policy.

These are just a few of the forces that could change the way a business would have to operate. All of these are external factors, over which an individual firm has no control.

An important question is: are the businesses aware of these changes?

In order to identify any changes that take place a business must be aware of its market (see Chapter 6), and generally have good communication links with the world of commerce. Organisations such as the Chamber of Commerce and the CBI are important here (see Chapter 5).

Changing attitudes and opinions

Once a business has made the decision that it needs to change, for whatever reason, it must then decide how to carry out those changes.

Any change in business will require changes in the way the workers, and quite often the managers, view things.

There are several views about how to change a person's opinions but ultimately it needs the skilful management of people, human resources. There are two schools of thought: the one-sided argument approach that provides one set of facts, and the two-sided argument approach that presents a series of points and then a set of counter arguments. The one-sided approach is thought to work better with unskilled and semi-skilled workers whilst the two-sided approach is believed to work better with those who are better educated, the professional groups.

Opinions can be casual and relatively easy to change but attitudes are often more difficult to remove or change. It is common to find the young, rebellious junior representative on the shop floor. This individual often works alongside the older more mature worker who used to be young and rebellious but now sees the management in a different light.

To change attitudes it is important to know why those attitudes exist. If the management wishes to change its method of production the shop floor may be totally against the new technology being used. Why is this so? It may be that management is trying to get rid of workers or earn more profit for themselves; in this case strategies designed to promote negotiation can be used.

The correct approach, for instance, could be to negotiate new working arrangements or a profit sharing scheme. People can be persuaded to change their attitude if they believe that they will benefit. It is therefore the job of a firm's management to persuade the workforce that any changes decided by, or forced upon, a company will in the end benefit the whole company.

Changing behaviour

It is assumed that attitudes strongly influence behaviour but this is not always the case. Many people strongly support charities such as Save the Children, the NSPCC, the RSPCA, Comic Relief and so on, yet how many of these supporters actually contribute to these charities.

Many studies show that the best way for a firm to change its employee behaviour is to outline the consequences of resisting change, for the firm and the workers, and then outline what practical measures the firm is to take to overcome this situation.

ACTIVITY 5

List five factors that have changed the way British industry operates in the last five years.

Look at your opinions of your school or college now and five years ago. Have they changed? If so, why? Has this changed your behaviour?

The BSE scare which has affected British beef is a good example of change affecting an industry. Try to work out how this situation has affected industry.

It also provides a good example of changing attitudes and behaviour of consumers. How has this happened? What does this prove?

The costs of change

There are a number of ways in which changes can affect a business. The most obvious is cost. New technology costs more money as does increased competition. A further cost could be felt by the work force. New technology can replace workers. Competition or a loss of a market could mean decreased output and a decreased demand for workers.

The ultimate cost for any business is bankruptcy. If a firm loses its market, or is unable to compete or purchase new technology, it could find itself with a rapidly declining demand for its product creating losses. These costs outline the importance of a firm and its workers adapting to change.

Training

The biggest fear of change within any company comes from the fear of **redundancy**. 'Will the new technology take my job?', is often the thought in many workers' minds. This is the point where training can be very important.

Training is defined as:

a programme of activities directed towards the gaining of skills for a specific job.

The essential role of any manager within a business undergoing a period of change is to make the workforce feel wanted; this is another form of motivation. A good training programme can do this. New technology may change a worker's job but it does not always have to be seen as a threat to that job.

A **training programme** should lay down clearly the objectives of the company and the plans that it has for its workers. These business and manpower objectives should then be turned into a series of training objectives. These three essential features will show what the company's intentions are and should help to motivate the workers and remove any fears they may have.

A training plan needs the support of the entire management, plus adequate resources, and should be evaluated at every stage.

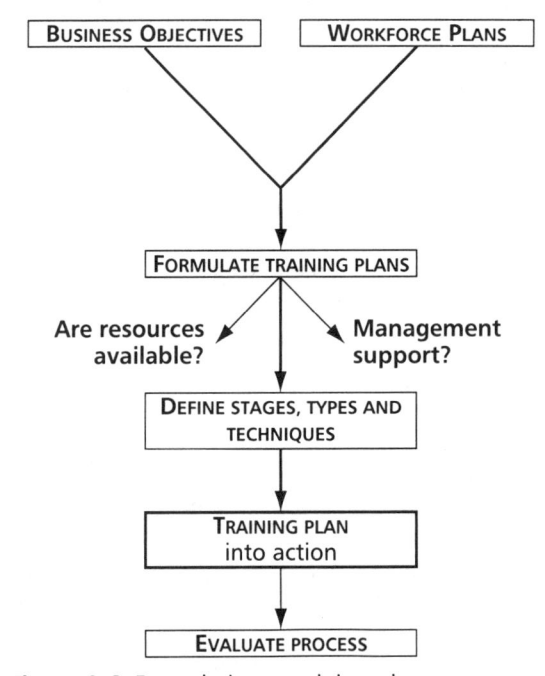

```
BUSINESS OBJECTIVES     WORKFORCE PLANS
         │                      │
         └──────────┬───────────┘
                    ▼
          FORMULATE TRAINING PLANS
  Are resources   ↙        ↘   Management
  available?                    support?
                    ▼
         DEFINE STAGES, TYPES AND
                TECHNIQUES
                    ▼
              TRAINING PLAN
                into action
                    ▼
              EVALUATE PROCESS
```

Figure 3.6 Formulating a training plan

Methods of training

There are a number of institutions that provide education and training (see section 5.4) but from the point of view of a business there are only three available methods.

On-the-job training is the oldest form of training. In this case the person training, the trainee, works alongside someone who has the skills required. Everyone at some time needs on-the-job training. This applies no matter what level of education a person has. It is cheap to operate and highly effective. It does have its limits. For example in a job using expensive materials mistakes can be made and money lost. It is also of no use when the skills needed are new to everyone in the company.

Off-the-job training takes place in specialist institutions, as listed in section 5.4, or within the business. These employ specialist instructors and remove the pressure of working at the same time. The costs of this type of training can be high but can more easily be estimated. If the training is provided by state-run institutions then costs may be lower due to economies of scale.

The Training Agency, now known as the **TEC**, is a government-run agency detailed in section 5.4.

Types of training

There are a number of different types of training. **Induction training** introduces new recruits to the business, its objectives, methods and philosophy as well as to fellow workers. An induction course can last from a few days to several months depending upon the company and the type of job.

Training for promotion is quite specific. The nature and length of such training will depend upon the type of job involved. It should include a variety of techniques, short courses, lectures, case studies, simulations, role play and exercises.

With respect to the role of training in a changing environment the most important types of training are **training in attitudes** and **training for change**.

Training in attitudes is a long-term process. It tries to extend the experience of the worker and so change his or her attitude. It might mean on-the-job training with a worker who has the desired attitude or it could involve off-the-job training using case studies, role plays, simulation and group exercises. At all times the trainee should benefit from a wider experience in controlled conditions.

Training for change requires detailed training plans. These might require the company to employ a specialist in the required area or to use specialist trainers in other institutions.

Recruitment

When changes occur within a business it may be that extra employees are needed to cope with the new jobs. The firm's present employees may not wish to re-train or be unable to meet the demands of the new jobs.

In these situations it is common for firms to offer voluntary redundancy or early retirement. The workforce may also be reduced by natural wastage, that is not replacing workers who leave. All of these situations enable firms to restructure their workforce.

The next stage in the process is to recruit new workers with the skills that are needed for the new market or the new conditions and situations that the firm finds itself in. **Recruitment** is a very important process which every firm has to go through.

The person appointed must have the skills required by the firm and match its needs exactly. This is the responsibility of the personnel department. Before any firm recruits a new worker, personnel must go through a number of stages.

Firstly it must produce a **job analysis**. This is a study of what the job involves. It contains the skills, training and tasks needed to carry out the job to the firm's satisfaction.

The second stage is to produce a **job description**. This outlines to potential applicants what is involved in the job. It provides a 'picture' of the job.

The third stage is to produce a **person specification**. This is intended to show the type of person that is required for the job. It outlines the type of personality required (happy, neat, flexible, etc), and characterises the person requires apart from their academic qualifications and training.

The recruitment itself can be internal or external. **Internal recruitment** allows a firm's worker to change his or her role. A worker may possess unused skills or have obtained qualifications since appointment. This type of recruitment provides a career path for employees and therefore also provides some motivation.

A firm knows more about its present employees' strengths and weaknesses than it does about outside applicants and in this sense internal recruitment is a good thing for all concerned. Training may also be shorter without the need for induction. However internal recruitment does limit the number of applicants and may create a vacancy elsewhere.

If a person's job changes and they decide to leave rather than re-train then appointing from within may cause resentment amongst the other workers.

External recruitment is to attract staff from outside the company. The method used is often determined by the type and importance of the job available and the size of the company. There are a number of ways of attracting staff externally:

- commercial employment agencies
- job centres
- recruitment agencies
- youth training schemes
- the careers service
- local schools and colleges
- the universities
- head-hunting
- TV advertising
- the national the local press.

Whatever method is chosen a firm's recruitment may be affected by the state of the labour market. If all the firms within an industry are looking for the same type of staff the demand will be high. It may be that there are few people available with the skills required. The firm must then look again at its strategy.

ACTIVITY 6

List all the skills that you, your friends and your family have. Who has the most skills? How did they obtain them?

Choose three of the methods used to recruit staff externally, (e.g. newspapers). For each method list the types of jobs advertised. Do you notice any patterns? Where would you look for a job and why?

Try to get hold of a job description and person specification for a post. What do you notice about these two? Try to create a picture in your mind of the type of person needed for this job. Write down the main points.

Fred and Harry decide on a recruitment and training policy

Fred and Harry's new employees did not all stay with the firm, despite the introduction of regular consultation and discussion. It was when one left that Fred and Harry began to think about how they should best recruit a replacement. Recruitment was easy – redundancies at Scallies and other builders had seen to that – but Fred and Harry needed to be sure that every employee was suitable.

They therefore drew up a job description. They needed people who had the right attitude and some experience in the building trade. They had come to the conclusion that they could offer some training if they found someone with the right attitudes, but who lacked some of the skills needed. They could supervise on the site – Harry really was excellent at this type of on-the-job training. Fred's computer course had shown him the sort of off-the-job training that could be done in the local colleges, so they were not worried about devising a training programme.

In fact, they were more in need of a person specification than a job description. The right person could be assessed, then a job analysis could be undertaken, and that person's skills matched with those needed to create their training needs.

Fred and Harry had already discovered that colleges and the local TEC were only too keen to help, so that they now expected to be able to assemble a committed and trained workforce.

Review terms

Redundancy; training; training programme; on-the-job training; off-the-job training; The Training Agency (TEC); induction training; training for promotion; training in attitudes; training for change; recruitment; job analysis; job description; person specification; internal recruitment; external recruitment.

Looking for a job at a job centre

Data Questions

Foundation level

1 Explain the meaning of the following terms:

  (a) redundancy
  (b) job description
  (c) training
  (d) recruitment.

2 (a) What sort of a person would Fred and Harry like to have work for them?

  (b) How could they find such a person?

  (c) What could they do if the person they appointed did not have all of the skills they required?

Intermediate level

1 Explain the meaning of the following terms:

  (a) redundancy
  (b) job description and person specification
  (c) training needs and training programme
  (d) recruitment.

2 Based on what you know about Fred and Harry and their firm, draw up a person specification for a new employee.

3 Outline what could be done to remedy a skill shortage.

Higher level

1 Explain the meaning of the following terms:

  (a) job analysis
  (b) job description and person specification
  (c) training needs and training programme
  (d) TEC.

2 What would you advise Fred and Harry to do to ensure that their next employee is suitable for their needs?

Coursework Suggestions

Idea

How closely does your education, your interests and character correspond to the job you want? What do you need to do in order to have more chance of achieving your ambitions?

Carry out the following tasks in order to discover this.

- Write a curriculum vitae (CV) of yourself, laying out your education, any work experience, interests and achievements.
- Perform a SWOT (Strengths, Weaknesses, Opportunities, Threats) analysis on yourself.
- What job do you want? Find out all of the requirements from a job description and a person specification.
- Compare your CV and SWOT analyses to these needs.
- What sorts of training do you need to do in order to meet those needs (i.e. educational, attitudinal, etc)?
- How would you gain that training?

4

Business Finance

The control of money within the business

**4.1 SOURCES OF BUSINESS FINANCE • 4.2 COSTS AND REVENUES
4.3 FINANCIAL RECORDS • 4.4 FINANCIAL CONTROLS**

This section should enable students to:
- appreciate the sources of loan capital
- comprehend the basis of cost, revenue and profit
- be able to keep financial records
- use records to analyse the health of a business.

4.1 SOURCES OF BUSINESS FINANCE

As the economy has developed, a whole range of specialist institutions have emerged to ensure that the financial system works easily and smoothly.

The commercial banks

These are institutions that collect money from the general public, look after that money, and use it by lending to others who may need it.

Mergers have left four major **commercial banks** – Barclays, Lloyds–T.S.B., Midland and National Westminster (NatWest) – and several smaller banks, such as the Bank of Scotland and the Co-operative. These are sometimes called high street banks, because you can find one in the main street of every town.

The role of a commercial bank is to hold money in accounts for its customers, and offer a variety of services. These include:

- **loans** and **overdrafts**, provided that the bank is satisfied that you will be able to repay them
- **cheque books**, **standing orders** and **direct debits**, to make payments easier
- **security facilities**, including night safes for businesses and strong rooms for the safe keeping of valuables
- **exchanging currency** for holiday makers and businesses dealing with foreigners
- **financial advice**
- **executor and trustee services** to handle estates after death.

The most likely source of finance for small businesses are the commercial banks, all of whom have small business units. They offer assistance by way of overdrafts or fixed term loans. They are far more likely to assist if the borrower is able to offer security, which is something the borrower agrees that the bank can sell to repay the loan if the business is not successful.

Merchant banks

Originally, these were firms of merchants specialising in the export of British goods. This involved the sending of money from one country to another, and the merchants gained a reputation for trustworthiness. Thus, their bills of exchange were always accepted.

As trade developed, other trading companies appeared, but their bills of exchange were not always so readily accepted, so the original merchants began to do this, for a commission. In this way, the established merchants became bankers specialising in bills of exchange.

Merchant banks still deal in bills of exchange, the issue of new securities, and act as advisors to large companies. Thus merchant banks are more likely to offer facilities for the larger businesses.

Building societies

Like the commercial banks, the number of **building societies** has recently fallen as a result of mergers. Two of the largest are the Halifax and the Woolwich.

The main function of building societies is to loan money to individuals to purchase their own homes. This accounts for about 80% of the combined funds of the societies. However some building societies will loan for the purchase of commercial properties, and most will increase the size of a domestic mortgage to provide business capital.

The borrower obtains a **mortgage** from the society. This is a loan. The borrower pays interest on that loan, and repays the loan and the interest over periods as long as 25 years.

If the borrower fails to pay, the society can take over the house and sell it to someone else so as to recover the money owed.

Building societies obtain the money that they loan out by borrowing from the public.

Building societies are now able to do more than just loan money for house purchase, and so they offer personal loans, cheque books and credit cards, and in many ways act like commercial banks. The distinction between them is starting to disappear. Indeed, the second largest building society, the Abbey National, became a bank in 1989, and others are following suit.

ACTIVITY 1

Find someone who has an account at a commercial bank and someone who has a building society account. Ask about the services available to each type of account.

List the services that your interviewees feel they both offer, and those that are different. What is the difference between the two accounts?

The Stock Exchange

The Stock Exchange deals with the buying and selling of existing shares in Public Limited Companies and securities issued by the UK Government and foreign governments.

It is important to remember that the money coming from the sale of a share that has already been issued goes to the owner of the share, and not to the company.

The London Stock Exchange

The value of the share reflects what buyers think about a company. If the price of a share is rising, then buyers think that the company is doing well. If it is falling, then buyers have less confidence in the state of the company.

✓ Review terms

Commercial banks; loan; overdraft; security; merchant banks; building societies; mortgage; The Stock Exchange.

ACTIVITY 2

If you were to start an insurance company, what factors would you take into account in order to calculate the premium to insure a house in your area against theft?

List all the factors that would affect the premium, and explain why each is important.

Fred and Harry seek another loan

Fred and Harry remembered the time they had first decided that they needed to expand. They had been working together for six months and wanted a new van and larger premises.

They had approached their bank for a business loan of £20,000, which would allow them to grow and provide extra working capital.

Their proposals had included employing a labourer, so that they could concentrate on their specialist tasks and not have to fetch and carry for each other.

The manager of Centrecounty Bank had been impressed by their business plan, which had been prepared by Jennie, and gave them a loan secured upon their yard and Fred's home.

Several years later, they again approached the bank with another proposal for expansion but, to their surprise, the manager was not helpful. He was no longer able to make the decisions that he had taken previously. Now, he had to refer to the Area Commercial Accounts Manager, who was not local and knew little about local people or local conditions. He was interested in ensuring that Centrecounty Bank did not enter into loans that held any risk.

Fred and Harry became another pair of small businessmen who felt dissatisfied with the decisions taken by banks. They felt betrayed, and could not understand why their request had been denied. They felt that the loan would have been properly secured, and anyway, they thought that making a profit involved risk so they expected that banks would take risks, just as they did themselves.

Data Questions

Foundation level

1 Explain the meaning of the following terms:
   (a) business plan
   (b) secured loan
   (c) working capital
   (d) specialist tasks.

2 What factors would a bank manager take into account when considering whether or not to give a business loan?

3 Why do businesses want to expand?

Intermediate level

1 Explain the meaning of the following terms:
   (a) business plan
   (b) secured loan
   (c) risk
   (d) working capital.

2 What factors do lenders take into account when considering an application for a business loan?

3 Discuss the relationship between risk and profit.

Higher level

1 Explain the meaning of the following terms:

  (a) business plan
  (b) secured loan
  (c) risk
  (d) working capital.

2 Why have many businesses been critical of the commercial banks in recent years?

3 Why do businesses want to expand?

Coursework Suggestions

Idea

Do building societies and banks differ in the services that they offer?

- Find out what they both do.
- It is essential to follow this information up: find out what their customers think about the quality of the service they both offer.

Use the Consumers Association reports, and newspaper articles.

Prepare some questions and put these to people who take accounts at banks and building societies, so as to discover how they feel about the differences in service offered.

Idea

You have been left £1,000 in a will and wish to invest it.

- What factors would you take into account in deciding how to invest the money?
- What options are available to you?
- Where would you invest it, and why?

4.2 COSTS AND REVENUES

Revenue

Revenue is the amount of money that a business receives for the sale of goods and services.

Total revenue is the price of each item sold multiplied by the quantity sold, or the total value of sales.

Total revenue = Price × Quantity

Costs

The total cost of running a business is split into two parts.

Fixed costs are those costs which do not change, no matter how much is produced. They are constant, and include such items as rent, rates and insurance.

Variable costs are those costs which change according to how much is produced. They are zero when nothing is made, but gradually increase as the quantity produced increases. They include wages, the purchase of raw materials and the cost of power.

Total costs = Fixed costs + Variable costs

Profit

All firms aim to make a **profit**. Profit is the difference between the revenue collected for selling goods and services and the costs of making those goods and services.

Total profit = Total revenue − Total cost

Total profit forms only part of the information that firms need to know to ensure maximum profits. It may be helpful to know the profit per unit, and whether total profit could be increased by producing a greater or smaller quantity of the product.

Profit per unit

Profit per unit is especially important if a firm is producing several different items, or have just begun to sell a new product. To calculate profit per unit, it is necessary to find the cost and the revenue per unit.

Quantity produced £	Fixed costs £	Variable cost £	Total cost £
0	100	0	100
1	100	20	120
2	100	38	138
3	100	50	150
4	100	60	160
5	100	65	165
6	100	74	174

Figure 4.1 Calculations to find profit per unit

$$\text{Average cost} = \frac{\text{Total cost}}{\text{Quantity}}$$

$$\text{Average revenue} = \frac{\text{Total revenue}}{\text{Quantity}}$$

If Total revenue minus Total cost gives Total profit, then:

Profit per unit
= Average revenue − Average cost

This can all be put together in one chart (Figure 4.2), which shows that the maximum level of profit would be £90, with a production of three units.

However, the maximum profit per unit is £31, with a production of two units, but this would give a total profit of only £62.

This gives two conflicting pieces of information, and the decision on how much to produce will depend on the aims of the firm.

Quantity £	Price £	Total revenue £	Total cost £	Total profit £	Average revenue £	Average cost £	Profit per unit £
0	150	0	100	−100	−	−	−
1	120	120	120	0	120	120	0
2	100	200	138	62	100	69	31
3	80	240	150	90	80	50	30
4	60	240	160	80	60	40	20
5	40	200	165	35	40	33	7
6	20	120	174	−54	20	29	−9

Figure 4.2 Table showing profit per unit

If the quantities were in thousands, rather than single units, the maximum profit is unlikely to be exactly £3,000, but somewhere around that figure. If this could be calculated, then the firm would have even more detailed information on which to base its decisions.

Maximum profit

The method to find maximum profit involves marginal costs and marginal revenues.

Marginal cost is the extra cost of producing one more unit. If it costs £120 to produce one unit and £138 to produce two units, then the cost involved in increasing production from one unit to two is £18. This is the marginal cost.

Marginal revenue is the extra revenue received from the sale of one extra unit.

If the total revenue from selling one unit is £120, but the sale of two units would give a total revenue of £200, then the extra revenue resulting from the sale of the extra unit is £80. This is the marginal revenue.

It is possible to calculate the marginal costs and marginal revenues and to plot a graph of them. Each marginal cost and marginal revenue represents the difference between the totals.

For example, between sales of one and two the marginal revenue is £80. This is not at a sale of one or two, but in between, so the graph would be plotted between one and two.

Quantity £	Total revenue £	Marginal revenue £	Total costs £	Marginal costs
0	0		100	
		120		20
1	120		120	
		80		18
2	200		138	
		40		12
3	240		150	
		0		10
4	240		160	
		−40		5
5	200		165	
		−80		9
6	120		174	

Figure 4.3 Marginal revenues and marginal costs

If the marginal revenue received from selling a unit is greater than the marginal cost involved in making it, then the profit is being made in the production of that unit. When the marginal cost is greater than the marginal revenue, then a loss is being made in the production of that unit.

Thus, to maximise profits, a firm should continue production up to the point where marginal revenue ceases to be greater than marginal cost.

ACTIVITY 3

Using the figures relating to marginal cost and marginal revenue in Figure 4.3 above, draw a graph to show the optimum level of output for the firm.

Then plot the average revenue curve to discover the selling price at this output.

Finally, plot the average cost curve to find the average cost per unit at this level of output.

Shade the area which indicates the area of profit, and calculate the total profit that would be made.

Break-even Analysis

It is possible to use some of the information relating to cost and revenue in order to calculate the minimum number of sales that a firm needs to make before it enters into profit.

Looking at Figure 4.4, it is clear that at an output of one unit, total cost is the same as total revenue, so there is neither profit nor loss.

At an output of two units, revenue is greater than cost, so a profit is being made. This is best expressed diagrammatically, as in Figure 4.5.

Quantity should be plotted on the horizontal axis and cost/revenue on the vertical axis.

Quantity £	Fixed costs £	Variable costs £	Total costs £	Total revenue £
0	100	0	0	0
1	100	20	120	100
2	100	38	138	200
3	100	50	150	240
4	100	60	160	240
5	100	65	165	200
6	100	74	174	120

Figure 4.4 Figures necessary for the calculation of minimum sales required

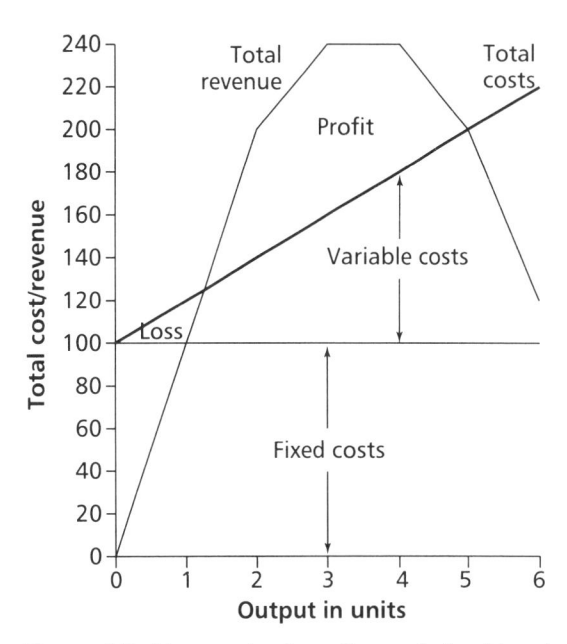

Figure 4.5 Diagram to show the analysis of break-even point

Draw the fixed cost curve, and then plot the variable cost curve above it. This will also be the total cost curve.

Now plot the total revenue curve. Where the total revenue curve meets the total cost curve, then the break-even point has been reached.

As long as total revenue is above total cost, then a profit is being made.

Review terms

Revenue; total revenue; fixed costs; variable costs; total costs; profit; profit per unit; average costs; average revenue; maximum profit; marginal costs; marginal revenues; break-even point.

Fred goes to college and learns about costs

Thornton College of Further Education
Department of Business and Management Studies

Courses for Small Businesses

These are specialist one-day courses designed to help small businesses tackle some of the problems that they face.

Monday 17th March	❏ Keeping costs down
Wednesday 19th March	❏ How to sell more
Friday 21st March	❏ How to charge the right price

Fred was impressed with the HNC that his wife had obtained from the college, and he felt that he could learn something that would help the business, so he decided to attend the last of these courses.

He was told all about fixed and variable costs, total costs and revenue, but none of it seemed particularly relevant to him until the break-even analysis was demonstrated.

At once, Fred realised that he had an exact method of costing out work so as to ensure that his quotations would make an appropriate profit.

He worked out their total fixed costs for the year, and divided this by 50, to represent the number of working weeks in the year. This would give the average fixed costs per week.

This was then divided by five to give the average daily fixed costs; these came to £50.

With Harry acting as the labourer, and Fred laying, the variable costs included the bricks themselves, the sand and cement, fuel for the mixer, and so on. He calculated the variable costs at £15 per 100 bricks. They also reckoned that they needed to make at least £50 each a day in order to make a decent living, but they would work for less if they were short of work.

On a normal day, he could lay at least 1,000 bricks.

Data Questions

Foundation level

1 Explain the meaning of the following terms:
  (a) fixed costs
  (b) variable costs
  (c) total costs
  (d) total revenue
  (e) quotations.

2 Assuming that the variable cost is £30 per 100 bricks, construct a chart showing: fixed costs, variable costs, total costs, average revenue and total revenue at outputs of 0, 100, 200, 300, 400, 500, 600, 700, 800, 900, 1,000, and 1,100.

3 Using this information, draw a break-even chart.
  (a) What is the break-even point?
  (b) How many bricks have to be laid so that the break-even point is reached, and Fred and Harry make £50 each?
  (c) How much would profit would they make if 1,100 bricks a day were laid?

Intermediate level

1 Explain the meaning of the following terms:

(a) average fixed costs
(b) variable costs
(c) daily fixed costs
(d) total revenue
(e) quotations.

2 Assuming that the variable cost is £30 per 100 bricks, construct a chart giving the information needed to draw a break-even chart.

3 Draw the chart.

(a) What is the break-even point?
(b) How many bricks have to be laid so that the break-even point is reached, and Fred and Harry make £50 each?
(c) How much would profit would they make if 1,100 bricks a day were laid?

Higher level

1 Explain the meaning of the following terms:

(a) average fixed costs
(b) variable costs
(c) average fixed costs
(d) total revenue
(e) quotations.

2 Construct and draw a chart giving the information needed to draw a break-even chart. What price would you recommend that they charge per 100 bricks? Explain your proposal.

Coursework Suggestions

Idea

There are several potential pieces of coursework that could be based upon this section, the most obvious of which is a break-even analysis for a firm, or even for one particular product. In the same way, the optimum output for a firm or a product could be calculated.

The difficulty is obtaining the information. Many firms, in reality, would not be able to provide the details needed, and those that could may be very reluctant to hand over such confidential data about their financial affairs.

It would be possible to spend a great deal of time and effort preparing to undertake such a project, only to discover that, in the end, the information is not forthcoming, so be very careful if you wish to look at this area that you are fully convinced that you will be given all the material you need.

4.3 FINANCIAL RECORDS

The most obvious reason why a firm keeps records is that no-one can remember everything, so firms write down the details of their financial affairs.

There has to be a record of the amount of money that has been received and where it has gone. This information is known as **book-keeping**, and is used to produce accounts, which provide information such as the level of profits.

Book-keeping

Accurate book-keeping is essential if accurate financial information is going to be prepared. The types of records kept are likely to vary according to the nature of the particular business, but the principles of record-keeping remain the same:

- a **cash book** to record all money taken and all payments made
- a **petty cash book** to record very small purchases
- a sales accounts book, or **sales ledger**, for all credit sales.

The cash book records all business receipts and payments, except for the very small payments that have been noted in the petty cash book, along with the date, from whom or to whom it is transferred.

Receipts go on the left, and payments on the right. A petty cash book keeps track of the small purchases, such as pencils or a light bulb.

RECEIPTS			PAYMENTS		
Date	Details	Amount	Date	Details	Amount

Figure 4.6 A simple cash book layout

Sales and purchase accounts

The same format is used to keep track of transfers between the business and each customer or supplier. When a good is supplied, an **invoice** is sent by the firm to the customer. This is a request for payment. When that payment is received, the fact is recorded alongside. At the same time, the payment would also be recorded in the cash book.

SALES ACCOUNT Account no. *1004* Customer *ABC Ltd*

RECEIPTS			PAYMENTS		
Date	Details	Amount	Date	Details	Amount
21.1	Invoice 301	120.00	22.1	Cheque	120.00

Figure 4.7 A simple sales ledger layout

Bank accounts

The bank will keep an account of all payments into and out of a firm's bank account. These statements of account will be sent to the business, and can be checked to see if either the bank or the firm has made any mistakes. Checking that figures agree is known as a **reconciliation**.

The monthly balance on the bank statement should be reconciled with the closing balance for the month in the cash book:

Closing bank balance + Items not credited − Cheques unpresented

= Closing cash book balance

Items not credited appear as credits in the cash book, but have not yet been credited to the bank account.

Cheques unpresented are payments sent and therefore entered in the cash book, but not yet presented for payment at the bank. If the two totals do not reconcile, a mistake has been made somewhere.

ACTIVITY

For the next week keep a record of your own income and expenditure, or that of your family, so that you have records similar to those that a business might keep.

How difficult have you found the record-keeping?

What has it taught you about your earning and spending patterns?

✓ Review terms

Book-keeping; cash book; petty cash book; sales ledger; invoice; reconciliation.

Restoration Builders Ltd. is established

Perhaps it was just as well that the bank had not offered Fred and Harry the financial facilities they wanted. A few days later, Elizabeth Snell, a partner at the firm of accountants where Jennie worked, contacted the partners. Her father had just died, and she needed help and advice in dealing with his estate.

He had been a local farmer, and had left everything to Elizabeth. She had no interest in farming, and the farmhouse, buildings and land would be sold. Elizabeth wanted to discover the costs involved in renovating the house and selling it separately from the land.

After an inspection, the following figures were produced.

Option 1
The farm was 120 acres, which could be sold at £2,000 an acre. This would include the house and all buildings. There were no ready purchasers, and it could take up to a year to find a buyer. Legal expenses would be £5,000. Estate agency charges would be £5,000.

Option 2
A neighbouring farmer was prepared to purchase 100 acres at £1,500 an acre, and would sign a contract at once. This was just the land, and did not include any buildings.

The farmhouse and a piece of land would fetch about £50,000 in its present state. The farm buildings with some land would make £10,000. The other land would raise another £10,000 at auction. Legal expenses would total £7,500, estate agency charges £5,000 and auction costs £1,000.

Option 3
Fred thought that by spending another £75,000 on the house, it could sell, with a couple of acres of land, for about £200,000.

The farm buildings were not worth a great deal, but they could be converted into three cottages for about £75,000. Each of these would sell for £50,000.

This would still leave a large area of ground away from the houses which could be sold at a later date. Legal expenses would be £8,000 and estate agency charges £6,000.

The birth of Restoration Builders Ltd.

Elizabeth was attracted by the idea of selling the land and converting the houses. She wanted Fred and Harry to do the work because of their excellent reputation, and came up with a proposal that was to change all of their lives. She suggested that the partners and herself should form a limited company, with the three of them as equal shareholders.

The new company would renovate the farmhouse and buildings, but she would own them and take the money that came from their sale. She would sell the farm land and, in order to purchase her part of the business, she would provide the unsold area of land which would become the new yard.

The sale of the existing yard, now worth £18,000, would provide the capital for expansion. Fred and Harry would be paid a wage of £20,000 each for their work, and the profits remaining would be split equally between the three directors. They agreed that at the end of the job, they would review their positions, and see if they wished to continue to trade.

Elizabeth pointed out to Harry and Fred that the stock which they had accumulated over their years together really ought to be valued and introduced into their accounts, and any materials taken away from sites ought to have a value. They were surprised to discover that the value of these materials amounted to £20,000.

Data Questions

Foundation level

1 Explain the meaning of the following terms:

   (a) partnership
   (b) limited company
   (c) shareholders
   (d) directors
   (e) profit.

2 Showing all of your workings, calculate the total revenue if Elizabeth chose:

   (a) option 1
   (b) option 2
   (c) option 3.

3 Showing all of your workings, calculate the total cost if Elizabeth chose:

   (a) option 1
   (b) option 2
   (c) option 3.

4 Showing all of your workings, calculate the total profit if Elizabeth chose:

   (a) option 1
   (b) option 2
   (c) option 3.

5 Make a sales and purchase ledger to show the expenses and sales that would take place in option 3.

Intermediate level

1 Explain the meaning of the following terms:

   (a) partnership
   (b) limited company
   (c) shareholders
   (d) capital
   (e) stock.

2 Showing all of your workings, calculate the total revenue, total cost and total profit involved in:

   (a) option 1
   (b) option 2
   (c) option 3.

3 Prepare a sales and purchases ledger which records the undated financial activities involved in option 3.

Higher level

1 Explain the meaning of the following terms:

   (a) partnership
   (b) shareholders
   (c) capital
   (d) stock
   (e) auction.

2 Showing your method, calculate the total profit involved in:

   (a) option 1
   (b) option 2
   (c) option 3.

3 Prepare a sales and purchases ledger which would record the undated but complete financial activities involved in option 3 and transactions leading to the establishment of Restoration Builders Ltd.

Coursework Suggestions

There are plenty of views on how business records should be kept. Every book on accounts gives clear instructions, and every accountant will advise clients on what should be done. There are plenty of commercial packages available to assist record-keeping. It is interesting to wonder to what extent small businessmen take notice of these. What sort of records do they keep? Would one of the more well-established systems help control the business?

Review the standard methods, explaining the advantages and any difficulties of using the systems.

Ask a number of small businessmen about their methods of recording financial information, and analyse the answers.

Explain the principles of proper book-keeping to those who use less orthodox methods, and examine their reactions.

Find out why they use their own methods, and why they do not use the standard methods. Find out if they think that the standard methods would provide better financial controls.

4.4 FINANCIAL CONTROLS

All of the financial records described in the previous section can be used to produce information about the financial state of the firm.

The trading and profit and loss account

The **trading account** is intended to discover if, as a result of trading, a profit or a loss has been made, and how much. It relates only to the purchases of goods bought for re-sale and the sales of the same goods. Other assets (see below), like a motor vehicle, which is needed to deliver goods, is not traded, and so does not appear in the trading account.

RECEIPTS			PAYMENTS		
Date	Details	Amount	Date	Details	Amount
			3.2	Purchases	1,250
11.2	Sales	2,500			

Figure 4.8 The trading account

Therefore, the trading account at the 11th of February can be summarised:

Value of sales	2,500	
Less purchases	1,250	
Profit		**1,250**

The **profit and loss account** extends the trading account so as to include any expenses that may have been involved in the sales. It would not include the purchase of an asset such as a motor vehicle, as this has a value and can be re-sold. It would include petrol, tax and insurance, and maintenance costs, and it would also include the difference between the cost of the vehicle and its current value. This is known as depreciation (see below), and can be included because it represents an amount of money that the firm has lost as a result of its business activities.

RECEIPTS			PAYMENTS		
Date	Details	Amount	Date	Details	Amount
			3.2	Purchases	6,000
9.2	Sales	4,000	9.2	Telephone	200
11.2	Sales	5,000	9.2	Electricity	200
2.3	Sales	3,000	1.3	Delivery	600

Figure 4.9 The profit and loss account

Therefore, the trading and profit and loss account at the 2nd of March can be summarised:

Sales	12,000		
Purchases	6,000		
Gross profit		**6,000**	
Less expenses			
Telephone	200		
Electricity	200		
Delivery	600		
		1,000	
Net profit			**5,000**

The balance sheet

The **balance sheet** shows the full **assets** and **liabilities** of a business so as to show its value.

All assets need to be valued at the end of each accounting period. Machinery, office furniture, vehicles, and so on, may last many years, and so are known as **fixed assets**. The fall in value of such assets is **depreciation**.

If a firm purchased a van for £10,000, paying by cheque, it has created an asset, but by paying for the van, it has reduced its assets at the bank by £10,000, so it has really substituted one asset for another. If the van was worth only £8,000 at the end of the year, it would have depreciated by £2,000. This depreciation would appear in the profit and loss account.

In the balance sheet, the amount of depreciation is shown as a deduction from the asset:

FIXED ASSETS			
Item	Opening value	Provision for year	Closing value
Van	10,000	2,000	8,000

Figure 4.10 The balance sheet

Businesses may possess unsold stock, hold cash, have balances in bank accounts, owe money, and are owed money themselves. This can be recorded as **current assets** and liabilities.

If there is unsold stock valued at £1,000, cash of £500 in the safe, a bank balance of £1,500 and invoices valued at £2,000 are unpaid, then the current assets would be as follows.

Current assets:

Stock	1,000	
Cash in hand	500	
Balance at bank	1,500	
Sundry creditors	2,000	
Total		**5,000**

If there was also an outstanding loan of £2,500, and unpaid bills of £1,500, then the current liabilities would be as follows.

Current liabilities:

Loan	2,500	
Debts	1,500	
Total		**4,000**

A conclusion can be reached:

Net current assets   **1,000**

The fixed asset and current assets can be added together to show the full value of the firm:

Total assets   **9,000**

It should be possible to check this amount by taking the value in the previous year, and then adding or subtracting the total amount of money that has entered or left the business. This is the part of the balance sheet known as the **capital account**.

CAPITAL ACCOUNT		
Opening capital	10,000	
Add		
Profits	2,000	
Capital introduced	2,500	
		14,500
Less drawings		5,500
		9,000

Figure 4.11 The balance sheet: capital account

Thus, the balance sheet is:

Fixed assets   + Current assets
            = Capital remaining in the business

ACTIVITY 5

Use the figures from Activity 4 to produce a trading and profit and loss account for the week you kept records.

Try to produce your own balance sheet.

Financial soundness

It is possible to assess the financial soundness of a business by using several simple formulae.

The current ratio

The **current ratio** shows how readily a business could pay its current debts and is measured by:

- current assets : current liabilities.

The bigger the ratio, the sounder the firm. The nearer the figure is 1 : 1, then the less able the firm is to pay its liabilities at once.

The liquidity ratio or acid test

This is an even tighter test of a firm's ability to pay its liabilities rapidly.

The current ratio assumes that if a firm had to settle all of its current liabilities at once, the firm would not be able to dispose of all its stock at the value given to it in the balance sheet. No doubt the firm could do this over time, but not at once. Thus, the liquidity ratio ignores stock and is measured by:

- current assets less stock : current liabilities.

This asks how much money there is to pay creditors, ignoring the value of stock. A low ratio suggests that there could be too much short-term credit in the business, while a very high ratio indicates that the firm has a good reserve of long-term capital.

Credit ratios

The credit ratio is intended to show how long a firm takes to pay its bills and is:

- creditors : purchases.

If a firm has creditors owing £10,000 and total purchases of £50,000, then the ratio is 1:5. This, in itself, is not very helpful. However if you multiply the first figure by 52 (the number of weeks in a year), and divide by the second figure, the length of time taken to pay a bill is shown.

$$\frac{1 \times 52}{5} = 10.4 \text{ weeks}$$

This means that the firm is taking over 10 weeks to pay its bills. Most suppliers offer credit facilities of 30 days or less, so it may appear that this firm is finding difficulties in paying for its purchases.

The debts ratio is intended to show how long the firm takes to collect money owed and is:

- debts : credit sales.

If the figures are £20,000 on total sales of £80,000, the ratio is 1:4. If you multiply the first figure by 52 (the number of weeks in a year) and divide by the second figure, the length of time taken to receive payment is shown.

$$\frac{1 \times 52}{4} = 13 \text{ weeks}$$

This means that it takes 13 weeks to receive payment, and, as most firms offer credit facilities of 30 days or less, this suggests that the firm is finding difficulties in receiving payment for its products. Of course, the figures will differ according to the nature of the business, but if it takes longer to receive payment than to pay, the firm could be in difficulty, especially if suppliers ask for prompt payment.

Business efficiency

It is useful to consider the trend relating to the profitability of a business, so as to see if it is becoming more or less profitable.

This can be done using the **gross profit ratio** which is:

- gross profits : total sales

and the **net profit ratio** which is:

- net profits : total sales.

If net profits decline, but gross profits do not, then overheads, such as rates, must be rising.

Return on capital

This assesses whether or not it is financially worthwhile being involved in the business and is represented by the ratio:

- net profits : owner's capital.

For example, suppose a business has been valued at £50,000, and makes a net profit of £10,000 a year, then the return would be 10,000:50,000, which is 1:5 or 20%. This might seem a good **return on capital**, but if you could gain 10% interest on the capital by leaving the capital in a building society, this would give £5,000, so the real return from purchasing and running the business would be only £5,000.

Cash-flow

Profit does not always mean cash. A business may show a profit, but be short of cash. **Cash-flow** is the money coming into and going out of a business week by week or month by month. Most business is seasonal, so the flow of cash is uneven. If a customer does not pay promptly, a problem over cash may be created. In the same way, bills are not regularly spaced out through the year. It is one thing to know that, at the end of a period of time, the business will receive a quantity of cash and a large profit will have been made. However, the business needs to have paid all of its bills in order to survive to the point where it receives its cash.

Thus, a business needs to plan its income and expenditure so as to ensure that its cash-flow can support the business. A cash-flow chart shows what has happened to the money within a business, and indicates how much is available at any time.

In the example shown in Figure 4.12, Muncher's restaurant is clearly profitable over the year, but its incomings and outgoings are very varied, and this can cause problems. It may be able to rearrange some of the expenditure so as to make the business run more smoothly. For example, the bank loan is repaid every three months. Perhaps the repayment date could be changed, or the payments could be made monthly. The heating and lighting bills could be paid monthly. Perhaps the landlord would allow different payment dates for the rent.

In this way, the payments of the business could be spread out better, so as to ease the burden in particularly expensive months.

74 GCSE BUSINESS STUDIES

Cashflow forecast for Muncher's Restaurant 1996–1997

	Feb.	Mar.	Apr.	May	June	July	Aug.	Sep.	Oct.	Nov.	Dec.	Jan.
Income	10,000	14,000	20,000	20,000	24,000	30,000	35,000	30,000	25,000	40,000	100,000	40,000
Expenses												
Food and drink	5,000	7,000	10,000	10,000	12,000	15,000	17,500	15,000	12,500	20,000	50,000	20,000
Wages	2,000	2,800	4,000	4,000	4,800	6,000	7,000	6,000	5,000	8,000	20,000	8,000
Rent			10,000			10,000			10,000		10,000	
Rates			5,000									
Heat and light			20,000			2,000			2,000			2,000
R & R	4,000							1,000	2,500			
Advertising	100	100	100	100	100	100	100	100	100	100	100	100
Entertainment	200	200	200	200	200	200	200	200	200	200	200	200
Phone			300			300			200			200
Rentals	500	500	500	500	500	500	500	500	500	500	500	500
Bank charges			500			500			500			500
Insurance	2,000											
Car and travel	200	300	200	200	200	200	200	200	200	200	200	200
Miscellaneous	500	500	500	500	500	500	500	500	500	500	500	500
Loan			2,000			2,000			2,000			2,000
Total	14,500	11,400	35,300	15,500	18,300	37,300	26,000	33,500	26,200	29,500	81,500	34,200
Monthly balance	(4,500)	2,600	(15,300)	4,500	5,700	(7,300)	9,000	(3,500)	(1,200)	10,500	18,500	5,800
Cumulative balance	(4,500)	(1,900)	(17,200)	(12,700)	(7,000)	(14,300)	(5,300)	(8,800)	(10,000)	500	19,000	24,800

Figure 4.12 Cash flow forecast for Muncher's Restaurant, 1996–1997

ACTIVITY 6

Work out a trading and profit and loss account for the restaurant.

Make sensible suggestions as to how the cash-flow could be altered, and then draw up another cash-flow chart.

Use whichever financial ratios you can to assess the restaurant.

✓ Review terms

Trading account; profit and loss account; balance sheet; asset; liability; fixed assets; depreciation; current assets; capital account; current ratio; liquidity ratio or acid test; credit ratio; gross profit ratio; return on capital; cash-flow.

The company's financial progress

Within six months the work was completed and the directors were able to review their position. The sales ledger showed the following entries:

Date	Description	Amount
1 July	R. Tilley (before the renovation work)	25,000
5 Oct	E. Snell (work on farm house)	75,000
3 Dec	E. Snell (work on farm house)	75,000

The purchase ledger showed the following entries:

5 July	Materials	5,000
15 July	Drawings for Fred and Harry	6,000
31 July	Wages	7,000
6 Aug	Materials	5,000
15 Aug	Drawings for Fred and Harry	6,000
31 Aug	Wages	7,000
4 Sept	Materials	5,000
15 Sept	Drawings for Fred and Harry	6,000
31 Sept	Wages	7,000
1 Oct	Dumper truck	10,000
15 Oct	Drawings for Fred and Harry	6,000
7 Oct	Materials	5,000
31 Oct	Wages	7,000
6 Nov	Materials	5,000
15 Nov	Drawings for Fred and Harry	6,000
31 Nov	Wages	7,000
5 Dec	Materials	10,000
12 Dec	Materials and equipment for new yard	10,000
15 Dec	Drawings for Fred and Harry	10,000
31 Dec	Wages	5,000

Data Questions

Foundation level

1 Explain the meaning of the following terms:
   (a) sales ledger
   (b) purchase ledger
   (c) wages and drawings
   (d) asset
   (e) stock-in-hand.

2 Prepare a trading account for the period shown in the ledgers.

3 Add to this the trading expenses to make a profit and loss account.

4 List any capital items that are mentioned and explain the meaning of the term 'balance sheet'.

5 How successful has the firm been in this period?

Intermediate level

1 Explain the meaning of the following terms:
   (a) bank statement
   (b) positive balance
   (c) drawings
   (d) asset
   (e) stock-in-hand.

2 Prepare a trading and profit and loss account for the period shown in the ledgers.

3 Explain the meaning of the term 'balance sheet'. Use the information in the above text to produce a balance sheet.

4 Examine the success of the firm.

Higher level

1 Explain the meaning of the following terms:
   (a) bank statement
   (b) positive balance
   (c) drawings
   (d) asset
   (e) stock-in-hand.

2 Prepare a trading and profit and loss account for the period shown in the ledgers.

3 Use the information in the above text to produce a balance sheet. Outline what additional information you would require to ensure its accuracy.

4 Assess the viability of the firm. What other information would be helpful and why?

Coursework Suggestions

This is a difficult area. You are unlikely to be given accurate information by most businesses, so unless you are absolutely sure that you wish to undertake coursework in this area, and you are equally sure that you will be given the information, then don't spend any more time even thinking about it.

Idea

However, if your parents own a business, or you are equally confident about the provision of the information, then you can investigate the health of the business by studying the accounts, and applying the appropriate ratios.

You can then offer comment on the business, and, if appropriate, offer advice so that it can improve its position.

5

The External Influences on Business

The environment in which all businesses make their decisions. The factors which affect the ways in which businesses can operate.

5.1 CENTRAL AND LOCAL GOVERNMENT • 5.2 THE EUROPEAN UNION
5.3 TRADE UNIONS, EMPLOYERS' ASSOCIATIONS AND OTHER PRESSURE GROUPS • 5.4 TRAINING, SUPPORT AND ADVISORY SERVICES
5.5 PROTECTIVE LEGISLATION

This section should enable students to:
- understand the role and functions of local and central government, and the basis of their expenditure
- identify the role of the EU in business activity
- understand the role and functions of trade unions, employers' associations and pressure groups
- appreciate the extent of consumer protection available in the UK, and the UK Government's role in ensuring safety and equal opportunities in the work place.

5.1 CENTRAL AND LOCAL GOVERNMENT

In all societies there have to be rules, so some type of agency is needed to uphold those rules. In the same way, the society has to be protected from outside attack, so some form of security system is needed. The agency and its systems require organisations: people are employed to do this and administration comes into existence. The police, armed forces, and civil service need to be paid for their work, so everybody in society has to contribute through taxation.

In the United Kingdom, the role of the **central government** has changed considerably over the years as it has accepted greater and greater responsibility for the well-being of the people and control of the economy.

The role of central government

The development of the state's responsibilities is a matter of history, but they fall into four distinct categories.

- The provision of essential public services. This is the most basic government function, and cannot be performed by anyone else. It involves the maintenance of the head of state, the legislative system and provision for law and order and external security.
- The control of sectors of the economy for economic, social or strategic reasons. This may mean that some industries receive financial support, or they may be state-owned, such as the postal service. The amount of government control is a political matter, and different parties have different views on the extent of government involvement.

- The pursuit of social policies. This can involve the amount and nature of expenditure on social services, such as education and health.
- The control of the economy as a whole. This includes the maintenance of employment, economic growth, and the balance of payments.

The control of the economy is effected in two ways – through fiscal policy and monetary policy.

Fiscal policy

Fiscal policy is related to the revenue that a government collects – taxation – and the way it is spent – public spending.

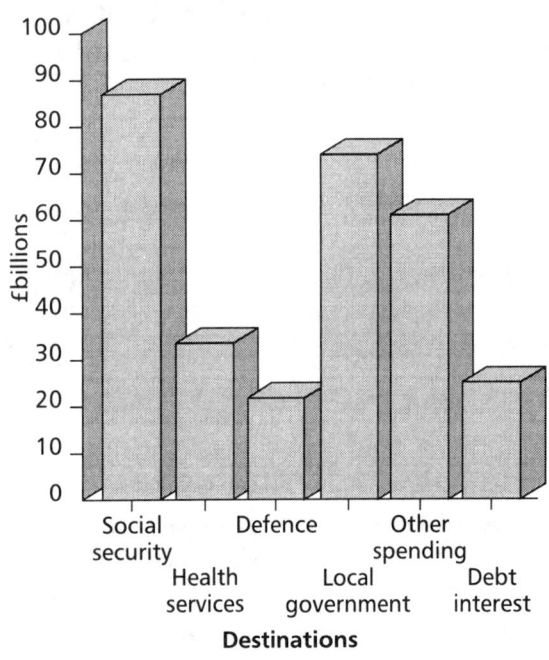

Figure 5.1 UK government expenditure

Source: *The Budget in Brief* HM Treasury, HMSO

In order to pay for its activities, the government has to obtain money from somewhere. The income of the government is called **public revenue** and comes from the general public in the form of taxation. There are two types of taxation: direct, and indirect.

Direct taxation

Direct taxation is so called because the individual pays money directly to the revenue authorities.

Income tax

Income tax, a tax on the income of individuals and firms, provides the UK Government with about one third of its income. In the UK, the more a person earns, the higher proportion of income is paid in tax. This is known as **progressive taxation**.

Proportional taxation is when everyone pays the same proportion of their income as taxation.

Regressive taxation is when the more a person earns, the smaller the proportion of taxation is paid.

National Insurance contributions

National Insurance contributions are intended to help pay for social security benefits. They are earnings related.

Capital gains tax

Capital gains tax is a tax on the profit that a person makes from selling their assets. Not all assets are included – the sale of a private house, for example, would not be considered for tax purposes – and gains below a limit are ignored.

Inheritance tax

Inheritance tax is payable on the wealth of someone who has died.

Corporation tax

This is a tax on the profits made by companies. In the same way as income tax, the **corporation tax** rate is fixed in the Budget.

Indirect taxation

Indirect taxation describes taxes on expenditure and so are paid by the individual to the provider of the good or service, who then passes the tax on to the revenue authority. It may be possible to avoid paying these taxes by refraining from buying goods and services that are taxed, but as most items are taxed, this is not likely.

Such taxes tend to be regressive, as they take a higher proportion of the income of the poor than the rich.

Customs duty

Customs duty is imposed on goods imported from outside of the European Union.

Excise duty

Excise duty is imposed on goods such as petrol, tobacco and alcohol, and produces about one third of the total revenue from indirect taxation.

Value added tax (VAT)

This is a general expenditure tax imposed on most goods, except food, and many services.

It is a system of taxation the UK had to introduce as part of membership of the European Union.

As far as the consumer is concerned, it is a percentage, currently 17.5%, which is added to the cost price of good or service. However, the process is rather more complicated, as VAT is charged at every part of the manufacturing process.

Suppose a sculptor buys a lump of rock from a quarry. The quarry charges the sculptor:

£1,000 plus 17.5% VAT = £1,175

The sculptor works of the rock and creates a sculpture of Mrs Thatcher. He sells it to a museum for:

£10,000 plus 17.5% VAT = £11,750

The quarry has produced a piece of rock which cost nothing, and was sold for £1,000, so £1,000 was added to the value of the rock, and the quarry must pay £175 in VAT.

The sculptor bought the rock for £1,000 (+ VAT) and sold it, after his work, for £10,000 (+ VAT), so he has added £9,000 to the value of the rock, and so he must pay £1,575 in VAT.

If the museum were to sell the sculpture to a grateful nation for £20,000 (+ VAT), then the museum would have added £10,000 to its value, and so would have to pay £1,750.

Other forms of income

These include income from loans that the government may have made, rent from Crown lands, and charges for goods and services such as medical prescriptions and dental treatment.

In addition, the government may itself borrow money.

ACTIVITY

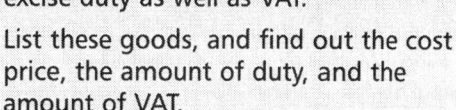

Some goods, like petrol, include an excise duty as well as VAT.

List these goods, and find out the cost price, the amount of duty, and the amount of VAT.

How much tax is there on the same product in other countries within the European Union? Why are there such differences?

Monetary policy

Monetary policy affects the amount of money that the banks and other financial institutions are able to lend. If individuals and companies are encouraged to borrow, then more goods will be bought, so more people will be employed to make the extra goods, and the economy will grow. Conversely, if borrowing is discouraged, then fewer goods will be bought, fewer need to be made, and so less people need to be employed.

Thus, monetary policy is a key instrument in the control of the economy and the level of economic activity in the country. It can operate in two ways: by acting on the liquidity of the banks and thus influencing the amount of money that they have to lend, and by changing interest rates so as to alter the attractiveness of taking out a loan.

Thus, the policy of a government at any time will have serious repercussions on the business world, with the availability and price of credit changing according to the economic climate.

The role of local government

Local government is responsible for activities that are local rather than national. However, local authorities have to act within a framework of rules laid down by central government.

The main areas of concern to local authorities include:

- consumer protection
- education, which means the operation of a system created by central government, and largely involves the building and maintenance of the schools, the payment of staff and the provision of equipment

- environmental health services
- leisure facilities
- libraries and museums
- personal social services for the elderly, infirm and handicapped
- planning permission for new buildings, or the change of use of existing ones
- police and fire services
- the maintenance, but not construction, of roads
- the provision of housing.

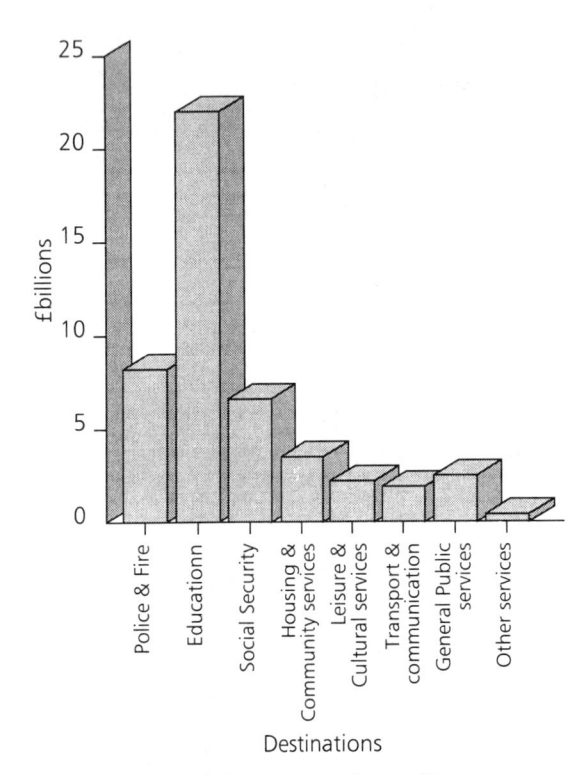

Figure 5.2 Local Government Expenditure

Local government revenue

Central government grants

Central government provides about three quarters of the money needed by local government in the form of central government **grants** and also imposes spending limits. The rest of the money is raised by the local authorities themselves.

Council tax

Domestic properties are valued and placed into one of eight categories, according to their value, and the same amount of **Council tax** is paid by the owner of each property in a band. Single occupants pay 25% less, and people on low incomes also pay reduced amounts.

The uniform business rate

Business property is valued, and the central government charges a proportion of that value each year. This is called the **uniform business rate** and is distributed to the local authorities according to their populations.

Other forms of income

These can include car park charges, admission to leisure centres, rents on council-owned property, and so on. Some local authorities try to attract business to their area by offering incentives such as low rates, and reduced rents on council-owned industrial estates.

ACTIVITY

How does your local authority affect your life?

List the council-owned amenities that you use. How many of them do you pay for? How do the prices compare with private firms who offer the same facilities?

Should the council provide these facilities free? If they did, the council tax would have to increase. Does this matter?

Review terms

Central government; fiscal policy; public spending; public revenue; direct taxation; income tax; progressive taxation; proportional taxation; regressive taxation; National Insurance contributions; capital gains tax; inheritance tax; indirect taxation; customs duty; excise duty; VAT; monetary policy; central government grants; council tax; uniform business rate.

The Budget and Restoration Builders

November approached, and Restoration Builders, like most other firms in the country, waited anxiously for the Chancellor to give his Budget Speech in the House of Commons.

Elizabeth was worried that there could be measures which would affect their trade. Newspaper pundits warned that the national recession would not be helped by the Budget.

THE FINANCIAL NEWS   13 November

Budget day blues?

The problems which face the Chancellor are enormous. Unemployment is higher than any government would like to face, but inflation is too high and the balance of payments figures show an alarming deficit.

If the Chancellor decides on tax cuts to bring about economic growth and reduce unemployment, he faces the danger of adding to the inflationary spiral and a spending spree would increase imports and worsen our trade deficit.

It is most likely that he will tackle inflation this year, and that is likely to mean further reductions in spending, which is not good news for the general public, nor is it good news for business.

Data Questions

Foundation level

1 Explain the meaning of the following terms:
  (a) the Budget
  (b) tax cuts
  (c) recession
  (d) imports
  (e) a spending spree.

2 Outline the sort of Budget that a firm such as Restoration Builders might like, and then explain how it could damage the economy as a whole.

Intermediate Level

1 Explain the meaning of the following terms:
  (a) the Budget
  (b) tax changes
  (c) balance of payments
  (d) trade deficit
  (e) recession.

2 Explain how the Budget could affect trade for Restoration Builders.

Higher Level

1 Explain the meaning of the following terms:
  (a) the Budget
  (b) economic growth
  (c) inflation
  (d) trade deficit
  (e) recession.

2 How can inflation damage a firm such as Restoration Builders?

Coursework Suggestions

Idea

Everyone has different ideas about the role of government, and the amount of government control.

List some of the main things that central (or local) government does, and conduct a survey to see how well people think they are done.

Find out how much each government service costs, so that you can tell those who are critical.

Find out how those who are critical believe the government should operate.

Governments can do whatever they are required to do, but everything costs money.

Your survey gives opinions; they need to be considered in conjunction with costs.

You should be able to collect data that will produce sensible results, and allow you to make effective evaluations.

Idea

How does the UK Government's provision of public and merit goods affect you, or your family, or your class mates, or any other group of people?

Make a list of the benefits that you receive. See if everyone is satisfied with them. See how much extra people would be prepared to pay to improve them. It is easy to express dissatisfaction with a service, but when it costs money to change, many people decide that it is not worth doing.

Thus, you can find out the benefits people receive, the level of satisfaction with them, and how strongly they feel about the need for improvements to benefits.

This would allow you to draw conclusions about how a group of people feel about government services.

5.2 THE EUROPEAN UNION

Origins

The Second World War left the countries of Europe needing to rebuild the homes and industrial buildings that had been destroyed. Industry had to change from the production of the needs of wartime to those of peace.

These tasks were made more difficult by the fact that the war had been expensive, so that no country had enough money to make all the changes as quickly as they would have liked.

In 1948, Belgium, Holland and Luxembourg established economic links, and these three joined with France, Italy and (West) Germany in 1952 to form the European Coal and Steel Community. This established a unified market in coal and steel for the six countries.

In 1956, the same six countries signed **The Treaty of Rome** to found the European Economic Community, which is now called the European Union. The aim was to move towards the elimination of tariffs among the members, together with identical import duties for other countries.

The UK did not want to join at this stage, partly because of a desire to maintain independence from other countries, and partly through ties with the Commonwealth.

Instead, the UK became involved in the establishment in 1960 of **The European Free Trade Association**, with Austria, Denmark, Norway, Sweden, Portugal and Switzerland. Finland joined later. This group's aim was the abolition of tariffs between member countries, but without the aim of a common import duty. This satisfied the wish of the UK to offer preference to Commonwealth goods.

However, trade with the Commonwealth declined, and the economies of the members of the European Community prospered, so the UK applied for membership in 1962, but was rejected. Denmark, Ireland and the UK joined in 1973, Greece in 1981, Portugal and Spain in 1986 and Austria, Finland and Sweden in 1995.

Purpose

The European Community exists to promote free trade and competition, economic integration and the harmonisation of law. A long-term goal may be political union.

The structure of the European Union

The European Commission consists of Commissioners appointed by the member governments. It administers European Union policy, including the finances.

The headquarters of the European Union in Brussels

The European Council of Ministers decides the policy of the European Union. One representative from each country attends. The representative will vary according to the subject under discussion, so as to ensure that those attending have a grasp of the issues. The heads of states will attend if the matter is of great importance.

The European Parliament has elected members from each country. It does not make major decisions, but it does have to pass the budget of the European Union, and so has some power. In 1979, the European Parliament delayed the budget, and it could use this as a bargaining tool once again.

The European Court of Justice is an international court that deals with matters of European Union law.

The European Union as a trade group

The Treaty of Maastricht was signed in 1992. Its aim was to move the members towards full economic union, with a single currency. This did not prove to be popular with the people of many of the member countries. In fact, the Danes rejected the Treaty in a referendum, and so it is uncertain whether the measures will be implemented.

The Single Europe Act 1992

The Single European Act was brought into being in 1992, and aimed to create a single market within the European Union by ensuring the free movement of people and goods within the Union. This means that there should be no customs duties charged on goods made and sold within the European Union.

ACTIVITY 3

Find out the difference between the UK Parliament and the European Parliament in terms of power and the politics of the members.

✓ Review terms

The Treaty of Rome; The European Free Trade Association; The European Commission; The European Council of Ministers; The European Parliament; The European Court of Justice; The Treaty of Maastricht; The Single Europe Act 1992.

Restoration Builders Ltd., the EU and export opportunities

Britain's membership of the European Union altered the position of the building industry. The European Council of Ministers was well aware of the recession, and its impact upon the economies of its member states. In several countries, it was the construction industry that was hardest hit. In order to attempt to alleviate the problem, the Council issued a directive stating that Value Added Tax on building materials and construction work should be suspended in all member states until further notice.

At about the same time, Restoration Builders received two letters – one from France, and the other from the USA:

THE BUILDERS GAZETTE

Boom on the way

The decision by the European Council of Ministers means that all building materials will be charged at a zero rate of VAT.

Costs will be reduced by 17.5%. Most builders are registered for VAT, and so they will be able to charge for labour at a zero rate as well. This means a considerable reduction in the costs of building work. Now is the time for the public to hire us, so it is up to us to find as much work as possible. As long as we can do the work in the promised time scales, then our trade is set to experience a boom.

Les Antiquités
27, Rue de Provence, Paris

Tel: 0039-998-776633

29th October 1996

Order to: Restoration Builders, Thornton

Please supply the kitchen set that you have advertised in the magazine 'Old Kitchens'. The advertised price is £2,500 + delivery.

I hope that you will be able to offer a trade discount of 10%. I assume that you will offer the normal credit period of 30 days after delivery. If you are interested in doing more business with us, please telephone.

British Antiques

Victoria House, 116th Street, New York City

29th October 1996

The Managing Director, Restoration Antiques, Thornton

ENQUIRY

We are a firm specialising in the sale of British antiques in north eastern America. Our trade is so good that we are now looking to buy items from the UK in order to meet market demand. At the moment, we are enjoying a strong demand for traditional kitchens and bathrooms, and we have been told that you are one of the major suppliers of suitable genuine antique articles.

We have never been involved in import-export, so we have no experience of it. Do you? Are there any problems with paperwork? What information do customs require?

We would be interested in buying a wide range of items, including stoves, fires, fireplaces, baths, hand basins, etc., and would be happy to fly over to discuss this further, provided that you feel you could meet our demand, which would be at least 12 of the above per month.

We look forward to hearing from you in the near future.

Yours faithfully,

Howard Thomas Jn

Data Questions

Foundation level

Explain the meaning of the following terms:

(a) European Union
(b) European Council of Ministers
(c) directive
(d) VAT
(e) trade discount
(f) import–export.

2 What problems would Restoration Builders have in dealing with British Antiques? Why would it be easier to trade with Les Antiquités?

3 Explain the likely effect of reduction to zero in the rate of VAT on the building trade.

Intermediate level

1 Explain the meaning of the following terms:

(a) directive
(b) market demand
(c) order
(d) zero rate VAT
(e) trade discount
(f) credit period.

2 What differences might Restoration Builders experience when dealing with British Antiques and Les Antiquités?

3 What is the likely impact on the economy as a whole of a zero rate of VAT in the building trade?

Higher level

1 Explain the meaning of the following terms:
   (a) directive
   (b) export licence
   (c) customs declarations
   (d) zero rated VAT
   (e) trade discount
   (f) credit period.

2 What are the likely financial and bureaucratic differences of dealing with a firm outside the European Union?

3 Reducing the rate of VAT within the building trade will increase demand, but this could also cause problems. Explain why.

Coursework Suggestions

Idea

How much do people in the UK know about the European Union? How much to they know about the effect on the UK economy of membership? Try to find out.

Devise a series of simple questions, such as the names of the members countries, the aims of the Union, and so on, and ask 20 people of different ages and occupations.

Analyse your answers so as to show how aware your interviewees are of the European Union.

Idea

The UK trades a great deal with the other members of the European Union.

Find a company near where you live that exports to Europe. Find out how the quantity and value of these exports has changed since we joined.

Is it easier to export to Europe than anywhere else? What are the differences? Has 1992 made any difference? What is the likely future?

5.3 TRADE UNIONS, EMPLOYERS' ASSOCIATIONS AND OTHER PRESSURE GROUPS

A pressure group consists of a number of people who want to change or influence public opinion, and, if necessary, the policy of a government. Perhaps the most obvious example is the trade union movement.

Trade unions

Trade unions are organisations of workers who have joined together to help each other gain better wages and conditions in the work place.

In years gone by, when wages were very low and working hours long, the unions were much needed. Groups of workers, acting together, were far more likely to bring about change than were individuals asking for improvements on their own.

In the third quarter of the nineteenth century, unions of skilled workers were formed, and towards the end of that century, unions for unskilled workers appeared.

Employers did not accept the unions readily, and the two sides often disagreed. Employers could threaten to dismiss staff, while the unions had their own methods of trying to force their wishes on employers.

The most severe of these was, and is, the strike, which means that the union members refuse to go to work until their demands have been met. Employers cannot make any money if no-one is working, and they still have expenses to pay, their fixed costs, so they are faced with losing more and more money the longer the strike continues.

In the late 1970s and early 1980s the amount of time lost through strikes grew, so Mrs Thatcher's Conservative Government passed several Acts of Parliament which were intended to limit the power of the unions, and so reduce the number of strikes.

The UK had certainly gained a bad reputation for strikes, but this was not altogether justified when compared with other countries.

**1975–85
Annual Average**

Holland	23
West Germany	28
France	139
Denmark	181
United Kingdom	478
Ireland	669
Italy	981

Source OECD: *Employment Gazette*

Figure 5.3 Number of working days lost through strikes per 1,000 employees

Number of trade unions

The number of trade unions has declined greatly in recent years, so that now there are now fewer than 300 trade unions in the UK, many of which do not have large memberships.

The biggest unions have been formed as the result of amalgamations between smaller union. One such is the Transport and General Workers' Union which has nearly 1.25 million members.

Most unions are affiliated to the **Trades Union Congress (TUC)**, which is the central body of the trade union movement. It holds an annual conference which decides on general policy, although the individual unions can ignore the decisions if they wish.

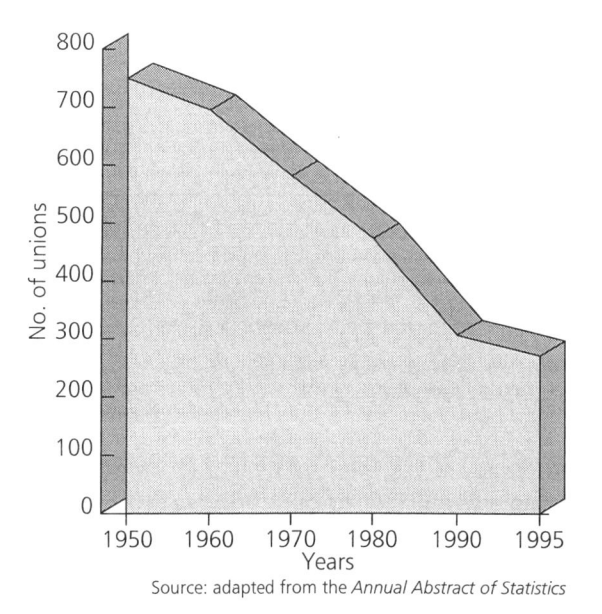

Figure 5.4 Number of trade unions 1950–1995

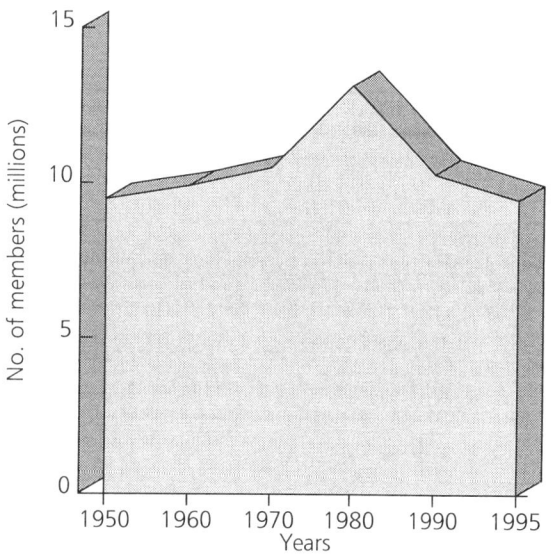

Figure 5.5 Membership of trade unions 1950–1995

Membership

The membership of trade unions has declined greatly in recent years but, nevertheless, about 40% of workers in the UK are members of trade unions. Some industries have more than this, and some less. For example, most coal miners are members of a union, but the hotel and catering industry does not have high membership. It is higher among full-time than part-time workers, among men than women, and in large rather than small firms.

Since the Employment Act 1990, an employer cannot refuse to employ someone who is not a member of a trade union. The functions of trade unions are to:

- improve the wages of members
- improve the working conditions of members
- ensure the provision of educational, recreational and social amenities for members
- influence national policy making.

> **ACTIVITY 4**
>
> Ask friends of relatives if they belong to a trade union. Find three that do.
>
> Note the names of the unions to which they belong, and the actual jobs that they do.
>
> Ask them why they are members, and if they can tell you one thing that the union has done or could do for them.
>
> Find someone who is an employer, and find out what he thinks about trade unions.
>
> Why do you think that members of trade unions and employers feel so differently about the unions?

Professional bodies

Professional bodies could be described as trade unions for the professions. The interests of doctors, for instance, are protected by the British Medical Association, while the Law Society looks after lawyers, and the Bar Council represents barristers.

Their role is to monitor activity concerning their professions, and ensure that the interests of their members are advanced.

> **ACTIVITY 5**
>
> Repeat Activity 4, but for members of professional bodies rather than trade unions.
>
> Ask the members of professional bodies what they think about trade unions.

Employers' associations

Just as employees have associations, called trade unions, so do the employers have their groups, known as employers' associations.

The most famous is **The Confederation of British Industry**. Most large firms, and many small ones, are members. It has an annual conference and regularly issues statements on behalf of its members, but it has little real power.

Many industries also have associations, to which firms within the industry belong, They give each other support and encouragement, but, again, they do not appear to have much real power.

Pressure groups

There are many other organisations within the UK which try to influence public opinion. These are known as pressure groups. They are as varied as the Lord's Day Observance Society and the National Council for Civil Liberties. They seek to educate the public, and are able to express minority views to appropriate government departments. Their opinions are often welcomed in the decision-making process because government likes to gain as much information as possible before taking decisions.

Chambers of Trade and Commerce

These exist to provide local companies with information and representations, and they are linked so as to be able to contact each other for mutual support and assistance. Most towns have a **Chamber of Trade**; some are not particularly active, with their main event a monthly luncheon. However, many others are far more energetic. The larger towns and cities have **Chambers of Commerce and Industry**, which offer wider services such as:

- business information on current market opportunities, legislation, finance and training
- advice on international trade, exporting and documentation
- trade missions worldwide
- consultancy support in management, innovation, technology, and so on
- a directory of local business
- regular seminars and workshops on current business issues.

All the local Chambers of Trade and Chambers of Commerce and Industry are connected to a central organisation, which acts as a source of information and a powerful trade body.

The Consumers' Association

The Consumers' Association is the charity which undertakes research and comparative testing of foods and services. Its trading subsidiary, Consumers Association Ltd, publishes these findings in the magazine *Which* and its other publications.

The Consumers' Association represents the consumer interest and campaigns for improvements in goods and services. It has been successful in its attempts to secure safer consumer goods and effective in achieving results on a wide range of issues including more and better information on labels, investor protection, increased competition in the market place and making suppliers of goods and services more responsive to consumers. They have published many books of interest to the consumer.

✓ Review terms

Trade unions; Trades Union Congress (TUC); professional bodies; employers' associations; The Confederation of British Industry; pressure groups; Chambers of Trade and Chambers of Commerce and Industry; The Consumers' Association.

ACTIVITY 6

You can do something very similar to Activities 4 and 5, but this time looking at other types of pressure groups.

Ask what societies, organisations and clubs people belong to. This will show that many are members of pressure groups, whether they realise it or not. For instance, most car owners are members of the AA or the RAC. They join for the obvious benefits of car repair and recovery.

However, the AA and the RAC also represent road users, and are regularly consulted by government on issues relating to transport. The size of membership is a demonstration of how seriously they are taken. Most members will not have made their views clear, but nevertheless, the AA and RAC will speak on their behalf.

When you have found out what organisations your group of interviewees have joined, trace their importance as pressure groups, and ask the members if they realise what kind of policies are represented by the organisation they belong to.

Complaints about Restoration Builders Ltd.

Sales from the yard had grown enormously. People came from miles away to find the bits that they thought would improve their homes.

All the goods were on show, and at the weekends a firm of caterers brought a van to provide refreshments for the visitors. Music was played and children's games organised so that families could visit the yard and the children would be amused while their parents inspected the wares.

This led to complaints from neighbours, because the yard was now open seven days a week, and it was felt that the traffic and the noise was inappropriate to the area. An action group was formed to try to restrict the opening hours and to see if the company's activities could be limited in any way. The group had found the local newspaper to be sympathetic and reports in the paper supported the group.

(continued on p. 90)

(continued from p. 89)

> ### THE THORNTON WEEKLY
> # The Sunday nightmare
>
> Sunday is supposed to be a day of rest, unless you live near Restoration Builders, claim residents.
>
> Non-stop traffic, blaring music, and screaming children are the main features of the weekend, says Colonel Tweed, a spokesperson for the Residents' Association. 'We moved into the country to enjoy the tranquillity, the peace, especially at weekends. Instead, the area is like a fun fair', he told reporters.
>
> The trouble comes from the sales area of Restoration Builders, which is open at weekends. They sell a wide range of antique items for the home and garden, such as water pumps, brass door sets, old fashioned stoves and stone sinks.
>
> We telephoned Harry Adams, a director of Restoration Builders who said that their work employed local people, and if the neighbours did not like it, then it was too bad.
>
> The residents complain that it is this attitude which caused the conflict.

This newspaper comment led to a crisis within the company. Elizabeth and Fred were angry with Harry. They felt that he should not have spoken to the press at all. Public relations was Fred's job. If he had had to speak, he should not have been so aggressive, so lacking in compromise.

Many of the employees were also unhappy. They were tired of the complaints, and many had reached the point where their motivation was affected. Everyone had to come to the yard at least once a day, and sometimes protesters were at the gate. This had led to several confrontations, and the police had investigated possible breaches of the peace by both the protesters and the employees.

Fred and Elizabeth were anxious to calm everything down, but Harry did not believe that this was necessary. However, they did agree to call a meeting of their employees to discuss the matter. It soon became obvious that the issue would have to be resolved, or some workers would leave and there could be a serious incident with the protesters. In addition, the bad publicity had led to the breakdown of discussions on the purchase of one property, and other vendors were worried about dealing with Restoration Builders Ltd.

Fred decided to have a quiet word with the editor of the local newspaper, for whom he had worked in the past. He explained their position, and added that he would consider withdrawing advertising from the paper if the adverse publicity continued. This was quite a considerable threat – every issue contained details of property that Restoration Builders wanted to sell, a discreet advert asking for approaches from potential buyers, a large advert offering their building services to the general public, and details of what was available from the yard. The total cost was about £25,000 a year, which represented a significant part of the paper's advertising income.

The membership of the protest group was small, as there were not many local residents, but they had gained the support of the local councillors and the town's Member of Parliament. In addition, the Lord's Day Observance Society objected to the activities on a Sunday, and the Town Council's Department of Environmental Health was monitoring the noise levels. The traffic division of the County Police Authority was concerned about the increased number of cars visiting the yard, and the increase in minor accidents in the area.

(continued on p. 91)

The directors agreed that the best way forward would be to invite all of the interested parties to a meeting, so see if some sort of compromise could be reached. They also invited representatives of the town's Chamber of Trade, of which they were a member.

Restoration Builders outlined their position. They were a local business, which, despite a national recession in the building trade, was growing. They were employing an increasing number of workers, many of who had previously been out of work. Their success meant that they dealt with other local firms, such as building material suppliers, and thus created greater local prosperity. In addition, people came from miles around to spend money, not only on their antique items, but also elsewhere in the town. They were contributing to the financial success of the area.

No-one disputed this, but the arguments from the residents and the police were powerful. Representatives of the local council suggested a compromise. There was an old school near the centre of the town which was due to close. It was a large building, and the playground could be converted into a car park. If Restoration Builders would undertake the necessary work at their own expense, then the council should be able to grant planning permission for the use of the property to be changed to the sale of old building items. This would solve the problem of the residents and the police, and it would move that part of the business into town, where other shops could benefit even more from the influx of visitors. The school could be leased to the firm at a low rent, so as to make it worthwhile.

Data Questions

Foundation level

1 Explain the meaning of the following terms:
   (a) opening hours
   (b) public relations
   (c) action group
   (d) motivation.

2 Outline:
   (a) the benefits of a firm belonging to the local Chamber of Trade
   (b) the role of a Residents' Association
   (c) the responsibilities of a local authority's Department of Environmental Health.

3 What were the main factors which persuaded Restoration Builders to seek an alternative site for their sales?

Intermediate level

1 Explain the meaning of the following terms:
   (a) advertising budget
   (b) local prosperity
   (c) recession
   (d) motivation.

2 Outline:
   (a) the benefits of a firm belonging to the local Chamber of Trade
   (b) the importance of good public relations for a firm such as Restoration Builders
   (c) the legal powers of a local authority in relation to a firm like Restoration Builders.

3 What more could opponents of the yard have done to prevent the noise and inconvenience?

Higher level

1 Explain the meaning of the following terms:
   (a) advertising budget
   (b) local prosperity
   (c) lease
   (d) planning permission.

2 Outline:
   (a) the power of a local Chamber of Trade
   (b) the problems faced by a local authority wishing to improve the environment
   (c) the role of groups such as the Residents' Association in the community.

3 What factors should a firm such as Restoration Builders consider in arriving at a policy on public relations?

Coursework Suggestions

Idea

Select a trade union.

- Find out when it was founded, and what its original aims were.
- Who has merged with it over the years?
- How has it changed in size?
- What are its current aims? How have they changed since it was founded, and why?
- What is its likely future?

Idea

Has there been a strike in your area recently? If there has, go to the library and read the newspaper articles about it.

Describe what happened, and give the different versions from the union, the employer and anyone else who wrote about it.

Why are there different accounts? Which is most likely to be true, and why?

5.4 TRAINING, SUPPORT AND ADVISORY SERVICES

Education and training

In response to complaints that our educational system did not provide industry with a suitably qualified workforce, changes have taken place in our educational system in recent years.

The Education Reform Act 1988 introduced a national curriculum to ensure that all children gained a thorough knowledge of English, Maths and Science.

At the same time, the National Council of Vocational Training was introduced to provide qualifications based on occupational competence, and today it is possible to obtain a General National Vocational Qualification (GNVQ) or National Vocational Qualification (NVQ) at various levels in many different vocational areas.

Training and enterprise councils

The Youth Training Scheme (YTS) was introduced in 1983. From April 1988, every organisation applying to participate in YTS has had to have Approved Training Organisation status. In May 1990, YTS was replaced by Youth Training, administered at local level by **Training Enterprise Councils (TECs)**.

For adults, the Job Training Scheme was replaced in 1988 by Employment Training, which rapidly attracted 200,000 participants. It offers up to a year's training, as well as training in the work place.

In 1996, there were 81 TECs in England and Wales and 22 LECs (local enterprise companies, the Scottish equivalent) in Scotland.

Each TEC has up to 15 unpaid directors, two thirds of whom are senior business leaders in the private sector, with the rest drawn from education, the public sector and trade unions. The chairman must be the chief executive or chairman of a private sector company with over 25 employees or an annual turnover in excess of £5 million. This is not a government appointment, but TECs do have contracts with government departments to deliver training and enterprise programmes. Their activities include:

- training for youngsters and adults
- business and enterprise advice for those about to set up, and support for established firms
- education of schoolchildren in work skills and the placing of teachers in industry to improve their business skills.

Business link

In July 1992 the President of the Board of Trade launched One-Stop Shops to offer a single source of business support. They were re-named **Business Link**, and backed by the Department of Trade and Industry. There are partnerships between other major support agencies, such as TECs, chambers of commerce, local authorities and private organisations such as banks.

They bring together the most important business services into one location, and seek out companies that they can help to grow.

The keys to Business Link are the personal business advisers, who encourage growth by establishing relationships with managers to diagnose problems and then produce and implement plans. The services offered include:

- business strategy
- financial management
- business regulations
- the single market
- training and development
- the Management Charter Initiative.

The Management Charter Initiative was established to encourage management training. By 1991, over 800 leading companies had pledged their support, but the initial impetus has receded.

ACTIVITY

Find out all you can about GNVQ:

(a) how many levels are there?

(b) what do the levels mean?

(c) how many subjects are available?

✓ Review terms

General National Vocational Qualifications (GNVQ); Training and Enterprise Councils (TECs); Business Link; personal business advisers; The Management Charter Initiative.

Reorganisation at Restoration Builders Ltd.

Moving sales from the yard to the old school would require significant reorganisation so Restoration Builders called in a firm of consultants to consider the changes. Restoration Builders was involved in three distinct areas of activity:

1 the purchase, renovation and sale of properties;
2 the provision of a complete range of building services;
3 the acquisition and sale of building artefacts to the public.

The consultants offered the following ideas:

1 The sale of building artefacts, whilst relying largely on items found in the building work, should be run as a separate business, with its own base and organisation.
2 The building work needs restructuring. The appointment of a full-time architect would ensure that plans could be produced as needed, and he could also undertake some site inspections.
3 The role of each director needs to be carefully defined.
   (a) Fred is happy as the front man for the company, and he is good at this, but his marketing skills need improvement.
   (b) Harry is probably the best site supervisor anyone has ever met, and he loves the role, but his wife would rather he appeared more important. This conflict needs to be resolved.
   (c) Elizabeth is only part-time, but she now appears to be the only person with the authority to buy anything. This is hindering the purchasing function, and needs modification.
4 Staffing levels need to be considered. It is clear that Jennie is over-worked, and needs secretarial assistance. A careful analysis of work sheets needs to be made, so as to discover if any other extra staff are needed.
5 All records need to be computerised. This issue is vital. A customer database must be created.
6 The company needs to develop a coherent marketing strategy. The shop needs careful attention, so as to ensure that it meets the needs of the customer.
7 Staff may need vocational training. It may be appropriate to take this opportunity to discuss with all employees their aims and ambitions. This will improve motivation, and may also indicate workers in need of training.
8 An effective communication system needs to be introduced within the firm.

Data Questions

Foundation level

1 Explain the meaning of the following terms:
   (a) director
   (b) staffing levels
   (c) work sheets
   (d) database
   (e) the needs of the customer
   (f) vocational training.

2 What part-time vocational training would be available for:
   (a) a school leaver who wants to learn a building trade?
   (b) an 18 year old, who has an 'A' Level in business studies and computing who wants to work in an office?
   (c) Fred?

3 What help might help be available for the expansion of Restoration Builders?

Intermediate level

1 Explain the meaning of the following terms:
   (a) marketing strategy
   (b) staffing levels
   (c) computerisation
   (d) customer database
   (e) the needs of the customer
   (f) vocational training.

2 What part-time vocational training would be available for:
   (a) a school leaver wanting a trade?
   (b) an 18 year old, who wants to work in an office?
   (c) a senior manager who needs specific skills?

3 What help could the local TEC offer Restoration Builders?

Advanced level

1 Explain the meaning of the following terms:
   (a) marketing strategy
   (b) purchasing function
   (c) front man
   (d) customer database
   (e) the needs of the customer
   (f) vocational training.

2 How can Restoration Builders make the best decisions on staffing levels and the training required?

3 How can Restoration Builders ensure that they are receiving the maximum amount of assistance possible?

Coursework Suggestions

Idea

Whenever there are changes in education, some employers do not seem familiar with them. Use the information that you have obtained in Activity 7, and ask a variety of employers questions such as:

- What does GNVQ stand for?
- What does GNVQ Level 2 in Business Studies mean?
- If you wanted a plumber, what qualification would you expect?

Thus, you can compose a statistical analysis of employers' awareness of these qualifications.

5.5 PROTECTIVE LEGISLATION

Consumer protection

Consumer protection legislation is designed to ensure that goods:

- correspond to their description. If they do not, the consumer is entitled to a refund, or goods that match the description, and possibly compensation
- match the sample, or a refund can be required
- are fit for the purpose for which they were supplied when the consumer relies on the skill and knowledge of the seller
- are of merchantable quality.

Trading standards officers are employed by local authorities to investigate complaints and make sure that the laws are followed.

The sale of goods

Legislation exists to ensure that when a contract is made to buy and sell a good, both sides are protected from exploitation. For example, goods should be of suitable quality.

The law relating to contracts for the **sale of goods** was originally codified into the Sale of Goods Act 1893. The latest legislation is the Sale of Goods Act 1979. The Unfair Contract Terms Act 1977 attempted to ensure that commercial contracts were reasonable. The Supply of Goods and Services Act 1982 extended the terms of the 1979 Act to contracts involving the supply of services and other areas not already covered.

Trade descriptions

The **Trade Descriptions** Acts of 1968 and 1972 attempted to prevent false descriptions of goods, misleading pricing and inaccurate statements applied to services. Imported goods should not appear to be domestically produced. The Consumer Protection Act 1987 incorporated these acts, and also dealt with the liability for defective goods.

Unsolicited goods

Some businesses started to send goods to potential customers, whether they had been ordered or not (**unsolicited goods**), and then issued invoices for payment. This practice often caused confusion, with the recipient assuming that the unwanted goods had to be paid for. The Unsolicited Goods and Services Act 1971 therefore maintained that anyone receiving un-ordered goods could ask that they be collected, and if they were not, then the goods could be kept free of charge.

Consumer credit

The **Consumer Credit Act** 1974 incorporated previous legislation relating to hire purchase, credit and conditional sales so as to attempt to prevent the exploitation of the consumer. Licences to operate consumer credit facilities have to be granted by the Director General of Fair Trading.

The Office of Fair Trading

The Fair Trading Act 1973 created the **Office of Fair Trading**, led by the Director General of Fair Trading whose role was to supervise consumer protection. The Office has two sections, one dealing with consumer affairs and the other with competition.

It also has a Policy Division, dealing with monopolies, mergers and restrictive trade practices, especially when they restrict competition.

Employment protection

There is a wide variety of legal requirements covering **employment protection** to be observed when appointing staff and, once appointed, employees have extensive rights to ensure that they are fairly treated.

Health and safety

The Health and Safety at Work Act 1974 was modified and extended by the Management of Health and Safety at Work Regulations 1992, which came into force on 1st January 1993. It set out general duties and obligations which applied to all persons at work except domestic servants in private households. The aim was to make more explicit the duties of employers, suppliers, the self-employed and employees with regard to **health and safety** and thus:

- ensure the health, safety and welfare of everyone at work
- protect the public against risks to health and safety caused by people at work
- control all dangerous substances, including preventing them being unlawfully acquired and used
- control the emission of offensive substances.

The employer must therefore maintain equipment, make sure there is no risk involved in the use, handling, storage and transport of goods, train staff in health and safety and provide a safe and healthy working environment. Employees should take reasonable care of themselves and others.

A Health and Safety Commission oversees the purpose of the Act, and a Health and Safety Executive enforces the law.

Activities classed as 'non-industrial', such as offices, shops, warehouses, restaurants and hotels are responsible to the environmental health department of the local authority. The 'industrial activities' are dealt with by health and safety officers who represent the Health and Safety Executive. Both sets of inspectors can enter any place of work to check, and have the power to:

- issue a prohibition notice to prevent an activity that is too dangerous
- issue an improvement notice to put right any breach of regulations
- prosecute anyone breaking the regulations.

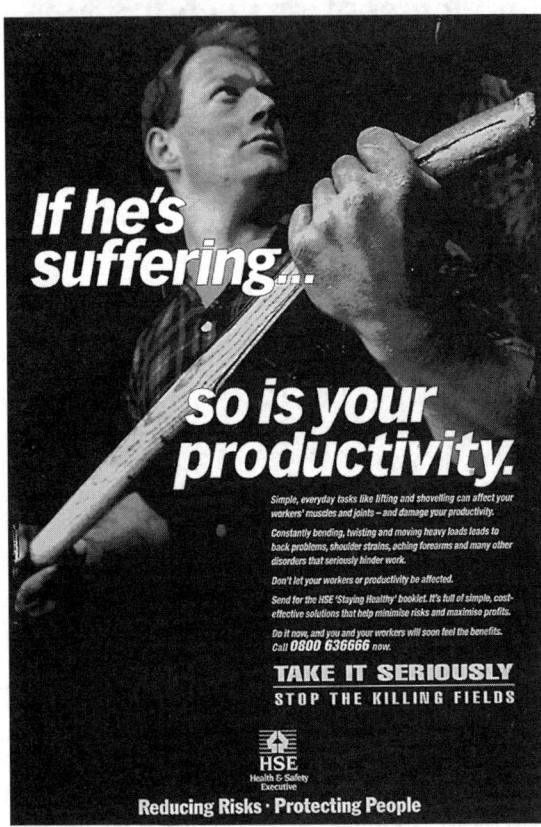

Advertising the benefits of health and safety legislation

Equal opportunities

Employers were forbidden to discriminate against existing or potential staff on the grounds of colour, nationality, religion, ethnic origins, sex or marital status, under the **Race Relations Act 1976** and the **Sex Discrimination Acts 1975 and 1986**. All cases under these Acts are brought by the **Equal Opportunities Commission** or the **Commission for Racial Equality** or the individual complainant. The Commissions may issue notices to prevent discrimination which can be enforced by a County Court injunction.

The Equal Pay Act 1970, which came into force in 1975, insisted that employers treat men and women identically in matters of wages, hours, sick-pay and holidays, where they do 'work of a broadly similar nature' in the same firm, or any firm owned by the same company.

An equal opportunities statement

The Employment Protection (Consolidation) Act 1978 defined the maternity rights of employed women. Under its provisions, women cannot be dismissed for pregnancy, and are allowed to return to their jobs at any time up to 29 weeks after giving birth.

Botticelli Group Statement of Equal Opportunity

The Botticelli Group believes that every employee should be treated with the same respect. Men and women of differing backgrounds and abilities bring value and potential to our organisation. Therefore, we encourage a culture of equal opportunities, in which success depends upon merit and performance.

There will be no discrimination against any person for any reason that is not relevant to the effective performance of the job at hand; all judgements about people for the purposes of recruitment, development and promotion will be made solely on the basis of ability and potential in relation to the needs of the job.

Every employee will be fully trained to do the job properly. And every employee will have the opportunity to develop further as a person and to pursue career opportunities consistent with ability.

Every manager and head is accountable for ensuring that this policy is put into practice fairly. Absolutely any employee who believes that there has been an act of discrimination should use the Botticelli Group's published grievance procedure to resolve the matter.

Unfair dismissal

The 1987 Act also regulated reasons for dismissal and length of notice. Workers can claim damages for **unfair dismissal** at an Industrial Tribunal if they are dismissed unfairly.

Contract of Employment

The Trade Union Reform and Employment Rights Act 1993 required that detailed written particulars of employment be provided for the employee. This document is known as a **contract of employment**.

The Employment Protection (Consolidation) Act 1978 ensured that employers make lump sum compensation payments to staff dismissed because of redundancy. Under the Wage Act 1986, staff have to be given full details of pay and deductions.

Review terms

Consumer protection; trading standards officers; sale of goods; trade descriptions; unsolicited goods; consumer credit; Office of Fair Trading; employment protection; health and safety; Race Relations Act 1976; Sex Discrimination Acts 1975 and 1986; Equal Opportunities Commission; Commission for Racial Equality; unfair dismissal; contract of employment

ACTIVITY 8

Think of any new products that you or your family have bought recently. Look at the advertisements and descriptions of them, and consider how accurate they are.

What laws do they conform to?

A customer complains to Restoration Builders Ltd.

62, Hadley Road, Hurlington

17th March 1996

The Managing Director,,
Restoration Builders Ltd, Thornton

Dear Sir

Last week I went to your shop The Old School, where I saw an old brass coal scuttle. Your assistant, Peter Yates, according to the name badge, assured me that it was Victorian and the receipt (no. 12956) includes the same description. However, I have been talking to someone who collects Victorian brass, and he assures me that it is reproduction, and worth a lot less than I paid for it. I bought it because it was Victorian, and so would like a refund. Please arrange for its collection, and the return of my money, together with £20 compensation.

Yours faithfully,

Monica Street (Mrs.)

(continued on p. 98)

(continued from p. 97)

Restoration Builders at The Old School
Internal Memo

From: M.D.
Date: 19th March 1996
Subject: Coal Scuttle, Invoice No. 12956

The purchaser of this item, Mrs Street, has complained that it is reproduction and not Victorian. She claims that you described it as Victorian, and that the invoice makes a similar claim.

Were such descriptions made?

I would also like to know who decided it was Victorian, and on what basis. If it is Victorian then we will reject her claims. On the other hand, if we misrepresented the good, then we will meet her demands.

We do not want a visit from trading standards officers, so please be even more careful when describing goods.

The Old School
Internal Memo

From: Peter Yates.
Date: 19th March 1996
To: Managing Director
Subject: Coal Scuttle, Invoice No. 12956

1. It was described as Victorian by Alisdair Oldham, who is our most experienced valuer. His specialism is Victorian brass, and he has recently published a book on how to identify the age of brass. He has a fine reputation within the trade. He still has notes on the scuttle, including the reasons for his valuation.

2. On the basis of his valuation, I did tell Mrs. Street that it was Victorian, and, at her request, I did include this in the invoice.

3. She said several times that it was a bargain, and she could sell it for twice as much. We follow company policy, and charge full market price; I would suggest that she has found out she cannot make a profit, and wants her money back.

Data Questions

Foundation level

1 Explain the meaning of the following terms:
   (a) receipt
   (b) refund
   (c) managing director
   (d) valuation
   (e) specialism.

2 If the scuttle was not Victorian, what laws might Restoration Builders have broken? What rights would Mrs Street have? What could Trading Standards do to solve the problem?

3 Using your knowledge of the legislation and the information provided, write a reply to Mrs Street.

Intermediate level

1 Explain the meaning of the following terms:
   (a) valuation
   (b) internal memo
   (c) misrepresentation of goods
   (d) valuation
   (e) specialism.

2 If Mrs Street had approached a trading standards officer, what could be done to solve the problem?

3 Assessing the information available, write a letter of reply from the managing director to Mrs Street.

Higher level

1 Explain the meaning of the following terms:
   (a) internal memo
   (b) misrepresentation of goods
   (c) trading standards
   (d) valuation
   (e) full market price.

2 What could a trading standards officer do to solve the problem?

3 Write a letter of reply from the managing director to Mrs Street.

Coursework Suggestions

Idea

Study a series of advertisements of goods and services. Find descriptions of the goods, for instance 'excellent condition', 'award winning', and so on.

Trace the description to examine its accuracy.

What redress is there if the description is inaccurate?

6

Business Behaviour

> The ways in which a business behaves in order to achieve its objectives
>
> 6.1 MARKET RESEARCH • 6.2 PRODUCT DEVELOPMENT 6.3 MARKETING AND THE MARKETING MIX • 6.4 THE PRODUCT LIFE CYCLE • 6.5 PRODUCTION METHODS
>
> This section should enable students to:
> - understand the need for market research
> - understand the importance of marketing as a concept and the marketing mix
> - identify the different stages of the product life cycle and its importance to a business
> - understand the need to develop new products and the best methods of production.

6.1 MARKET RESEARCH

If a business wishes to be successful, and it is assumed that this is the aim of every business, then it must be sure that it will sell all the goods or services that it produces.

A business cannot automatically assume that whatever it produces or provides will sell. The firm needs to find out:

- if there is market for their good or service and
- which consumers are wishing to purchase their good or service.

A further influence is the economic environment, which may affect people's ability to purchase the good or service provided.

A firm basically needs to known if there is a market for its product. What does the consumer want? Do markets exist for other products? Who are the consumers?

This kind of information is vital if a company is to be successful but it is not always readily available. Much of this information has to be obtained by the company itself, or by a specialist working for the company.

The gathering of such information is called **market research**. The purpose of market research is often defined as:

- keeping those who provide goods and services in touch with the wants and needs of those who buy the goods and services.

Sources of information

There are three broad areas in which market research can take place, these being internal information, external primary information and external secondary information.

```
         MARKET RESEARCH
           /         \
      External      Internal
       /    \
   Primary  Secondary
```

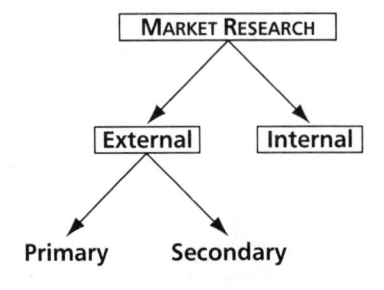

Figure 6.1 Sources of information

Internal information

Many firms have a great deal of information within their filing cabinets or on their computer files. This is **internal information** (data). It will include records of goods sold and information from salesmen and the marketing department.

This type of information is often forgotten but can be extremely valuable to an established business. However it is limited, as it only looks at the company's present situation and provides information on present customers.

External information
Secondary information

External information comes in two forms, primary and secondary. Secondary information is in the form of published materials. This is information collected not by the business who uses it but by other groups and organisations.

The value of secondary information is that it can provide a very broad picture, such as the output of the whole country, and can be added to a firm's internal data.

As technology improves the amount of secondary data continues to grow. The Internet has opened up a new and very powerful source of information, through which almost any subject can be investigated.

SECONDARY DATA:
- Government statistics
- Agencies and trade associations
- Libraries
- IT databases
- Consumer panels and associations

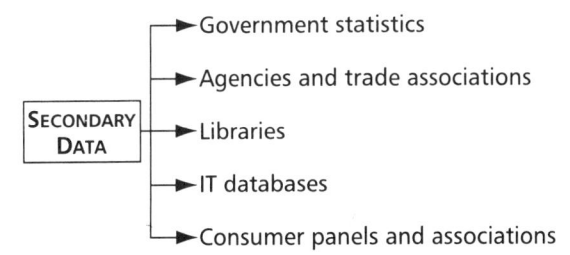

Figure 6.2 Sources of secondary information

Primary information

A major problem with secondary information is that after the data has been collected and then published it is often out of date. Alternatively it may not be exactly what the company needs.

Primary research actually involves going out to find the information needed; new and specific information that meets a firm's needs directly.

Primary information, data, is usually collected by using a **survey**. People are asked for their responses to a number of questions or issues, usually through the use of a printed questionnaire. There are two types of survey, a **census** and a **sample**.

A census involves asking questions of everyone in a particular market: an example is the national census that takes place every ten years. This method is expensive and time consuming and in most cases not very practical.

A sample involves asking questions of some of the people in a particular market, a group that represents the views of the entire market. The problem with this approach lies in selecting a sample of people that does accurately reflect everyone's views. The answers they give must be reliable and not biased otherwise the whole exercise is pointless.

There are a number of ways in which samples can be chosen; these either involve probabilities or choices made by the firm collecting the information. Some of the most common types of sample are as follows:

- **Random sampling** – the people interviewed are chosen completely at random.
- **Systematic sampling** – the people interviewed are chosen from a list at regular intervals (e.g. every tenth person on the electoral role, every fifth customer, etc).
- **Cluster sampling** – the people interviewed would be based in certain areas. For example a firm may look at its customers in the Midlands and divide this region up into smaller areas. They would then sample from one area they believe is representative.
- **Quota sampling** – the people interviewed are chosen because of certain characteristics (e.g. 50 male and 50 female; 25 aged 19 or under, 25 aged 20 to 30, 25 aged 30 to 60 and 25 aged 60 or over). Income levels or socio-economic groups could also be used.

For all these sample methods there are arguments in favour and against: two of the most powerful arguments are the cost involved and the accuracy of the information collected.

> **ACTIVITY 1**
>
> Visit your school or college library, find what information is available that would help a business. Ask the librarian for help.
>
> What government statistics are available? Can you find the average number of cars per house? The average income per house in different regions?
>
> If you set up a company selling burglar alarms, what information provided in the government statistics would be useful?

Questionnaires

The questionnaire is a very important means of collecting information. It is a list of questions designed to find out information about people's values, attitudes, opinions and beliefs.

Two types of question are used, **closed questions** and **open questions**. A closed question is one which restricts the answers of the person completing the questionnaire. The most popular closed question is the one with two answers, yes or no.

Open questions allow the person completing the questionnaire the freedom to answer the question in any way they like.

A good questionnaire should have the following features:

- be reasonably short
- only ask questions that provide the information needed
- not ask personal questions
- not be offensive
- have a logical format
- ask questions that are clear and easily understood.

Questionnaires can be completed in a number of ways: face to face, over the telephone and through the post.

The face to face contact is by far the best as it allows the interviewer the chance to explain any points that are unclear. However the interviewer or researcher can produce a biased response by the way they ask the questions or the things they say.

Telephone interviewing is now extremely popular because it is cheap and can reach a large number of people in a short space of time. The problem with this method is that many people are annoyed when they are interrupted at home and can quite easily give untrue responses to end the interview as quickly as possible.

The postal questionnaire, often found in new products, is also quite cheap but gives a variable rate of response. Some people cannot be bothered to answer the questions and others hate filling in forms.

There are other sources of primary information such as observation, recording events such as shopping habits, and opinion polls.

The costs of market research

Whilst market research is extremely valuable for a business, if it is done on a large scale by a specialised market research company it can be extremely expensive. A business needs to consider

Filling in a questionnaire face to face with the interviewer

the value of market research against its cost. How important is the research to the survival or growth of the company?

A firm could decide to use its own employees to conduct the research, as this would be much cheaper than using an outside agency. The problem with trying to conduct research cheaply is that there is a greater chance of the results being inaccurate and so the money will be totally wasted.

It is also important that a firm realises that market research is not a single operation but a continuous process. Markets and customers change over time and this must be monitored if a company is to operate effectively in any market.

Good market research will help a company to reduce the risks it takes in the market and help decision-making. It could help the firm to avoid a large loss by producing the wrong product, or producing it in the wrong shape or colour.

For small companies, market research by an outside agency is often far too expensive and they have to rely upon secondary information. This is one of the reasons why the larger companies, who can afford research, are successful.

The benefits of market research

Accurate market research can be extremely important for a business, and provide information for use in a number of different situations.

Good market research should identify a market for a business. Even where research shows that a market is swamped with suppliers, it may reveal that there are certain segments of that market still not catered for.

A market exists when buyers or sellers come together. The firm, which is the seller or supplier, needs to find buyers. Market research will identify these buyers. A market segment exists when a whole market, such as car buyers, can be broken down into smaller, more defined groups. An example would be those car buyers interested in purchasing 'off road' or 4×4 vehicles. This valuable information may provide a specialised market for the firm, a niche market.

It is not unusual for market research to identify overseas markets as well as markets at home; this includes market segments.

A very important feature of market research is that it can identify the characteristics of the buyers within a market. Socio-economic groupings are used as a means of classifying the community. These groups are:

- A and B, which represents the minority of high income groups
- D and E, which represents the low income, low skilled workers, and
- C1 and C2 which represents the upper and lower middle classes within the middle income range, often working in a profession such as nursing or teaching.

These groupings, although very general in a period of rapid social change, do give the firm a general idea of the customers to whom it can sell its goods. Knowing the characteristics of the buyers also helps to plan the way the goods are designed, packaged and marketed.

Good market research should tell the firm everything they wish to know:

- what good or service to produce
- what type of person is willing to buy it
- how the product should be designed, packaged and marketed
- where geographically the good will sell.

ACTIVITY

Try to find a copy of a questionnaire. Mark all the open questions and then the closed questions. Which questions are used more often?

Why do you think that some questions are used more often than others? Do the open questions ask for facts or opinions? Do the closed questions ask for facts or opinions? Does this explain why they are open or closed?

Produce your own short questionnaire. It could be about what your friends watch on television, or what they eat or their views on a particular topic. Get at least ten filled in and use the results to come to some conclusions. How easy was the questionnaire to produce? Did you get the results you expected?

Review terms

Market research; internal information (data); external information; secondary information; primary information; survey; census; sample; random sampling; systematic sampling; cluster sampling; quota sampling; closed questions; open questions.

Restoration Builders Ltd. uses a questionnaire

The directors decided that the most immediate task was to sort out a marketing strategy before the school was altered, so they approached Forrester and Associates, an advertising agency with a local office and a national reputation. The agency's first brief from Restoration Builders was to recommend how best to convert the old school into a shop.

The agency stated it would be able to identify the particular socio-economic groupings who used the yard most, and use this information to discover the particular needs of this market segment, so as to suggest the most suitable shop structure to satisfy these needs. The information was obtained from market research. A questionnaire asked 1,000 customers at the yard:

a) Were they single visitors, couples or families?
b) Would they buy something or were they just looking?
c) Did they use the refreshment facilities?
d) Were they looking for anything in particular?
e) How had they heard about the yard?
f) How often did they visit the yard?
g) Did they also visit the town?
h) Would they continue to come if the yard was relocated in the town?
i) What would they like from the move?
j) What sort of help would they like when looking at the goods?

The answers were analysed, and the conclusions were as follows.

Type of visitor:

Single 15%   Couple 35%
Family 40%   Groups 10%

Purpose of visit

Just looking – will buy if something attracts us 50%
Have come to buy a particular item if it is here 50%

Frequency of visit

First visit 10%   Second Visit 25%
Regular visitor 65%

Origin of visit

Newspaper advertisement 10%
Other advertisements 10%
Reputation 50%
Advice from builders, etc. 30%

Refreshment facilities

Use on this visit 50%
Use on previous visits 100%

Percentage of people using town facilities

Single visitors 1%
Couples 60%
Families 50%
Groups 100%

Relocation

100% of visitors to the yard said they would still come if it was relocated to the town. Most said that it would be a day out. Many expected to lunch in the town. Most would visit antique shops.

They hoped to find adequate parking facilities. Of those who came to buy specific items, most hoped that there would be someone who could help them. Many wanted to buy items from a particular era, and they needed reassurance that their choices were historically accurate.

Data Questions

Foundation level

1 Explain the meaning of the following terms:

   (a) market research
   (b) questionnaire
   (c) advertising agency.

2 Outline the main findings of the questionnaire.

3 What could Restoration Builders do with the information so as to satisfy the wants of the customers and also ensure that sales are as high as possible?

4 What use is market research? How good a piece of market research is the information provided?

Intermediate level

1 Explain the meaning of the following terms:

   (a) market research
   (b) marketing strategy
   (c) marketing segment.

2 What were the main findings of the questionnaire?

3 How could Restoration Builders use the information so as to satisfy customer demand and maximise sales?

4 What does Restoration Builders really want to know? How likely is the survey to provide the answer?

Higher level

1 Explain the meaning of the following terms:

   (a) marketing strategy
   (b) socio-economic grouping
   (c) market segment.

2 How would the findings of the questionnaire assist Restoration Builders in its decision-making?

3 Assess the effectiveness of the survey undertaken by Forrester and Associates.

Coursework Suggestions

Idea

Market research is a difficult task to carry out. You could try to conduct your own. Choose a topic in which you are interested and devise a questionnaire. Now take your questionnaire and interview people.

- What are your results?

The important part of this idea would be to then reflect upon your results. Are they accurate? Are they biased?

- Was the questionnaire a good one?
- How many people did you interview and why?
- Did you select a sample?

Evaluate the whole process you followed: was it a good practice or were there too many errors?

Even if this was not a formal item of coursework it would be an excellent investigation into the methods of collecting data. Your data collection for actual coursework should benefit.

Idea

Visit a local shop or small firm. Do they do any market research? Do they pay for a firm to do any market research?

- If not why not? How do they know what the market trends are?
- Has this caused them any problems with sales or changing fashions?

Offer to do some market research for them. Compare your results with what they expected. Ask how would this change their future output.

A note of caution: do not be too ambitious with this idea. A large market research project will take a long time and could make finishing your coursework quite difficult.

6.2 PRODUCT DEVELOPMENT

Business markets are very dynamic, which means that they are constantly changing. A successful business must be aware of these changes and be able to adapt to them. One of the greatest business challenges is what to do when a product comes to the end of its life (see section 6.4), market research is often able to alert firms to the fact that a product is becoming out-of-date.

Product development is not just concerned with the creation of new goods or services; more often it aims to change those that already exist.

The definition of product development is:

an activity leading to a product having new or different characteristics or consumer benefits, ranging from an entirely new product to the modification of an existing one.

Changing the characteristics of a product can involve anything from altering its design or the colour of its packaging to after-sales service (see section 6.3).

Whenever the development of a product takes place there is a process involved, a number of stages through which the company must go in order to ensure that the changes are successful.

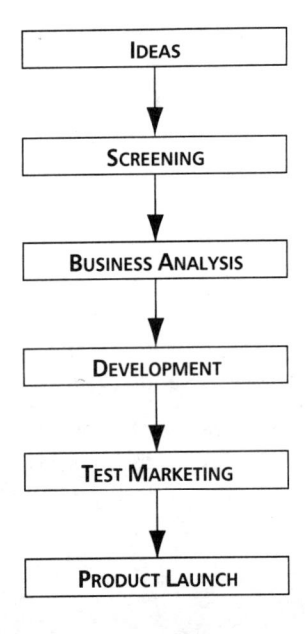

```
       IDEAS
         ↓
     SCREENING
         ↓
   BUSINESS ANALYSIS
         ↓
    DEVELOPMENT
         ↓
   TEST MARKETING
         ↓
   PRODUCT LAUNCH
```

Figure 6.3 Product development stages

Ideas

The first stage in the development process is when new **ideas** for prodcts, or **product changes**, are created. These can come from several sources.

Market research is one on the most common sources for identifying the need for new products or changes to existing ones. Testing the market to see what the consumers want often throws up new ideas for products. Equally, a firm may often find that a product that they thought was selling well could sell even more if modifications were made.

Research and development (R and D) is another source of new ideas. Large firms such as ICI spend huge amounts of money on R and D. An army of researchers devote all their time trying to devise new products or looking for ways to improve existing ones. The soap powder industry is a classic example of this; they have new and improved powders, liquids, stain digesters, colour powders and liquids, biological powders and so on.

Some firms have **brainstorming** sessions or a creative ideas department. The creative ideas department would monitor trade journals, look at changing statistics such as demographic trends, and put forward ideas for new products.

Screening

Not every idea for a new or improved product will work. It is therefore necessary to have this second stage to evaluate the ideas and decide which ones to accept and which ones to ignore. The **screening** stage involves a checklist of questions which need to be asked if the idea is to be successful.

Such questions could be as follows.

- Is the product or service legal?
- Does the product or service fit in with the company's objectives?
- Does the technology exist to produce the product or service?
- Does the company have the technology to produce the product or service?
- Can the product or service be easily promoted?
- Is there a large and growing market?
- Is there any competition in the market?

These are just some of the questions that could be asked, producing a checklist. The answers to these questions could then decide which ideas would be accepted and which would be rejected.

Business analysis

The third stage of the process is to **analyse** how successful those ideas that have been accepted are going to be. At this stage a business will analyse things such as the potential sales, the costs of production, the strength of the market and any similarities between the idea chosen and past products.

Even though an idea has been chosen it will not necessarily be successful, or as successful as the company wants it to be in order to recover all the money that has to be spent on a new project.

The screening stage will sort out the ideas that are acceptable from those that are not; and the analysis stage will put the acceptable ideas into an order of priority and separate them according to the potential profits that they can make. The most profitable ideas will then go on to the next stage.

Market research could again be part of this stage, investigating potential sales, size and growth of the market.

ACTIVITY 3

Make a list of all the new products that have come onto the market in the last year. They must be completely new!

Now make a list of products that have been altered, changed or added to, for instance new, bigger size, new improved and so on.

Now compare your two lists. Which is the greater? Why do you think that one list is longer than the other?

Development

The fourth stage is to take an idea and develop this into a product. This will involve the work of the R and D department. It could mean the design and building of **prototypes** or models, technical developments in a laboratory and possibly the testing of the product under controlled conditions.

Some testing with potential consumers may also take place but this would be carefully controlled.

Test marketing

For many products the costs of launching a product nationally are so high that **test marketing** is the ideal solution. It reduces the risks and the cost of failure, in some cases saving firms millions of pounds.

The greater the amount of money put into the new product, the firm's investment, the greater the need for thorough testing. Also the more original the product the greater the need for testing.

There are a number of ways that test marketing can be carried out. Representative towns and cities can be selected and the product sold to shops and wholesalers in the normal way but only in this restricted area. Full promotional campaigns would be used. This process is often used by large national retailers; they test a new product or design in one of their large stores and then decide if it is to be sold in all of their stores.

A further method is to get a selection of stores to agree to sell the new product. The number of stores and their geographical location can be decided. At the end of the agreed period the sales are assessed.

The launch

The final problem is the **launch** of the product, the **commercialisation**. At this stage the problems of development should have been solved and all the information obtained during the test marketing should have been used to improve and refine the product.

The major decision at this stage is 'what is the best way to market the product?' This is very important. A good product, successfully tested but badly marketed, could fail. Marketing is yet another cost, often running into millions of pounds, and needs to be carried out properly.

Timing is extremely important, as is the location of the launch. Most firms choose particular cities and then spread around the country. Other launches start in a region, such as the south east, and then spread to other regions.

Whatever the strategy adopted, it is important to remember that the launch, the marketing, of a product is as important as the product itself which in turn is as important as the market research that first indicated that a need or such a product existed.

The launch of Vauxhall's Vectra
By kind permission of Vauxhall Motors Limited

Launching the product: the very best way to enter the market

The launch of Lever Brothers' Domestos Multi Surface Cleaner
By kind permission of Lever Brothers Limited

ACTIVITY 3

Use your list of new products from the previous activity.

How did you know about the new products? Was it through advertising and promotion, did you just discover them or did someone recommend them?

Do the same exercise for the new improved products you listed. Are there any conclusions you can gain from your observations?

Can you think of any products that were launched but were unsuccessful, for instance the Sinclair C5. Can you make any suggestions as to why these products were unsuccessful?

✓ Review terms

Ideas; product changes; research and development; brainstorming; screening; analyse; market research; prototypes; test marketing; launch; commercialisations.

Recommendations based on the questionnaire at Restoration Builders Ltd.

Forrester and Associates
Marketing and Advertising Consultants

Client: Restoration Builders Ltd., Thornton

Report: The development of the Old School into an antique artifacts establishment

Introduction: Many firms seek to expand their activities by product development, but it is not possible to produce new or modified antiques. However, it is possible to sell a wider range of products, and to modify the method of selling. It is on these two areas that we recommend you concentrate.

The questionnaire which we undertook for you some time ago made clear what the public wants, and so we are confident that the following suggestions are worth your while to screen. If you are happy with the principles that we have proposed, then we would undertake a full business analysis before you proceed. Although this will take a little time, and may appear to be costly, it will ensure that, from its launch, the Old School Shop is able to meet customer demand.

1. Classify the items and have individual rooms for each category. This will make it easy for customers to find what they want, and for those just looking to decide if they are interested or not.
2. Ensure that someone is in charge of each room and has some idea of the history of the items. This will require training.
3. Employ someone with expertise in the area of old building materials and associated antiquities. This could be full or part time to begin with. Although fairly expensive, it would ensure that the items sold were authentic, and this would increase the reputation of the shop. The service could be supported by the use of famous experts at the weekend. This would generate good publicity and large crowds; many of these people would probably not buy anything initially, but some are likely to return on another visit as purchasers.
4. Refreshments are needed. It is suggested that coffee, tea and snacks be offered in the first instance, in an old-fashioned room so as to emphasise the nature of the business. A small museum which would amuse children could be included.
5. Liaise with local antique shops. Find out their specialisms, so that you can direct customers to them – and they can then send people to you in return.
6. Use another room as a showroom to show the types of kitchens and bathrooms that you can create.

Data Questions

Foundation level

1 Explain the meaning of the following terms:
   (a) product development
   (b) questionnaire
   (c) screen
   (d) business analysis
   (e) customer demand.

2 Outline the various stages of product development and explain the role of each stage.

3 How sensible are the suggestions proposed by Forrester and Associates?

Intermediate level

1 Explain the meaning of the following terms:
   (a) product development
   (b) launch
   (c) screen
   (d) business analysis
   (e) specialism.

2 Outline the various stages of product development and explain the role of each stage as it relates to the development of the Old School Shop.

3 How appropriate do you consider the suggestions made by Forrester and Associates?

Higher level

1 Explain the meaning of the following terms:
   (a) product development
   (b) launch
   (c) screen
   (d) business analysis.

2 Relate the various stages of product development to the development of the Old School Shop.

3 Critically assess the proposals made by Forrester and Associates.

Coursework Suggestions

This is an extremely difficult area to investigate and is best avoided. To produce a successful item of coursework for this area you would need to get a firm to agree to you investigating one of their new products at one of the stages listed; this is very unlikely.

Equally unlikely is that a firm will discuss why one of their products has been unsuccessful. The result is that your information will all be secondary and based largely on guesswork.

If you insist upon following this as a coursework topic, then consult your teacher and continue to consult him or her at every stage of your work.

Idea

Some possible approaches might be to look at a product that was launched and then disappeared quickly. Why was this so? What were its initial sales? How long did it last? What did people think of it?

Idea

Look at a 'new improved', 'new larger size' product. What do people think about the changes? Have these changes improved sales? How would people change the product if they could? Has it improved the product or is it a sales gimmick?

6.3 MARKETING AND THE MARKETING MIX

Marketing is not advertising, as many people believe, nor is it market research or selling. Advertising, market research and selling are part of the marketing activity of a company but not the whole process.

Marketing is a whole company philosophy, which affects every part of a business and every person with a business. Simply stated, marketing affects everyone.

A very simple definition of marketing is that it is:

providing the right goods at the right price in the right place at the right time.

However, this is very basic and not very accurate. A better definition is provided by the Chartered Institute of Marketing.

'Marketing is the management process responsible for identifying, anticipating and satisfying consumer requirements profitably.'

Marketing puts the consumer at the centre of a company's activities. It is about discovering the needs of the consumer, identifying needs, and satisfying those needs in a way that earns the company as much profit as possible. Part of identifying consumer needs is to realise that these needs change over time. Marketing should therefore anticipate any changes, now and in the future, in order to continue to satisfy the consumer.

Marketing has become even more important to businesses over the last 40 years. Greater competition, the rapid growth in technology, constantly changing fashion and trends, emphasised by television and newspapers, along with an increase in people's income, have all increased the need for a business to have a good marketing policy.

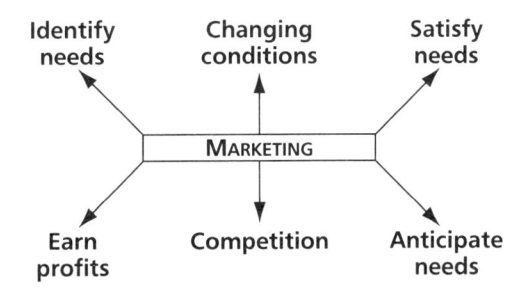

Figure 6.4 The marketing environment

The marketing process

The **marketing process** of a company is a continuous system. It starts with **market research** and **product research**, to find out what the customer wants and needs.

The next stage is to decide upon a plan. This will include the company's objectives and a plan for the company's marketing activities.

The next stage is to put the plan into practice, organising all the activities.

The final stage is to check constantly that the plan is operating properly. This provides feedback, further information to be added to the market research that continues to take place.

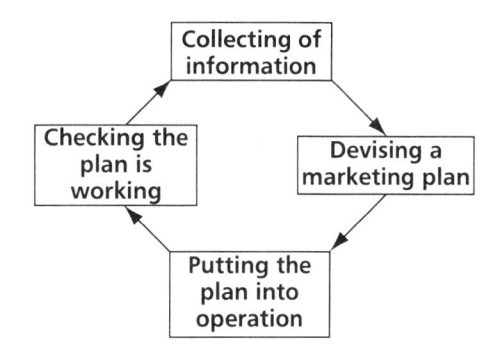

Figure 6.5 The marketing process

The objectives of marketing

The marketing objectives of a company should also be the business objectives; marketing should enable the company to achieve its objectives. Any marketing objectives should include some of the following:

- to target a market or part of a market, a **market segment**
- to maintain or achieve a certain **market share**
- to develop a range of products
- to improve the image of the products or the company as a whole.

These objectives are naturally linked and in trying to achieve one it is possible, and desirable, that others are achieved at the same time.

The four Ps

Effective marketing should produce the right product, at the right price, at the right time in the right place. In order to achieve this the four Ps, **Product**, **Price**, **Promotion** and **Place**, are important.

The product is everything from the design, and including the packaging, through to the after-sales service and guarantee.

The price must take into account the competition and the demand for the good by the consumer. If the consumer is not prepared to pay the price then it is wrong.

Promotion includes everything that is normally thought of as marketing, sales promotions, advertising, free gifts, trials and so on.

The final P, place, is equally important. If the good is not available at the right place, shop or city, then it will not sell.

ACTIVITY 5

Identify three or four new products. Ask your family or teacher if they can do the same. Compile a list of ten products that have been introduced in the last five years.

Take your list and place these goods into three columns: changing needs, changing technology and changing tastes and fashions. So, for example, was the development of 'Internet' due to changing needs or technology, or both?

Environmentally-friendly products are now produced by almost all companies. Consider how this movement started: was it the company's idea or was pressure applied from elsewhere? Discuss this with a friend or your teacher. Does this mean that a company's marketing can be deliberately changed?

Product

The concept of a product goes well beyond what most people see. There are certain tangible features to a product such as:

- shape
- colour
- size
- design and
- packaging.

There are other features of a product such as any guarantee, after-sales service, the availability of spare parts and the customer care policy.

There are also several intangible benefits. These include the reliability of the product and the reputation of the company or brand.

A consumer does not buy a product for a single need. A product is purchased for a range of features that meet a customer's needs. The range of factors is known as the **product concept**.

Companies themselves often produce a range of products, known as a **product portfolio**, to cover as many of the consumer's needs as possible. For example car manufacturers often produce small cars as well as estates and large luxury models.

Price

The price of a good is the amount of money that has to be given up to own the good, or use the services offered. This is possibly the most complicated of the four Ps. It is not always a straightforward decision.

The price set will depend upon a number of factors (see Figure 6.6) and will be different in different situations. For example, a new product might be priced differently to one that has been on the market for a long time.

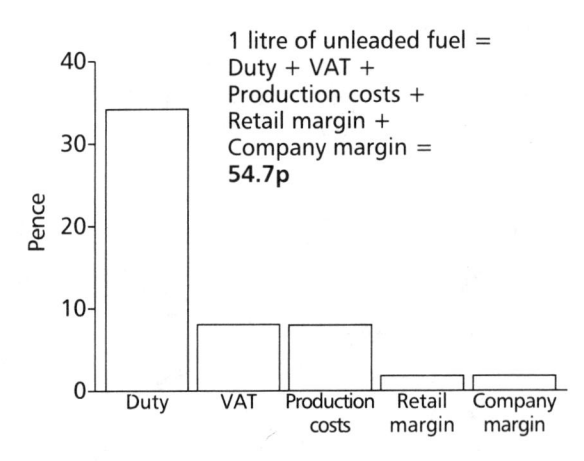

Figure 6.6 The factors affecting price – the price of petrol

To begin with, the company must decide what it wants to achieve. Is it:

- maximum profit
- a return on its investment in developing the new product
- to be competitive?

The price may be influenced by the government, the competition, shareholders, employees and retailers.

The pricing policy used by the company can be short term or long term. Long-term pricing policies include **cost-plus pricing** and **demand-orientated pricing**.

Short-term pricing policies include **promotional pricing**, **destroyer pricing** and **price skimming**.

Promotion

Promotion is about the process of communication. The process of promotion is to send messages to consumers through the media, and by other means, to create awareness and understanding of why they should, or might wish, to purchase a particular good or service.

The way in which this message is sent will vary according to the type of message and the intended audience, the market. Promotion involves a strategy, a **promotional mix**. A popular way of describing this mix is to use the letters AIDA.

- A – a customer's **attention** is captured and they are made **aware** of the product.
- I – an **impact** creates an **interest**.
- D – the customer is persuaded that they need the good so creating a **desire** or **demand**.
- A – **action** is taken: the good is actually purchased.

The methods that a firm can use to promote its goods and services are many and varied. **Advertising** is the most common method used.

Advertising itself can be done in a number of different ways.

- **Printed media** forms the largest sector of the media in the UK. This sector includes all newspapers, magazines, the trade press and professional publications and thus allows consumers to be targeted. However all adverts are static. They rely on printed words and pictures, often only in black and white.
- **Broadcast media** includes commercial television, commercial radio and, more recently, satellite television. Advertisements can therefore be dynamic, with coloured moving images and/or a dialogue. The drawback is that this media is expensive.
- **Outdoor media** includes billboards, advertising on buses and trains and posters. Again they are static but they are also cheap and can provide an image that is repeatedly seen day after day.
- **Direct mail** and film trailers in **cinemas** provide other means of advertising.

Apart from advertising, **sales promotion** is a method of attracting a customer's attention. This type of promotion would include free samples, trial packs, coupons, competitions, price reductions and charity promotions.

A more recent addition to methods of promotion has been **telesales**. People are employed to discuss products with, and make offers to, customers over the telephone.

ACTIVITY 6

Visit your local superstore or shop. Look at the different types of promotion that exist. Make a list of as many different types as you can find.

Which is the most popular type of promotion? Why do you think this is so?

Choose ten items that you or your parents have purchased recently. They can be large or small items, but a mixture would be best. Make a list of the reasons why they were purchased but ignore price and promotion. Which is the most important feature of a product in your house?

Place

'Place' refers to getting the goods to the right place at the right time. The method of distribution is therefore very important. Place is about the distribution method that the firm uses.

When discussing the distribution for any good there are a number of choices.

To begin with should the goods be transported via road, rail, air or by boat? For some goods the answer is obvious but this is not always the case. Air transport is very quick but expensive. Using the rail network is relatively cheap but limited by the freight lines available. Road transport seems to be a favourite; it is relatively cheap and the road network in the UK is good.

Once the method of transport has been decided the next decision is how will the goods reach the consumer? Here there are several different options.

- The goods can be sold directly by the **manufacturer**. This can be done via mail order, factory shops and so on.
- A second alternative is to sell the goods to a middle person such as a **wholesaler**. The wholesaler then sells them on to a retailer or directly to the public, such as the Makro chain.
- Some independent retailers, such as VG, Spar, Mace and Happy Shopper, have formed their own wholesale organisations, and buy from the manufacturer to supply their own shops.
- The goods can be sold directly to the **retailer** without a middle person.
- Finally, the goods could be sold to an **agent** who would then sell either directly to a retailer or on to a wholesaler.

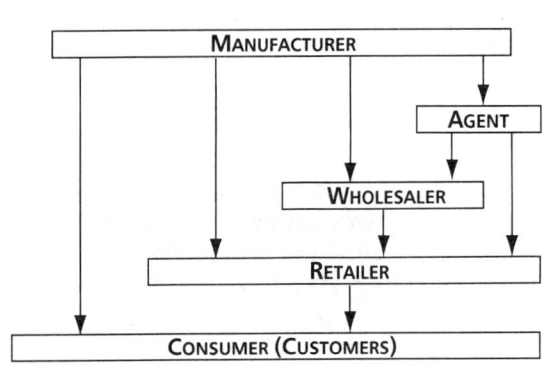

Figure 6.7 The distribution process

The marketing mix

The elements of the four Ps, product, price, promotion and place, all have a different scale of importance depending upon the product that is being sold.

A business must make decisions upon each of the elements, such as what pricing policy to use and how to promote the product, and must also decide which element of the four Ps is the most important. This is the true meaning of the marketing mix.

For some products the price, and therefore the pricing policy chosen, is the most important. This would be the case in a highly competitive market. However for other products promotion would be the most important. This would occur in a market where the price was as low as possibly, or where firms do not wish to compete on price.

For a product such as a Rolls Royce neither price nor promotion are important. In this case the product is by far the most important element in the marketing mix. Price in this case is possibly the least important.

It might even be the case that all the elements are equally important.

The successful business, with a successful marketing policy, will know which of the four elements is the most important and which is the least important. If they get the mixture wrong and concentrate upon promotion when the product is the most important element, then their marketing policy will fail. They will not sell as many goods as they want to and ultimately the company will not be successful.

Figure 6.8 The marketing mix

ACTIVITY 7

Try to find one product that is distributed using each of the methods shown in Figure 6.7. Is there a difference in the prices charged? If so, why?

Use the ten items you chose in Activity 6. Now state which of the four elements is the most important for each product.

For each product place all four elements in order of priority, that is the most important first and so on. Can you find any reasons why they are in this order?

Restoration Builders Ltd. decide on the organisation and marketing of their Old School Shop

Forrester and Associates' recommendations were accepted by Restoration Builders, and eventually the Old School Shop was established as a centre for the sale of building artifacts. It was altered and stocked so as to meet public demand.

The main products sold were furniture, fires and fireplace equipment, brass items, bathroom goods and kitchen items, and so five rooms were devoted to each of these, and a sixth room for everything else and an assistant was recruited for each. They each had specialist knowledge of their range of goods.

Cecil Mountford, a local history teacher who had taken early retirement, was appointed as the full-time expert. He had always been interested in old buildings and their contents, and had attended courses at the local college to improve his knowledge. He was prepared to accept a fairly low wage, as he was excited at the prospect of doing the job, and his pension meant that he was not short of money.

The prices were to be decided by each assistant, and checked by Cecil. They were to discuss any disagreements, and should refer to the general manager only if they could not agree.

He used his teaching experience and knowledge of his young grandchildren to help design and equip the refreshment area with attractions of particular interest to children.

The opening had to be one that people remembered. Forrester and Associates suggested that the promotion of the shop should include:

- regional newspaper advertising
- advertisements in specialist journals and magazines so as to create a wider audience among people interested in the goods
- leaflets delivered with the local newspapers to ensure that everyone in the area was aware of the change
- a celebrity from the world of antiques to open the new shop. This last item would attract local, regional and perhaps even national publicity. Obviously, the extent of the reports in the press an on radio and television would depend upon world events, but should be worth much more than the fee of the celebrity.

Review terms

Consumer needs; marketing process; market research; product research; market segment; market share; product; price; promotion; place; product concept; product portfolio; cost-plus pricing; demand-orientated pricing; promotional pricing; destroyer pricing; price skimming; promotional mix; AIDA; printed media; broadcast media; outdoor media; direct mail; sales promotion; telesales; manufacturer; wholesaler; retailer; agent.

Data Questions

Foundation level

1 Explain the meaning of the following terms:
   (a) public demand
   (b) specialist knowledge
   (c) newspaper advertising
   (d) leaflets
   (e) full-time work.

2 What are the four parts of the marketing mix? Identify each part of the marketing mix from the text above.

3 Design the advertisements promoting the Old School Shop for the local newspaper and a specialist journal. Why are they different?

4 Design a leaflet for the shop, and then explain how you decided what information to include, and why the leaflet is different from the advertisements.

5 Do you think the idea of using a personality to open the shop is a good one? How would you make sure the event received maximum publicity?

6 How good do you think Forrester's ideas on advertising will be? How could you find out if any of it worked?

Intermediate level

1 Explain the meaning of the following terms:
   (a) public demand
   (b) specialist knowledge
   (c) newspaper advertising
   (d) pension
   (e) early retirement.

2 Identify and explain the various parts of the marketing mix in the text above.

3 If you had to design the Old School Shop advertisements for the local newspaper and a specialist journal, how would you make them different and why?

4 Design a leaflet for the shop, explain how you decided what to include, and why the leaflet is different from the advertisements.

5 Is the idea of using a personality to open the shop a good one? How would you maximise publicity for the event?

6 Assess the likely effectiveness of the advertising proposed by Forresters and suggest how you could measure this.

Higher level

1 Explain the meaning of the following terms:
   (a) public demand
   (b) specialist knowledge
   (c) newspaper advertising
   (d) specialist journals
   (e) early retirement.

2 Apply and explain the elements of the marketing mix as it relates to the Old School Shop.

3 If you had to design the Shop advertisements for the local newspaper and a specialist journal, and also a leaflet, how would you make them different and why?

4 Is the idea of using a personality to open the shop a good one? How would you maximise publicity for the event?

5 How could you assess the effectiveness of the advertising?

Coursework Suggestions

Idea

Imagine that you have a new product to put onto the market. This could be a new soap powder, a new piece of computer software, a new car, in fact any product that you wish.

Now consider how you would market this product. What marketing mix would you use and why?

Consider the competition in your market. What is the most important feature? How large is the competition? Are there any special features in this market?

Consider all these factors, and more, and design your marketing policy. Make sure that you state all your research and observations and give reasons for your policy.

Idea

How do local businesses promote themselves? If possible find a local business that will help you. Look at their promotional methods and see if you can improve upon them.

Look at the present methods and cost them. Then look at the alternatives and produce a promotional package for these methods.

How many extra sales might your ideas produce? Could the firm afford your ideas? Do not forget to ask customers why they buy the product or use this company. Will extra promotion make any difference? Try to work within a sensible budget.

6.4 THE PRODUCT LIFE CYCLE

When a business produces a new product and intends to sell in large numbers for a very long time, it should provide the company with a stream of revenue and profit.

The problem is that not all products are successful and even if they are, many are only successful for a short period of time and then seem to disappear or go out of fashion.

Everyone can remember the Sinclair C5 and skateboards; both were popular for a short period of time. Equally we all know of CDs and CD players; both are still very popular.

The length of time a product exists in the market is determined by **demand** for the product which in turn is influenced by fashion and trends, income, the availability of substitutes and so on. New products are constantly entering the market and so take some of the sales away from the old established products. Some old products will disappear as new products are introduced.

This means that every product has a life span. This life span starts when the product is first sold onto the market and ends when no-one wishes to buy it any more. This is known as the **product life cycle**.

The life cycle of a product can be split into four distinct stages: **introduction**, **growth**, **maturity** and **decline**.

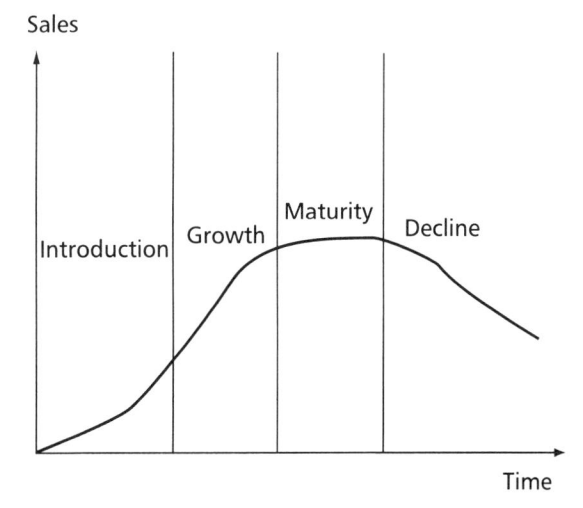

Figure 6.9 The product life cycle

The introduction stage

This is the point at which the product is first put onto the market. The product is new and few people know that it exists. This is the point of time when promotion is very important. Sales will be low but very gradually increasing. Profits will also be quite low; the firm might even be making a loss. During the introductory stage the firm will be trying hard to establish the product in the market and trying to recover some of the money that it has paid out on developing the product.

The growth stage

This is the point at which the product begins to take off. Sales begin to increase quite rapidly, with each increase being greater than the one before. Consumers are aware that the product exists and it begins to gain a good reputation.

Profits will increase during this stage, or if the product was previously making a loss this will now become a profit. The expenditure on promotion will decline as the product becomes well known and more of the development costs, if not all, will be recovered.

The increase in sales during this stage of the product's life will enable the firm to produce on a larger scale and benefit from **economies of scale**. This will result in even larger profits. The success of the product during this stage, as well as news of the increasing profits, will attract new companies with similar products into the market.

Towards the end of this stage the growth of sales will begin to slow down as there will be fewer and fewer new buyers in the market. Sales will still increase but at a slower rate.

The maturity stage

This stage naturally follows on from the slow down in the growth of sales experienced in the growth stage. At this stage sales will level out. Very few, if any, new consumers will enter the market and there will be a great deal of competition from similar branded products. Many firms will be competing in the market for the same customers, all with products that have minor differences.

This is the stage where the less successful competitors will go out of business. The market will not be able to take any further products of the same type; the market is said to be **saturated**.

The decline stage

Towards the end of a product's life, sales will start to decline. There are several reasons for this: changes in consumer tastes and fashions, the introduction of new technology and competition, often from overseas.

A decline in sales will mean that too many products are being produced and prices and profits will need to be cut. Some firms will leave the market and stop producing the product. Weak products often take up a great deal of a firm's time and so it is not profitable to continue to produce them at this stage.

Extending the product life cycle

The life cycle of a product may last for a few months or for many years. The Betamax video and eight-track tapes are examples of short life cycles whilst Mars bars are an example of a very long life cycle.

A firm does not have to accept the life cycle of its product. It can do various things to try to lengthen the product's life.

The way to extend the life of any product is to try to make it appear as if it is different or new. If the consumer believes that this is not the same old product they will again be interested and purchase the product.

Whatever a company decides to do in order to make the product appear to be different, and so extent its life, it will need to change its **marketing mix**. This may mean changing the emphasis of the marketing mix or changing parts of one or all of the elements of the mix. Possible changes in the marketing mix might include:

- changing the product; this could include minor design changes, alterations in the packaging or colour, longer guarantee periods or better after-sales service
- changing prices to match the competition; possibly even better finance deals, for instance 0% finance
- altering the pattern of distribution, selling in different types of retail establishment
- changing the style of promotion, possibly emphasising the reliability of the product or the image of the company.

Any or all these methods could be used. They could also be used at different stages. The most common turning point is towards the end of the growth stage, when the growth of sales begin to slow down and firms begin to feel that new life is needed. This is the time when we hear of 'new improved' this or 'bigger' that or the 'new shape'. The other time to rejuvenate the product is during the maturity stage; however, many firms feel that this is too late.

ACTIVITY 8

Produce a list of products that you use. Try to estimate at which stage in their 'life cycle' they are at present.

Produce a list of all of the ways a company can use to extend the life of a product. Now try to find ten products that you know of that have had their lives extended. Match the methods you listed to the ten products chosen.

The product portfolio

If a company has only one product on the market and that product comes to the end of its life, then that company will be in trouble unless it can extend the product's life. It may not be able to do this forever and so eventually the company will close down.

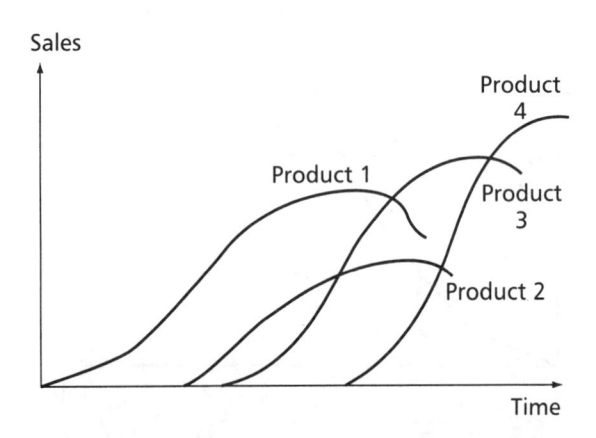

Figure 6.10 The product portfolio

An alternative is that the company has a range of products on the market; all at different life cycle stages. This is known as a **product portfolio**.

If a company has a well-managed product portfolio then it will have some products being introduced, some in the growth stage, others in the maturity stage and yet more in decline. As each product reaches the end of its life, it can be replaced with a new product at the beginning of its life cycle.

Using this method the company has a steady stream of products, all producing revenue, but it is not reliant upon one product, or one market. Changes in tastes, fashions, technology or income can all be overcome due to the product range.

Of course, a product portfolio is not always possible, especially if the firm is small and unable to produce more than one product. In this case the firm is very vulnerable to any changes in the market.

ACTIVITY 9

Choose a large company and list all the products that it produces (you may need some help with this).

Take a piece of paper and split it into four quarters. Name these four, introduction, growth, maturity and decline. Now place each of the products from the large company into the appropriate quarter of page.

Have any of the products that you first listed been updated? How has the company done this? Have they tried to extend the life of any of the products and failed? Why have they failed?

Review terms

Demand; product life cycle; introduction; growth; maturity; decline; economies of scale; saturated; marketing mix; product portfolio.

Restoration Builders Ltd. makes marketing experts ponder

MARKETING NEWS

The end of the product life cycle?

All students of marketing know all about the product life cycle. A new product has a rarity value which boosts price. As sales increase, prices stabilise and then fall, and finally the product ceases to be of interest to the customer and disappears.

Restoration Builders may have forced us all to reappraise our understanding of this. It has for years sold old building materials and house and garden utensils and has been so successful that it has just opened the first shop in the country entirely devoted to such goods.

Take as an example, an older coal-fired kitchen stove – the sort that were first made in the 1850s. They provided heat for the kitchen, an area for pans, and ovens for baking and roasting. They became so popular that tens of thousands of them were manufactured over the years, and it was every housewife's desire to have one. However, when gas began to be used for cooking demand fell rapidly; by the turn of the century there was no demand for them, and manufacture ceased. The product had run its life cycle.

Suddenly, almost a century later, they are back in demand, especially from families moving into the countryside and seeking to create an authentic, old-fashioned atmosphere. Mostly, they are used only for decoration, but some are used for their original purpose. As more and more families buying country homes decide to introduce such alterations, so firms like Restoration Builders benefit, as they are the only suppliers of scarce authentic items. No-one is going to make these stoves again – and even if they do, market research indicates that customers prefer to buy the original whenever possible – so the only source of supply is from buildings that are being altered or demolished, and have no further need for them. Thus, 100-year-old stoves are fetching a premium price, just as though they were a new product when the traditional marketing view would have been that their product life cycle had ended.

For Restoration Builders, marketing has never been easier. The public want quality old products. Restoration Builders have them and have somewhere to sell them from. All they need to do is tell their potential customers what they have and they are more or less able to name their price. For them, the marketing mix has never been easier, even if their success makes us examine our theories.

Data Questions

Foundation level

1 Explain the meaning of the following terms:
  (a) demand
  (b) supply
  (c) market research
  (d) scarce product
  (e) customer choice.

2 Outline the stages of the product life-cycle: use the old kitchen stove as an example.

3 How does the revival of demand for the stove fit into the product life cycle?

Intermediate level

1 Explain the meaning of the following terms:
  (a) demand and supply
  (b) premium price
  (c) market research
  (d) scarcity and choice.

2 Use the old kitchen stove as an example to outline the stages of the product life cycle.

3 What does the revival of demand for the stove tell us about the product life cycle?

Higher level

1 Explain the meaning of the following terms:

(a) product quality
(b) premium price
(c) marketing mix
(d) scarcity and choice.

2 How does the revival of demand for the kitchen stove fit in with the theory of the product life cycle?

Coursework Suggestions

Idea

Is there a product that you think is in maturity or decline stage? How could the life of this product be extended?

Draw up a policy to extend the life of the product. Interview consumers to find out why sales are declining.

- What do the people really want?
- What has changed in the market?

Alternatively choose a local shop or small firm. Find a product for which sales have decreased.

Produce a plan to extend the life cycle of this product. Find the exact state the product is in by looking at past and present sales.

Make it realistic and use a budget. Can the shop or firm suggest a budget? Can you be sure that any decrease in sales is not simply a temporary thing? Make sure you cost your ideas.

Idea

Do smaller firms really consider their product portfolio? You could test this question by visiting a local store or small firm.

- Do they have a range of products?
- What are the sales figures?
- At what stage of the product life cycle is each product?
- Do they chart a product's life cycle?
- Are new products being developed, or are they looking for new products to make or sell?

These are just a few of the questions you could ask and investigate. Is the information available? If not, why not?

Make sure that you answer the question 'do small firms really consider their product portfolio?'

6.5 PRODUCTION METHODS

Whatever the marketing mix of a company the quality of the product produced will be important. Consumers will not buy a badly-produced product no mater how cheap it is, or how well it has been marketed.

The decision of how to produce the good is therefore very important.

Which production method?

This decision is determined by a number of variables. For example, how large is the market? What factors of production are available and what do they cost? Is the latest technology available? And so on.

Each product is unique and so these different factors will lead the firm to a decision.

There are a number of ways in which a firm can organise production. These include **job production**

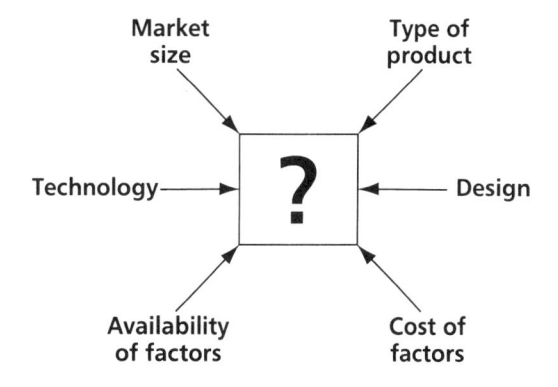

Figure 6.11 How to produce?

and **specialisation** (division of labour), of which **flow production** and **batch production** are examples.

Job production

Job production is the production of a single item at a time. It is used when the product is highly specialised or the demand for the product is small. These two factors often coincide; a highly specialised product usually has a limited demand.

Production is organised so that one job is completed at a time and often by only one or two highly-skilled persons.

The use of machinery is limited and the labour costs are usually quite high, but the workers are generally highly motivated and organising production is straightforward.

This particular method of production is normally adopted by new firms when they are starting up.

Specialisation

Specialisation is a method of production that allows people to produce that good or service, or part of it, at which they are best. Jobs and processes are divided between workers and this gives specialisation the alternative title of **division of labour**.

The benefits of division of labour were first noticed by Adam Smith (1723–90), in his book The Wealth of Nations (1776). He described how a pin-making factory employing ten men could increase its output from 200 pins per day to 4,800 pins per day. This was achieved by splitting the process of pin making into 18 different operations with men specialising in one or two operations.

The great advantage of specialisation is that output is greatly increased because everyone is more efficient at their job. This allows goods and services to be produced on a large scale.

The fact that larger quantities can be produced with the same amount of labour and capital means that these goods are cheaper to produce. They could sell at a lower price or earn more profit for the company.

Figure 6.12 shows that the basic advantages gained from the division of labour are economic. They all lead to reduced costs and greater output. By contrast the disadvantages are social, affecting the workers rather than the companies.

It is quite likely that the disadvantages of the division of labour could affect the company. If the workers are affected and unhappy they will not be motivated (see section 3.2). A workforce that is not motivated will have an effect on the level of output and the quality of the final product.

Although the division of labour has the benefit of increasing output and decreasing prices, it does have limitations. It is only of some use if the demand is high. Some goods and services are only demanded in small quantities and so this process is of little use.

At the same time not every good or service can be broken down into smaller processes. For example, services such as hairdressing and dentistry would be difficult to divide into smaller tasks and

Advantages

Practice makes perfect
constant repetition increases people's proficiency

Time and money is saved
less training, less capital required

A greater use of machinery is possible
this cuts costs and reduces inefficiency

Less time is wasted
no moving from job to job and collecting different tools

Division of Labour

Disadvantages

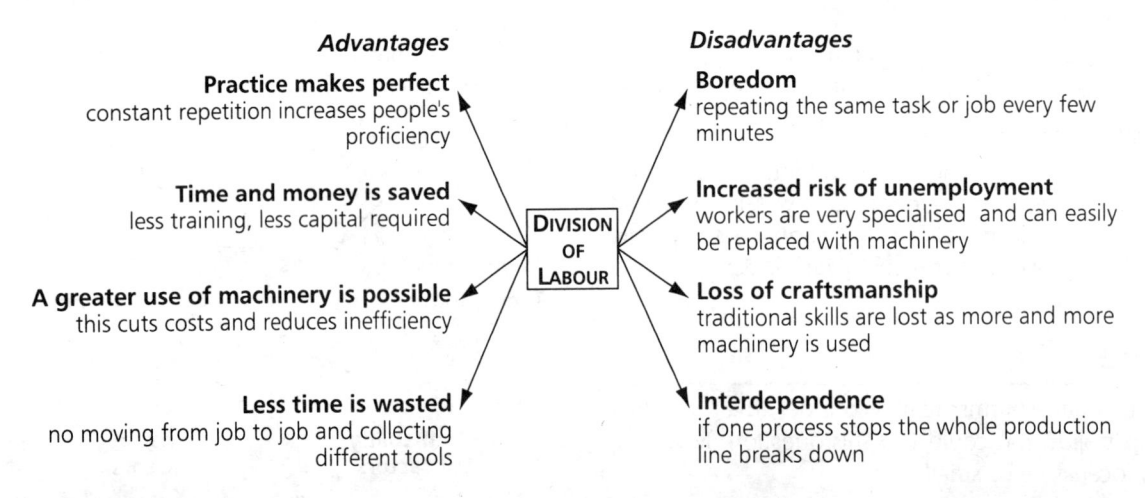

Boredom
repeating the same task or job every few minutes

Increased risk of unemployment
workers are very specialised and can easily be replaced with machinery

Loss of craftsmanship
traditional skills are lost as more and more machinery is used

Interdependence
if one process stops the whole production line breaks down

Figure 6.12 Division of labour

mass produce. The same would be true of the services your GP provides.

Batch production

This is a form of specialisation. Production is divided into a number of operations and each operation, or process, is carried out on all of the products in a batch. The batch then moves on to the next operation, or process, until the batch of products is complete.

Production can be in small or large batches and each batch can be slightly different. A large number of products are produced in this way, especially in the manufacture of canned food.

This process has many advantages over job production. It has a greater flexibility whilst still producing standardised products, and requires less-highly-skilled workers. The machinery required is more standardised than in job production and so the costs are lower.

With any process there will be disadvantages and batch production is no exception. Careful planning and coordination is needed and because each process requires little skill the workers are not as motivated as they would be with job production. As each batch has to be taken step by step through the production process, there are raw materials and partly finished items **(work in progress)** lying idle. The money invested in these is money that could be used elsewhere.

Flow production

Flow production is the typical example of specialisation. Production is organised so that different operations, or processes, can be performed one after the other by different people.

A car factory is a classic example of flow production; vehicles move along a conveyor belt, or along a line, with different operations being performed at each stage. At the end of the line the finished article is then driven away.

Flow production can only really be used when mass production is needed and where the product can be produced in a continuous line.

The advantages and disadvantages of this method are outlined in Figure 6.12, but a number of other points are important. This type of production does allow a greater use of technology, especially computer-controlled machinery, and the product will be standardised.

However, to set up such a production line is very expensive and any breakdowns along the line will bring the whole production line to a standstill. Worker motivation, as previously discussed, will also be a problem and this may affect quality.

Quality

Quality is an extremely important part of any production process. A poor quality product will not last and consumers will not purchase the product again. This will mean that the firm will be limited to first time purchasers and very quickly the market will disappear.

The consumer requires a product that is at the right price and is value for money. If there is a choice between two products of similar price the consumer will choose the one that is of the better quality. Many products in the past have failed because of poor quality production.

Whenever specialisation is used, quality becomes an issue. Badly motivated workers tend to produce poor quality goods.

One solution to this is to have **quality control** as part of the production process. This could involve a separate department, or a different set of workers, whose sole aim would be to check the quality of the product. These checks might be at different stages of the production process or at the very end.

ACTIVITY 10

Produce a list of ten products that are produced on a large scale, mass produced, and five products that use job production.

Choose five products that are mass produced, and see how far production can be broken down. What is the maximum number of processes for the production of each of these products?

Produce a list of five goods and five services for which it is not possible to use specialisation. List the reasons why specialisation cannot be used.

A very good example of the effectiveness of quality control is the car maker Jaguar. Towards the end of the 1980s and early 1990s Jaguar had problems with the quality of its cars, despite producing what was considered to be a very exclusive motor car. The result was that sales abroad, especially in the USA, began to fall.

Jaguar introduced a very strict system of quality control and the standard of the cars improved. At the same time sales in the USA and other countries began to increase again.

There are a number of ways that the quality of a product can be controlled. **Total quality management (TQM)** is the modern way to ensure a quality product is produced. This method aims to avoid problems before they happen. The manufacturing process is investigated at every stage by those people involved in the process. Everyone is responsible for the quality of his or her own operation.

Quality chains are an important part of the quality process. Each stage of production supplies the next step in the process. If the worker is satisfied with the product that is passed on, then the quality is satisfactory.

The one problem with controlling the quality of the production process is that it costs money because it slows down the whole system. The point is that if the quality of the product is not up to standard, it will not sell anyway. Therefore any costs should be more than repaid if the product sells well.

Quality assurance

A company may use a variety of methods to ensure that the product that it produces is of the highest quality but how is the consumer to know that these methods are enough and whether they are working? Every company will claim that its products are of the highest quality. Some may even say this when it is not true.

The consumer needs some way of knowing if a product is of a high standard or is below the standard that is generally believed to be acceptable. Firstly there are two very important laws, the **Sale of Goods Act 1979** and the **Consumer Protection Act 1987**. The Sale of Goods Act states that goods must be of a quality fit for their normal purpose, and the Consumer Protection Act covers the safety of products. These laws ensure that the goods are of **merchantable quality**.

As well as the law there are a number of independent bodies and trade associations that give their own special approval to the products of companies that have attained the standards of quality that they have set.

These independent bodies and associations include the **British Standards Institution (BSI)**, the **Consumers Association**, which produces the monthly magazine Which, and the **BEAB (The British Electrotechnical Approval Board)**.

Each of these bodies have their own mark of approval; the BSI awards the **kitemark**. Obtaining these trademarks provides the consumer with a guarantee that an independent third party has checked and approved the quality of the product. This is **quality assurance**.

ACTIVITY 11

Find ten products carrying a trademark that is an approval of quality, such as the kitemark. Ask your parents or your teacher for help.

Obtain a copy of the Consumer Protection Act 1987 and the Sale of Goods Act 1979 from your school or library, or the consumer advice bureau in your area. What products do these acts cover?

List 12 products that would be covered by both Acts. Find some of these products in your home or a shop (ask permission to do this). Can you tell from the products that they are covered by the law?

✓ Review terms

Job production; specialisation; division of labour; batch production; work in progress; flow production; quality; quality control; total quality management; quality chains; Sale of Goods Act; Consumer Protection Act; merchantable quality; British Standards Institute; Consumers Association; BEAB; kitemark; quality assurance.

An advertisement for Restoration Builders Ltd.

Restoration Builders at Thornton

Individual kitchens for individual tastes, created by a mix of tradition and modern computer technology

> *No batch production here. Everything is hand made to your requirements. A single order, a single job, a single production.*

Using all old fashioned materials

- sycamore
- oak
- ash
- pine
- granite
- stone
- tiles from Georgian mansions
- genuine Victorian stoves,
- handles,
- basins,
- taps

Crafted by hand by old fashioned specialist tradesmen to your individual taste.

- *Modern technology*
  which ensures that the kitchen is perfectly planned.

- *Expert design*
  to make sure that everything is exactly where you want it.

- *Total quality ensured*
  because everything is hand-built and individually inspected.

- *Our workers are craftsmen*
  and they care. Long before anyone thought of quality chains, men generations ago would talk about their work and try to achieve perfection. Ours still do.

- *Costs*
  are higher than for mass-produced kitchens, but if you are an individual, you want an individual product. We will create exactly what you want, and it will last, as did the kitchens of our ancestors.

From the very start, which is talking to us about what you want, until the very end, which is if you ever want to change your kitchen, you are in a market of one. Your satisfaction is our aim. Our service does not end when we have finished the job – it will always be work in progress.

Showroom at The Old School Shop, Thornton
Work guaranteed for five years
For a free brochure telephone 01987-654321

Data Questions

Foundation level

1 Explain the meaning of the following terms:
   (a) batch production
   (b) job production
   (c) specialist tradesmen
   (d) total quality
   (e) brochure.

2 What does the advertisement tell us about the production process at Restoration Builders?

3 How could this production process cause problems for Restoration Builders?

Intermediate level

1 Explain the meaning of the following terms:
   (a) computer technology
   (b) job and batch production
   (c) total quality
   (d) specialist tradesmen
   (e) design.

2 Outline the production process at Restoration Builders.

3 What problems could this process cause?

Higher level

1 Explain the meaning of the following terms:
   (a) market of one
   (b) job and batch production
   (c) quality chain
   (d) modern technology
   (e) design.

2 Assess the production process at Restoration Builders.

3 Consider the implications of such a process on the viability of Restoration Builders.

Coursework Suggestions

Idea

Try to find a local firm that will help you.

Investigate their methods of production: do they use specialisation? If so, why, and if not why not?

Investigate the differences or problems the company might encounter if they changed their method of production.

Investigate the market for their product: is it large enough for mass production? Would the customers prefer a hand-built high quality product?

Has the company considered job production, batch production or flow production?

Idea

Look at the quality control procedures of a local firm, or if this is not possible try to look at the quality control procedures in your school or college.

Has the organisation considered Investors in People? What quality control procedures are in place? What are the costs of quality control? What are the costs of not controlling quality?

Could a quality control process be put in place? Could the process already in place be improved?

Assess the costs of a quality control process or putting one in place and compare this to the loss of customers and output.

7

Business Studies Coursework

Simple guidelines and advice on how to complete coursework

7.1 COURSEWORK TITLES • 7.2 PRESENTATION, EVALUATION AND ANALYSIS OF DATA • 7.3 COURSEWORK SOURCES AND GENERAL GUIDELINES

This section should enable students to:
- choose a coursework title that they find interesting and manageable
- collect data efficiently and present it clearly
- relate theory to real business situations
- produce a report that fulfils the original coursework objectives.

7.1 COURSEWORK TITLES

Almost every subject at GCSE requires both coursework and an examination. Business Studies is no different. It is important that you complete your coursework, but it may be possible to make it easier if you follow a few simple guidelines and read the advice given in this section.

Some teachers and parents believe that it is necessary to spend a great deal of time on coursework, but this is not true. Coursework represents only 25% of your total mark. In other words, the examination is worth 75% of the total mark, and so is far more important in determining your final grade.

This does not mean that coursework is not important, and can be ignored. The marks gained from your coursework assignment can have a real effect on your final grade. The important point is that you plan your time correctly. Do not spend more time on your coursework than you do studying the rest of the course. If you ignore parts of the syllabus you will not cope with the examination and even if your coursework is excellent you may not gain the grade you require.

Do not neglect the rest of your work to concentrate on your coursework

The various examination boards make different demands for coursework. They may ask for one, two or even three items, each from a different part of the syllabus. Some examination boards state the areas of the syllabus that must be used for coursework and many of them state the maximum number of words that can be used. It is important before you start that you know all of these facts.

> **Do not neglect the rest of your work to concentrate on your coursework.**

Figure 7.1 Important advice on coursework

Each examination board publishes **marking criteria**. These 'marking schemes' are not a secret and you should be given a copy. These will tell you how many marks are available for the different skills that are being tested, and how the marks are awarded. If you know the different areas and skills being tested and how the marks are given you should be able to produce a piece of work that is more likely to score high marks.

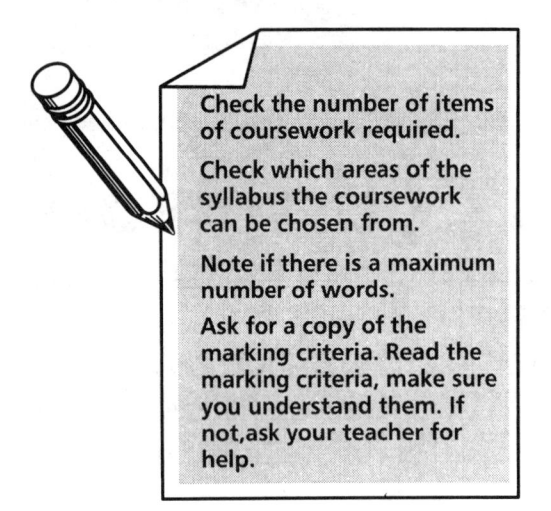

- Check the number of items of coursework required.
- Check which areas of the syllabus the coursework can be chosen from.
- Note if there is a maximum number of words.
- Ask for a copy of the marking criteria. Read the marking criteria, make sure you understand them. If not, ask your teacher for help.

Figure 7.2 Know about your coursework

Try to avoid working from other subject areas. Remember the business context is *very* important.

Figure 7.3 Advice on choosing a coursework topic

Starting coursework

All coursework has to be completed by the candidate, and this can cause teachers some problems. The amount of assistance which a teacher can give is limited by the regulations of the examination board. If too much help is given the candidate may be penalised. This has led to many teachers actually setting the same coursework for every student. In this situation every student will receive the same help and guidance and the regulations can be closely watched.

This approach is also thought to be easier for some students who are happier being told what to do. If this is the approach of your centre then the rest of this chapter can still be of some use. It will help you to understand how and why your title has been set, and how it should be answered.

In those schools and colleges that allow a free choice of topic, after negotiation, students have both an easier task and a harder task. A free choice allows students to choose something that really interests them and will be enjoyable to complete. The problem is that the choices are so enormous that trying to find a good topic with a business context can be difficult.

Remember that the subject content is business studies and so whatever topic is chosen the business context must be strong and clear. Many students produce work that could be used for Humanities, Careers or other subjects. These items of coursework do not score as many marks as they should.

Choosing a topic

A first step when deciding upon a coursework title is to look at those areas of the course that you find most enjoyable or seem to be easier for you to deal with. These larger topic areas can then be broken down to produce a more specific and specialised area. Remember, coursework has been designed to allow candidates to show how well they understand the theory of business studies and how it works in the real world.

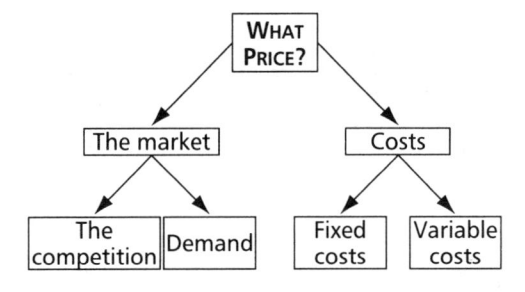

Figure 7.4 An example of breaking down a topic – pricing policy

Figure 7.4 gives an example of how the topic of a firm's pricing policy can be broken down into smaller topic areas.

If one part of this simplified example is chosen then this too can be broken down even further. For example, you might have noticed that petrol prices have changed recently, or that different stations tend to charge slightly different prices for their petrol. This could be an area that you would like to investigate. Possible titles might include: 'Why is it that businesses charge different prices for the same product?' or 'What has caused the recent price changes for petrol?'. Demand and the factors affecting it could be a reason. Figure 7.5 breaks this down into smaller sections.

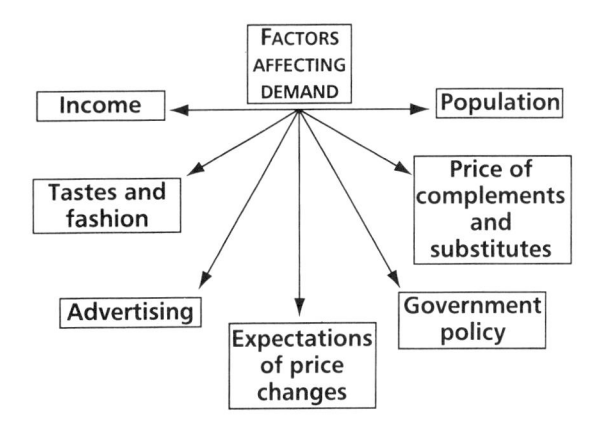

Figure 7.5 An example of breaking down a topic – factors affecting demand

The result of this is that you could investigate income within particular areas to see if they influence the price of petrol locally. You may or many not find a connection but you will have collected information, analysed it and drawn conclusions using the correct theories within a business context.

An alternative method of selecting a topic for coursework is to look at local, or national, issues. Is something happening in your local area that has implications for businesses? For example, is there a new road, bypass or motorway? Is a new shopping centre or leisure centre going to be built? Is the local authority trying to encourage industry into your area? Has a local business been particularly successful or has one recently closed down? If it is a local issue, there will be plenty of information available, so this could be worth considering when you make your decision.

What are your hobbies or interests? The local football club is a business and your youth club could not exist without money from somewhere; these could both be subjects worth investigating.

Is there nothing for young people of your age to do at night? You could look at the possibility of providing entertainment that people actually want. Investigate what they want and whether a business would make a profit by providing it.

Remember that the key to choosing a suitable topic is finding something that interests you, because if you enjoy doing it, then it will not be such hard work. Discuss your ideas with your teacher, to make sure that you are not attempting something that is too large or too difficult.

Whatever method is used to select a coursework topic it is important that the subject material is in a business context and that information is available. If possible the information should be primary rather than secondary.

For example if the topic chosen is 'the influence of the European Union on business' all the information will be from books and leaflets; this is secondary information, and there is little scope for an original approach.

It is far better to collect information yourself from surveys and questionnaires; this is primary information and you can draw your own conclusions that may be original.

- Consider – local issues; personal issues; hobbies and interests
- Remember – is the topic business studies? Is data available? Is it primary or secondary?

Choosing a title

Many students believe that coursework is just an essay, so they set themselves a task such as *'Government Industrial Policy'*. Not only is this title too broad, it allows little scope for originality and leads to a purely descriptive piece of work.

Choosing a title is the second step you must take before starting your coursework, and is probably one of the most important steps. The wrong title can cause you a great number of difficulties, as already shown.

One approach is for your title to ask a question or set a problem to be solved. For example:

- Why do large firms locate in the High Street?
- What factors influence the prices firms charge for second-hand cars?
- How has information technology affected the retail sector?

This sort of title creates a problem which has to be solved by you. The question needs an answer, proved with evidence that you have collected and analysed.

This will give your coursework an aim. If you begin to describe rather than analyse and evaluate, then you will not answer the question set. The most common problem with coursework is that candidates simply describe a situation or repeat theories and fail to analyse and evaluate.

An alternative approach is to make a statement that has to be proved or disproved. Again it will force you to work towards a statement based upon evidence collected and analysed. For example:

- The increased demand for environmentally friendly products has increased firms' costs and decreased profits
- The most successful petrol stations are those with the best facilities and not those with the lowest prices

These statements have to be proved or disproved. It does not matter whether the statement is correct or not, simply that you work towards an answer and can prove it right or wrong. The statement forces you to produce an answer and if you begin to describe you will not achieve your objective.

If this type of approach is contrasted with the approach producing titles such 'Marketing' or 'Business Finance' it can be seen that the latter is too general and too vague. What about marketing or business finance? There is no aim to these titles, nothing to prove and no question to answer. The result is a long essay, or piece of work, on everything connected with marketing or business finance. This sort of title produces coursework that scores very few marks. It is descriptive and lacks analysis and evaluation, where the majority of marks are gained.

When you decide upon a title you should at the same time have some ideas of your own about a solution. This solution can be in the form of an answer to the question or an explanation of the problem. This solution is known as a **hypothesis**. Either of the two statements discussed previously is in fact a hypothesis, but it is helpful to have such a statement even when you are asking a question or setting a problem. It gives your work an aim: you are trying to prove your hypothesis. Whilst doing this you will solve your problem or answer your question.

Forming a hypothesis is not an easy task. A hypothesis turns problems and questions into a form that can be tested. It requires a certain knowledge of the syllabus area being investigated, backed by a sound grounding in the theory of business studies.

> **Remember**
> Coursework is not an essay.
> Your coursework title should ask a question or set a problem to be solved.
> Alternatively, formulate a hypothesis (a statement to be tested).
> Avoid titles such as 'marketing' or 'business finance'.
> Ask for help if you need it!!

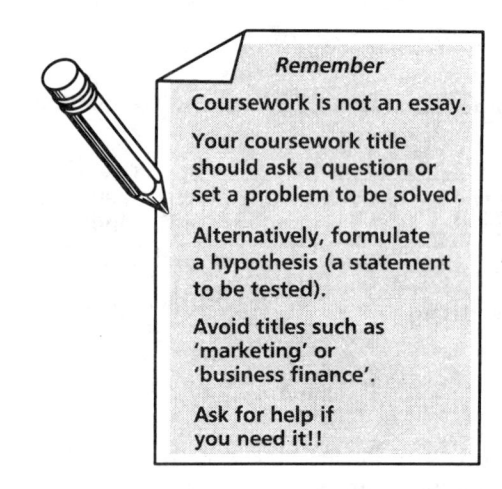

Figure 7.6 Advice on choosing a coursework title

7.2 PRESENTATION, EVALUATION AND ANALYSIS OF DATA

Coursework is not an essay; you should not produce a continuous piece of written work. This is an area where many candidates fail. They believe that an item of coursework is just a long essay, losing many marks because of this. Try to produce a report. This means that you should try to split your work into sections which should deal with the following areas:

- the background to the report
- the findings of the report
- the conclusions.

If your coursework is to look like a report then it should include charts, maps, diagrams and photographs if they are appropriate. This makes your work appear more interesting and also shows that you can communicate in other ways than writing. However do not put in pictures or diagrams if you do not refer to them or they are not needed. Again this is a common mistake; pictures or meaningless leaflets are put into coursework without any reason. This is just a waste of time.

There is no need to type or wordprocess your work, and you will receive no extra marks if you do so. However, the general impression of a well presented, neat and tidy report is far better than something scrawled on a few sheets of tatty paper. Think about the impression you are giving to others of yourself and your work. An added advantage of using a wordprocessor is that you can change your work easily if you wish to. You would not have to rewrite the whole piece but simply change the work at whatever place you wish to and print out a complete copy again. This saves time and effort and allows you to keep improving your work up to the deadline date.

If you are pleased with your work, which you should be, take the time and the trouble to show it at its best. Are your diagrams and charts neat and accurate? Are the pages numbered? Is what you are saying clear?

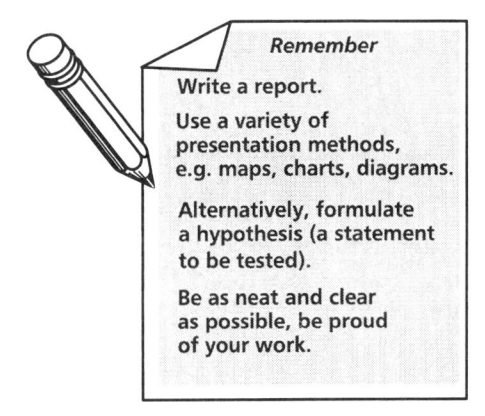

Remember

Write a report.

Use a variety of presentation methods, e.g. maps, charts, diagrams.

Alternatively, formulate a hypothesis (a statement to be tested).

Be as neat and clear as possible, be proud of your work.

Figure 7.7 Presenting your work

Organisation

Your work should be organised so as to obtain the maximum marks possible. You can only do this by looking at the marking criteria, which are fairly similar for each examining board. Make sure that you have seen these criteria, and if you do not understand them, ask your teacher to explain them to you. You cannot play any game properly unless you know the rules. The marking criteria are the rules of the examination and it is far more important than a game; it is part of your future and you must know exactly what is expected of you.

All the examination boards have the following four assessment objectives:

1. Knowledge/Use of Information
2. Application
3. Select/Organisation/Interpret
4. Evaluation/Judgement

This tells you something about what is required, but not enough. Each board has split these areas further, saying how many marks can be awarded for the level of skills demonstrated in each.

The Southern Examining Group for example, adds the following information.

- **Knowledge/Use of Information** describes the ability to use knowledge in relation to a business context. This is worth a maximum of 8 marks.
- **Application** describes the ability to apply concepts, theories, terms and knowledge to resolve problems and issues. This is worth a maximum of 14 marks.
- **Select/Organise/Interpret** all describe the ability to organise and analyse information in order to use it to resolve the problems or issues. This is worth a maximum of 22 marks.
- **Evaluation/Judgement** describes the ability to draw reasoned conclusions, distinguish between evidence and opinions and present it in a precise and logical manner as a solution to problems or issues. This is worth a maximum of 16 marks.

This list is very much more helpful, as it gives the maximum number of marks available for each assessment objective, and tells you in general terms what each objective requires.

The marking criteria set out four points that need to be remembered. They should be the guidelines which all of your coursework follows.

You need to present information within the context of business studies.

You need to apply your knowledge of business studies to the topic.

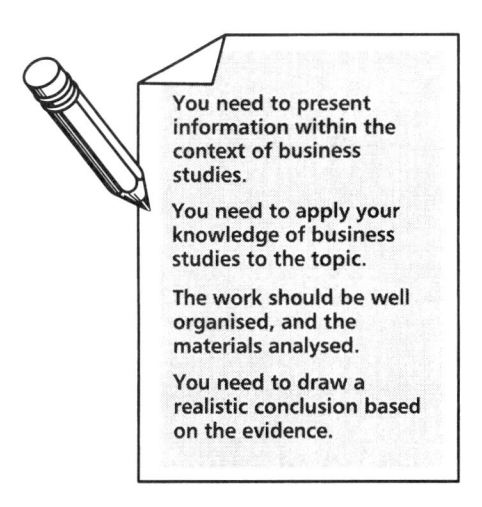

The work should be well organised, and the materials analysed.

You need to draw a realistic conclusion based on the evidence.

Figure 7.8 Coursework guidelines to follow

Each of these areas carry a different number of marks, so they should be given a proportional amount of thought, time and importance.

There are many different ways to organise your work, but one possible approach is given in Figure 7.9.

Title
Aims
Method
Information
Analysis
Conclusion
(Bibliography)

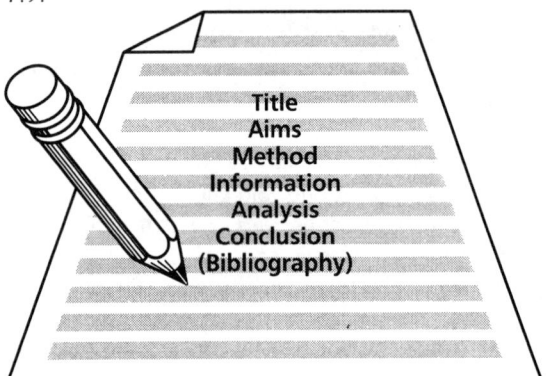

Figure 7.9 One method of organising your work

The necessary elements can be outlined:

- The **title** should pose a problem or ask a question; alternatively it should set a hypothesis to be tested.
- The **aims** are not essential but it is useful to say what you intend to do.
- **Method**, again is not vital, but it is useful to say how you went about your study.
- **Information**: this is self explanatory, but you must make sure that you do collect some information.
- **Analysis** of the information is vital, using the correct terminology and methods.
- A **conclusion** finishes the assignment and allows you to answer the question set or prove the hypothesis correct or incorrect.

Finally, a **bibliography**, which is a list of the books you used, or a **list of sources**, completes your work. A list of sources allows you to show how much work you have done and thank those people that have helped you. This list can include people you have interviewed as well as books and magazines or journals that you have used.

Presentation of data

The presentation of data is very important in a coursework assignment. Section 3 in the mark scheme given earlier is 'Select/Organise/Interpret'. This requires information to be selected and then presented in an appropriate format so that it can be used to solve the problem set in the question. Presenting data in the right way is therefore very important.

There are a number of different ways in which data or information can be presented:

- tables
- pie charts
- bar charts
- line graphs
- pictograms
- maps.

The secret is to make sure that the best method is used. For example if comparing profits over a period of time a line graph or a bar chart would be the best but a pie chart would be totally wrong. If you wished to look at manufacturing output around the UK then a map would be useful unless you only wished to compare the rates, in which case a bar chart could be used. Pie charts are often useful to look at shares of things. For instance, out of 100 people how many shop locally, how many at Sainsbury's, how many at the Co-op and so on?

When presenting data always think:

- What am I trying to show?
- Is this the best possible way to show it?

Do not use the same data to produce different charts or tables, it simply wastes your time. Also, never put any information into your assignment that you are not going to use. Too many assignments have leaflets and pictures that are of no use and are never mentioned. The rule is, if you do not use it, do not include it. It will not gain you any extra marks.

Analysis of data

Once your data has been collected and presented, the next stage is to make some sense of the results.

Look at Figure 7.10. This information is from an imaginary survey conducted by a group of GCSE students aged 16. It is the prices of four different products that they use, purchased from four different shops.

They chose shower gel, a pad of A4 writing paper, a can of Pepsi Max and a king size Mars

Price in pounds

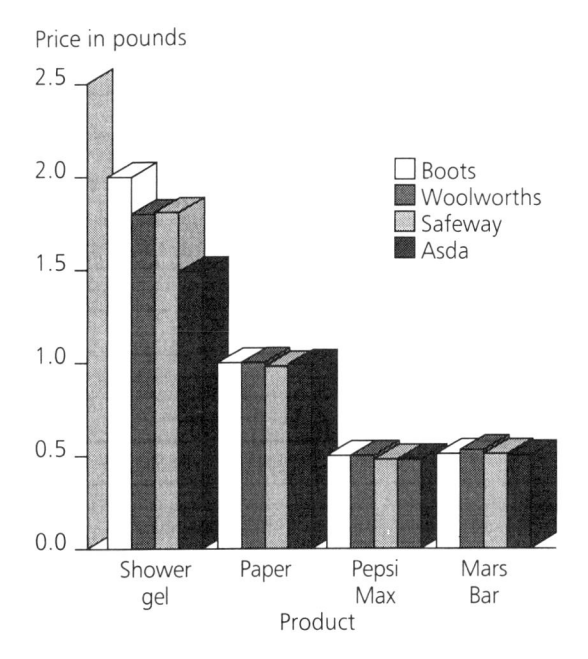

Figure 7.10 Student price survey

bar. The shops they chose were Boots, Asda, Woolworths and Safeway. A very simple hypothesis could be that 'shopping at a superstore is cheaper than shopping at a chain store'.

Analysis of the data collected should present a clear picture of what the information is saying. The data shows clearly that the most expensive item is shower gel, and the cheapest item is a can of Pepsi Max. Asda is the cheapest for shower gel, king size Mars bars and Pepsi Max. Safeway is the cheapest for paper and Pepsi Max, along with Asda. Boots is the most expensive for everything except king size Mars bars. The prices of paper, Pepsi Max, and king size Mars bars are all very similar with a difference in price of 2p for paper, 3p for Pepsi Max and 5p for king size Mars bars. The biggest difference is found with the shower gel. The price range is 51p which is a 33% difference using the cheapest price, and a 25% difference using the most expensive price.

If all four items are purchased, Asda works out the cheapest at £3.45, followed by Safeway at £3.77, Woolworths at £3.84 and then Boots at £4.02. It is noticeable however that no single store is cheaper for all four items. But the two superstores do work out cheaper overall.

Whilst this is a very simplified example it does give some idea of how simple data presented clearly can be analysed to highlight the main points. The next stage would then be to draw some conclusions but you must always remember that any conclusions you draw are only as good as the information collected. Therefore the next logical step is to evaluate your information.

Evaluation

Evaluation of the information collected is something that the majority of students fail to do. It is not an easy exercise and because of this gains high marks when it is carried out.

In the example in Figure 7.10 the information seems to be supporting our simple hypothesis. It would be easy to agree that shopping at a superstore is cheaper than shopping at a chain store. But is the information really saying that? On three of the items the price difference is very small; it is only the large price difference on the shower gel that actually makes Asda that much cheaper. If the shower gel is removed then the total expenditure for the three items is very close together: a difference of 9p between the most and least expensive. In this case the information does still support the hypothesis even though the difference is small.

Another stage in the evaluation of your data is to ask 'how accurate is the information collected?'. Four stores have been chosen: are they representative? Why not more stores and shops? Only four products have been chosen, why? Are these really the products that a 16 year old would buy?

The use of only four stores is a weakness; more should have been used, including corner shops, mini-markets, other superstores, the Co-op, etc. However if you live in a small village or near to a small town these might be the only shops that you could visit. In this case you are limited by your situation and should say so. If you had the chance to visit other stores you could list those you would have liked to have visited and why. Do not be afraid to admit that your research has limitations and weaknesses. In this situation it might be the best you could do and so your information is acceptable.

The products chosen are also a problem. Most young people would not buy their own shower gel, if they use it, or their own writing paper. These two products are not really representative. This is an error but it is too late to change it. Again do not be afraid to admit your mistake. You can discuss what products you should have chosen, or how you could have got a better sample of products. You must then decide whether you are going to continue and make some decisions or simply state that the information is not good enough to draw any conclusions. In this simple case the information is not good enough to test the hypothesis. If it was decided to formulate a conclusion then it should be stated that it is based upon information or data that is not totally accurate.

> *Remember: this hypothesis was only intended as an example, to illustrate several important points, and would need to be altered to produce a good business studies project.*

The main point about this chapter is to advise you to go through the process of collecting information, presenting it in a visual format, analysing the information to explain what it is telling you, evaluating the information to see if it is accurate and unbiased and drawing conclusions. Even if the conclusion is that 'my information is inaccurate and proves nothing', you have still completed the process and used your skills. Therefore you will gain credit for all your efforts. It does not really matter that you cannot answer the question set or test the original hypothesis.

You should remember:

- Your work needs a structure: title, aims, method, information, analysis and conclusion.
- Present your data clearly.
- Do not include leaflets, pictures or newspaper clippings unless you are going to use them.
- Analyse your data: what does it tell you? What are the main points?
- Evaluate your data: is it accurate? How could it be improved? Is it biased?
- Draw some conclusions: test the hypothesis or answer the question or state that your information/data is too inaccurate to draw any conclusions.

7.3 COURSEWORK SOURCES AND GENERAL GUIDELINES

The subject that you have chosen for your coursework and the question that you have asked, or the hypothesis you wish to test, will determine the sort of information or data that you need. This in turn will determine the sources that are best for you to use.

It is not possible in this chapter to list all the sources that you might need for your work. The following list is an attempt to set out at least some of the possible approaches that you may take when collecting your information.

Notes and books

You will receive little or no credit if you simply copy out your notes, or even parts of books. This does not mean that you cannot use them. In fact, the notes and books that you have are likely to be full of useful information, which may well include the correct business terminology that you should use, as well as the concepts and theories that you will be using. They may also contain facts and figures that you want to use. One problem with any book is that the figures may not be up to date, so do not rely on them.

Newspapers and periodicals

These will comment on what is happening at the time, so you can collect up-to-date facts and opinions by referring to them. Editorials often comment on events, and the letters pages contain the views of people who wish to express their opinions. The normal news pages deal with what is happening, and often quote the statements of others as well.

Specialist publications

There are so many of these that it would be impossible to list them. Of particular note are the publications of the Central Statistical Office (CSO). If you want accurate figures on almost anything from the crime rate to the output of the economy, this is where to look. Other specialist publications might be provided by your local Chamber of

Commerce, or your local Training and Enterprise Council (TEC).

The library

Your school or college library will have a selection of books and newspapers. The papers are often kept for a long period of time, so you may be able to refer back to specific events if you know when they happened. Some libraries keep press cuttings of important events, so these may be available to you. Some national newspapers are now available on CD Rom with articles for the past year.

Librarians are there to help you, so if you do not know where to look for the information that you need, ask for assistance. They will tell you what is available on the topic and where it is in the library.

Prominent people

Local dignitaries often like to be approached for help. If you think that, for example, your local MP can help you, then write and introduce yourself, your work, and ask politely for the help that you need. Keep a copy of your letter. You may want to include it and the reply in your work.

If someone refused to provide information, or even ignored your letter, do not be afraid to point this out. Suppose your title was 'The regeneration of industry in my area', then the view of your local MP would be important. If you did not receive a reply then it would be entirely appropriate to say that your study would have been improved by a contribution from the MP, but he failed to reply to your letter. This means that you cannot be criticised for failing to gain the views of someone at the centre of the problem.

Firms

Small shopkeepers may be fed up with students asking them questions, especially when a lot of the questions refer to how much they sell and how much profit they make. They also do not have a great deal of time to spare to help you. This is understandable.

However, many larger firms have information officers who will provide answers and some of the largest companies employ people just to answer queries, so it is worth your while writing to head office with your question. Always keep a copy of your letter, and, once again, if you are refused information, make sure that you point out that it was refused. In this case, offer a comment on why you wanted it and what you would have done with it.

People

You may wish to interview someone because they have a particular knowledge of the subject that you have chosen. Make sure that you have prepared your questions in advance. This means that you must have worked out what you expect to learn in your interview. Take notes as the meeting progresses. You may think that you will remember everything that was said, but you will not.

You may wish to find out the views of a group of people. This can be done by constructing a questionnaire, a list of questions. When you compile your list of questions, make sure that you are clear about your objectives. Ask yourself what you intend to discover. Having decided that, then consider each question and make sure that it will contribute to your main objective. The phrasing of your questions is important. The language should be clear, so that the people you are asking can understand. You can have yes/no answers, or a rating scale, for instance:

1 = very dissatisfied
2 = somewhat dissatisfied
3 = nearly satisfied
4 = satisfied
5 = very satisfied.

You can also ask people to offer comments, but these do not always produce good results, and can be difficult to analyse.

Surveys often take a great deal of time, but they can produce some excellent material, although the analysis of the results can be time consuming. It is important that you ask a representative sample of people. If you want to know what people in your area think about the building of a new out-of-town shopping complex, then just asking your school friends would not tell you what other people think. You need to have men and women, young and old, married and single, employed and unemployed, and so on, in order to ensure that you have a representative sample.

Visits

It may be appropriate to make a visit to a site or an area to help your work. Indeed, it may not be possible to undertake the study if you do not. It may be possible to take photographs to illustrate your work. Certainly you should make some comments on your visit in your work, so that your efforts can be appreciated.

Your teacher

Your teacher is there to help you. There are rules about the amount of help that can be given, but your teacher is able to help you select a topic, and offer advice on what sources you should use. When you are doing the work, you can approach your teacher if you run into problems, or if you find it difficult to keep to the agreed topic. If you do find such problems, do not hesitate to go to your teacher. You will have wasted a great deal of time and effort, and not scored the marks you deserve if you do not. The teacher will make a record of any assistance given, and will inform the examining board, but there is not likely to be any penalty. Even if there is a penalty, it is better than simply not finishing the work.

The guidelines in Figure 7.11 form a checklist that you can follow but you should also refer back to the more detailed notes in the chapter if you need help.

If you have read this chapter and follow its advice throughout your project then your finished work should be both of a high standard and something that you can be proud of. Hopefully you will also have enjoyed completing it and you will certainly have learned something about business studies.

Review terms

Notes and books; newspapers and periodicals; specialist publications; the library; prominent people; firms; people; visits; teaching staff.

Useful addresses

Bank Education Service
10 Lombard Street
London EC3

General Guidelines
Choose a topic that interests you.
Do not neglect the rest of the course.
Pose a question/set a hypothesis.
Present your information clearly.
Use visual materials.
Do not include leaflets/pictures that are not relevant.
Analyse your information – what does it tell you? What are the main points?
Evaluate your information – is it accurate? Is it biased? How could it be improved?
Answer your questions/test your hypothesis.
Draw your conclusions
List your sources or use a bibliography.
Wordprocess if you can.
Do not spend time on a detailed artistic cover.
Put it in a simple folder or a single plastic wallet.
Good luck!

Figure 7.11 General guidelines for your report

Barclays Bank Review
54 Lombard Street
London EC3

Central Statistical Office
St George Street
London
SW1P 3AQ

Economic Briefing
Information Division
HM Treasury
Parliament Street
London
SW1P 3AG

Economic Briefing
Promotions Unit
Central Office of Information
Hercules Road
London
SE1 7DU

Economic Review
Philip Allan Publishers Ltd
Market Place
Deddington
Oxford
OX5 4SE

The Economics and Business Education
Association
1a Keymer Road
Hassocks
West Sussex
BN6 8AD

The Economist
54 St James Street
London
SW1 1JT

HMSO Publications Centre
PO Box 276
London
SW8 5DT

Lloyds Bank Review
71 Lombard Street
London EC3

National Westminster Bank Review
41 Lothbury
London
EC2P 2BP

Business Review
Phillip Alan Publishers
Market Place
Deddington
Oxfordshire
OX15 0SE

Business Studies magazine
Periodicals Division
128 Long Acre
London
WC2E 9AN

8

The Examination

A concise guide on approaching examinations

8.1 THE EXAMINATION PAPER • 8.2 SAMPLE SPECIMEN MATERIALS
8.3 SAMPLE EXAM PAPER (WITH OUTLINE ANSWERS AND ADVICE)

This section should enable students to:
- understand the examination rules and instructions
- plan their time effectively
- choose the right questions to answer
- understand exactly what each question is asking them to do.

8.1 THE EXAMINATION PAPER

All of the examination boards make their GCSE awards as a result of candidates undertaking pieces of coursework and a written examination. Thus, if you want to pass your GCSE, you have to take an exam. Some people are better at exams than others, but everyone can improve their performance by following a few simple rules.

Read the instructions

First of all, make sure that you know how many questions to answer, and whether there are any compulsory questions or not.

That may appear to be obvious, but every year some candidates do not conform to the rules, and so lose marks. Make sure that your teacher has shown you the past papers, or, in the case of a new syllabus, has checked to see the question requirements.

Look at the instructions on the front cover of the examination paper, just to be sure that you have remembered the instructions.

It will say something similar to the instructions shown in Figure 8.1.

General Certificate of Secondary Education

BUSINESS STUDIES
Time Allowed: 2 Hours

ANSWER ALL QUESTIONS.

INFORMATION
Mark allocations are shown in brackets.

Figure 8.1 Sample examination paper instructions

Now you are sure about what is expected of you. You must attempt all the questions.

Allocate your time

There is little point in devoting an hour to a question that is worth only ten marks, and five minutes to a question that could score fifty.

You need to look at the questions, and then allocate your time so that you can match the time that you spend on each part of the paper with the number of marks that can be gained.

The information on the front cover of the examination paper will tell you about mark allocations. They are shown in brackets after each question.

For example, the 1996 sample paper issued by SEG consists of two sections.

Section I consists of three questions, each of which is sub-divided. The questions largely require you to extract information from the text or use the text as a stimulus to aid the recall of information.

Section II contains about three questions, some of which may be sub-divided. These questions pose a greater demand for opinion, evaluation and judgement.

Thus, your questions and marks look as in Figure 8.2.

Section I
Question 1 – 24 marks
Question 2 – 10 marks
Question 3 – 6 marks

Section II
Questions 4, 5 and 6 – the marks vary for each question at each level, but come to a total of 60 marks.

Total marks 100 and time available 2 hours or 120 minutes.

Figure 8.2 Allocation of marks on an examination paper

40% of the total marks can be obtained from Section I and the other 60% from Section II, so you should spend 48 minutes to complete Section I, and allow 72 minutes for Section II.

The questions and marks available allow you to calculate a time allocation as shown in Figure 8.3.

Section I
Question 1 – 24 marks – 29 minutes
Question 2 – 10 marks – 12 minutes
Question 3 – 6 marks – 7 minutes
Question 4 – 20 marks – 15 minutes

Section II
This can be calculated in the same way, according to the marks for each question.

Figure 8.3 Calculating the time available for each question

You now have a clear idea of the best way of scoring marks in the time allowed.

Whichever examining board you are studying, and whatever examination you are taking, you can perform a similar analysis so that you are in a position to score the maximum marks possible and to use the time available to your best advantage.

You should always remember to:

- work out how long to spend on each part of the questions
- use your watch to make sure that you keep to the time scale that you have allocated
- practise answering questions within time limits to make this easier.

Select your questions

If there is any choice, many candidates like to have sorted out what to answer before starting the paper. This is not a bad idea, as it means that you can devote all your time to writing after making your decisions.

On the other hand, other candidates like to finish the compulsory questions before making their choices, as they feel that they can concentrate better on one area and do not have to worry about the others while writing.

Either way, you are going to have to make some choices eventually.

The worst mistake that can be made is if you like a particular topic, and see that it is on the paper, and so decide to do it without reading the questions properly. No matter how much you think you know, you need to be sure that you can actually answer the questions set.

You should always remember to:

read the paper carefully.

Make sure that you can actually answer all the parts to a question before putting pen to paper.

It is often a good idea to read through all the questions once, and then go through each part again, ticking those you could do, and putting a cross where you could not answer a part.

This may leave you with a paper that shows you what to answer. If it does not, go through it again, indicating, again with ticks and crosses, those you would feel most and least happy to attempt.

The questions with the most ticks – or the least crosses – are the ones that you should select.

Look at the exact requirements of the question

When the paper was set, there would have been long discussions about what was wanted from every part of every question, and the wording would have been adjusted accordingly. Thus, the instruction in the question tells you how to respond.

Looking at a typical examination paper reveals such instructions as:

- give
- select
- name
- list
- identify
- summarise
- describe
- discuss
- calculate
- outline
- what
- explain
- why
- how
- assess
- comment on
- evaluate

All these words have a meaning. Some are preceded by the word 'briefly'. This is another instruction.

It is vital that you respond adequately to such instructions, otherwise you may not produce the answer which is required.

Some of the words are similar in meaning, and expect a particular type of response.

They can be split into three categories:

1. Those that seek to discover what you know, or if you can extract information from data that is given to you. These will usually include words such as give, name, list, identify, select, what and which.
2. Those that seek to discover if you have understood a subject area or some data. These include calculate, summarise, describe, outline and explain.
3. Those that seek a judgment from you. These include discuss, why, how, assess, comment on, examine and evaluate.

Moreover, most, if not all, GCSE examination papers involve the use of material on which some of the questions are based. This is known as data response.

The questions are preceded by information, which can include graphs, charts, and diagrams as well as the written word. You are usually required to show that you can select particular points from this information. After that you may well be asked to demonstrate that you have understood the text. Then you may be required to evaluate the material.

- Check which examination you are sitting.
- Ask for a past or specimen paper.
- Read the instructions; do you understand them?
- Check with your teacher that you understand exactly what you have to do in the exam.
- Use a dictionary to find the correct meanings of the words used in the questions, e.g. summarise, assess, evaluate, etc.
- Practise some past questions under timed conditions.
- Ask for a copy of the mark schemes provided by the exam board.

8.2 SAMPLE QUESTIONS WITH OUTLINE ANSWERS

A sample of the kind of data response material you will be required to read in your examination follows on the next pages. The questions ask you to extract information from this text.

Specimen case study

THE FINANCIAL NEWS

Restoration Builders to go Public

Latest news is that the large building firm Restoration Builders is to seek a quotation on the Stock Exchange, and thus become a public limited company (PLC).

Apparently, the founder Fred Norman, and his original partner Harry Adams, have reached the age where they want less direct involvement with the firm.

Shares

They want to sell part of their shares in the company in order to, in Fred's own words, 'enjoy the proceeds of our hard work', but they would continue to contribute as consultants.

Reputable

It is likely that the shares will be fully subscribed, as Restoration Builders has a fine reputation, both as an employer and for satisfied customers.

Prospectus

Restoration Builders Ltd

We wish to seek a quotation on the Stock Exchange so as to provide capital for further expansion, and to arrive at the true worth of the company.

Thus, we are offering 10 million shares at £1 each, which is their par value.

It is true that Fred Norman and Harry Adams are going into semi-retirement when this deal is completed, but the system that they have established means that this will cause no dislocation to the business. Indeed, as they sit back and review the company, their contributions will lead to further efficiencies.

The company is famous for its excellent relationship with the workforce – no strikes, no stoppages, and one of the lowest staff turnover rates in British industry. This is the result of a clear, long-established pattern of practice.

The workforce

Our communication system was established years ago. All senior managers meet every Friday afternoon to review the week's events, the progress of work in hand, and any possible new business.

Supervisors are informed, both verbally and in writing, on the following Monday, of decisions relevant to them. They also receive reports of anything else relevant to the business.

Once a month, all work finishes early and there is a general meeting of all workers to outline events and answer questions.

Many employees are members of appropriate trade unions which are recognised and also consulted on a regular basis so as to deal with any complaints before they become major problems.

Promotion has always been on merit, with equal opportunities for all, and there has never been any suggestion of any form of discrimination. As a result, employees have always felt themselves part of a closely knit team of workers, resulting in high motivation and morale.

Company records are extensively computerised, and there is a detailed database of customers. Accounts and stock control is also part of the company's computer package.

The organisation

The company operates in three distinct areas, each of which is run as a separate business, with the directors effecting coordination if necessary.

1. The purchase, renovation and sale of properties.
2. The provision of a complete range of building services.
3. The acquisition and sale of building artefacts to the public.

The directors all have a coordinating function – Administration and Finance, which means that records of all the firm's activities are held centrally; Marketing and Publicity, so as to ensure that the image of the firm is maintained; Operations, so as to ensure that the business runs as a whole.

However, each section has a manager who is responsible for that section, and each section has administrative and support staff to make sure that it runs efficiently; it has supervisors and workers, so the work can be carried out. The managers are in charge, and can take major decisions. They meet with the directors once a week and can seek advice if they need it, but they are responsible. The centralisation of administration, etc., is to effect economies of scale rather than to interfere, and each manager would, as a matter of routine, be consulted on, for example, national advertising. They have their own budgets for local, sectional advertising.

Thus, there is in place an organisational structure that works, is effective and provides continuity.

Restoration Builders Ltd.: Trading and Profit and Loss Account for the financial year ending April 5th, 1996

	(£)	(£)	(£)
Takings			
Building work	1,780,000		
Sales of property	1,070,000		
Sales of artefacts	1,150,000		
		4,000,000	
Less purchase of			
materials	350,000		
property	600,000		
artefacts	50,000		
		1,000,000	
Gross profit			3,000,000
Less expenses			
Wages	1,000,000		
Travelling expenses	500,000		
Rates	50,000		
Heating, etc.	50,000		
Bank charges	50,000		
Professional fees	100,000		
Insurance	50,000		
Advertising	250,000		
Repairs and renewals	150,000		
		2,200,000	
Net profit			800,000

Restoration Builders Ltd.: Balance sheet as at 31 December 1996

	(£)	(£)	(£)
Fixed Assets			
Premises (Head Office)			850,000
Plant & Equipment			450,000
Vehicles			150,000
			1,450,000
Current Assets			
Stock		700,000	
Work-in-progress		200,000	
Debtors		100,000	
Cash at Bank		50,000	
		1,050,000	
Less current liabilities			
Trade creditors	200,000	200,000	
Working capital			850,000
Net assets			**2,300,000**
Financed by			
Share capital			500,000
Retained profits (1996)			800,000
Reserves			1,000,000
Capital employed			**2,300,000**

The database at Restoration Builders keeps a record of every customer, their requirements, and the possibility of future business. For example, the firm paints a private house. Houses should be painted every three years, so just before the three years is up, the computer will produce the details, and the householder will be approached to see if he wants the job doing again.

Restoration Builders
The Yard, Country Road, Thornton

Tel: 01241-734562

17th October 1996

Mr and Mrs F Grosse,
13 Roman Way,
Thornton.

Dear Mr and Mrs Grosse,

It is almost three years since we had the pleasure of painting your house. The paint manufacturers recommend that for optimum protection to woodwork, houses should be painted every three years.

We would be honoured to repeat the work, and would be happy to provide a quotation. As you are an established and respected customer, we promise that, if the amount of work required is the same, the price will not be more than 10% higher than three years ago.

Moreover, we are now able to offer credit facilities, so that your invoice price can be made by standing order or direct debit and spread over a 12 to 36 month period.

If you would like further details, or if there is any other work you would like done, please contact us.

Assuring you of our best efforts at all times.

Yours sincerely,

A Huddart

Alex Huddart
Repeat Sales Division

Restoration Builders
The Yard, Country Road, Thornton

Tel: 01241–734562

17th October 1996

The Training Adviser,
T.E.C.,
Help Street,
Thornton.

Dear Sir,

At Restoration Builders, our recruitment policy is to employ the person who we feel will fit in best with everyone else who works here. We are determined to have a happy workforce, so we would not offer a job to anyone who could not make friends with everyone else. We insist that all our workers have good social skills and that they are polite and thoughtful with our customers.

Of course, we do not always find that applicants with the right attitude have the skills that we require.

This means that our staff need training. In the past, we have relied on such things as BTEC courses at the local college, but we are finding that this is not always sufficient. Some staff need immediate training in particular areas. For instance, someone may be an ideal employee, but might need to be better able to use IT. We can train them ourselves, or we can pay for the training.

Do you, or any other government agency, offer training schemes designed specifically for a single employer, such as ourselves? What sort of costs would be involved, and what grants, if any, are available?

I look forward to your reply.

Yours faithfully,

Elizabeth Snell

Elizabeth Snell
Finance and Administration Director

8.3 SAMPLE EXAMINATION PAPER

General Certificate of Secondary Education

BUSINESS STUDIES
Time Allowed: 2 Hours

ANSWER ALL QUESTIONS.
INFORMATION: Mark allocations are shown in brackets.

SECTION I Answer ALL questions
1. Explain the meaning of the following terms:
   - (a) Public Limited Company (3 marks)
   - (b) Trading Account (3 marks)
   - (c) Equal opportunities (3 marks)
   - (d) Motivation (3 marks)
   - (e) Company records (3 marks)
   - (f) Stock control (3 marks)
   - (g) Database (3 marks)
   - (h) Quotation (3 marks)
   - (i) Advertising budget (3 marks)
   - (j) Credit facilities (3 marks)
2. Draw a chart to show the organisational structure at Restoration Builders. (6 marks)
3. (a) What are the advantages and disadvantages of becoming a Limited liability company? (6 marks)
   (b) Why would a private limited company want to become a Public Limited Company? (6 marks)

SECTION II Answer THREE questions
4. Study the financial information, and then give reasons on whether or not you would recommend that someone buys shares. (20 marks)
5. Restoration Builders can identify former customers on its database. How else can modern technology be used to assist the marketing of goods and services? (20 marks)
6. Assess the effectiveness of the internal communications and information system developed by Restoration Builders. Could it be improved? (20 marks)
7. If Restoration Builders were to order specific courses for particular employees, how would they decide what training each individual needed? (20 marks)
8. Comment on the suitability of an employment policy that takes into account social rather than professional skills. (20 marks)

Possible answers

Question 1

These require brief descriptions only. For example:

(a) a public limited company is a business which enjoys limited liability (that must score 1 mark) but which is sufficiently large (probably worth another mark) that its shares are freely traded on the Stock Exchange (another mark). You could offer an example such as Marks and Spencer PLC – this could also attract a mark. Thus, with three marks available, you must have written enough to score all three.

Question 2

There is no single correct answer, but the chart should show the managing director in overall charge, with directors of administration and finance, marketing and publicity and operations.

The three sections – property purchase and sale, building services and the sale of building artefacts should be identified – each with a manager who is responsible to the directors, but in charge of administrative and support staff, supervisors and workers.

Question 3

(a) This is fairly straightforward, and requires a simple answer – explain the meaning of the term (this must be worth about 2 marks), and give the main advantage, that the owners of the firm do not run the risk of losing their homes and possessions if the firm fails (again, possibly worth 2 marks). List the disadvantages – that there could be a loss of trust, and suppliers would ask for personal guarantees anyway (worth 2 or 3 marks).

(b) You would probably gain 1 mark for any reason, another for a brief explanation, with a third mark for a full explanation, for instance to gain capital (1 mark) to expand (1 mark) and thus improve profitability (1 mark), increase market share (1 mark), and so on.

Question 4

Clearly, marks will be awarded for the quality of the financial analysis. There is a trading account and a balance sheet, so they must both be considered.

As far as the trading account is concerned, you should look at the gross profit. Are they making a profit on their trading activities? The gross profit should then cover the expenses with some money to spare. In this case expenses are less than gross profit and so a net profit of £800,000 is made. The relationship between the cost of the materials they use and the price they sell the finished goods for is also important. In this case they make a 300% profit; in other words, the cost of the goods is one quarter of the price they sell them for. Are there any unusual expenses, or are any particularly high?

For the balance sheet, you should look at the company's assets and liabilities. Can the company cover its debts? Do the assets of the company cover its liabilities? Can the company cover its current liabilities with its current assets? This is important if the debts need to be paid quickly. How is the company financed? Are there any large loans or mortgages outstanding? What is the cash situation? Large amounts of cash in the bank are a waste, but if there is too little the company might have problems when they wish to purchase raw materials and so on. This is a cash-flow problem.

The highest marks cannot be awarded unless a sensible conclusion has been reached (20 marks).

Question 5

You are likely to gain a mark for each example, and probably four or more for the quality of the explanation, so do not just make a list, but give a clear and concise account of how the idea can be used. For instance, your answer could include a suggestion such as: 'Word processing software enables companies to write personal letters to a large number of people at very low cost. Thus, letters advertising a product can be sent by direct mail to potential purchasers who have been identified from a database.' This is the bare bones of the idea; a more detailed explanation should be given if the examiner is to feel confident that you have thoroughly understood the entire process.

Question 6

The information provided suggests that the system is very successful. It should be outlined, but not simply copied from the text. On what does the success depend? – Honesty and trust. If you are critical, you need to know that you will never be penalised. Thus, you are relying on the existing staff – and the two most senior men are retiring, so the process could be in difficulty. Any suggestions on an employee-based assessment scheme would be valid.

Question 7

Your answer could be presented along the following lines. 'Look at each employee. Identify their strengths and weaknesses. Consider their job. What are the requirements? How do their strengths and weaknesses coincide with the requirements? What is needed to meet these requirements? This gives you the training needed at that particular time. Regular appraisal of each employee is necessary to ensure that training is adequate for the job.'

Question 8

The good candidate will be able to consider the concept in the light of a careful consideration of the theory involved, while weaker candidates will simply comment on how they feel about the notion. Other answers will fall between the two.

Comment on the suitability of an employment policy that takes into account social rather than professional skills.

You must remember:

- **to look at the wording of the question**
- **to decide exactly what the question requires**
- **to plan your answer**
- **to draw a conclusion.**

Index

accounts department 27
acid test 72
administration department 27
advertising 125
advertising media 113
agents 114
assets 71
attitudes
   changing 55
   training in 57
authority 29

balance sheet 71
bank accounts 68
bank loans 33, 60, 62
bank statement 68
banks 60
batch production 123
BEAB (British Electrotechnical Approval Board) 124
behavioural theories 32–3
benefits in kind 50
bills of exchange 61
board of directors 24
body language 44–5
bonus payments 49
book-keeping 67
books, use in coursework 134
brainstorming 34, 106
break-even analysis 65, 66
British Standards Institution (BSI) 124
broadcast media 113
budget 81
building societies 61
business aims 31–3
business analysis 107
business behaviour 100–26

business efficiency firm 30
business environment, changes in 55
business expansion, problems of 47
business finance, sources of 60–76
business growth 32, 36–42
   methods 38–40
   reasons for 36
Business Link 92–3
business organisation 23
   internal 26–31
business reorganisation 93
business role 12–17
business sectors 14
business size 24, 33, 36
business structures 23–6

capital 2, 13
capital account 72
capital gains tax 78
capital goods 15
capital intensive production 3
cash book 67
cash-flow 73–4
census 101
central government see government
chain of command 28
Chambers of Commerce and Industry 88
Chambers of Trade 88
change
   costs of 56
   training for 57
Channel Tunnel 19
charities 55
charts 45
cheques 68
choice 1–8
climate 18

cluster sampling 101
commercial banks 60
commercial economies 38
commercialisation 107–8
Commission for Racial Equality 96
communication 28, 43–8
   barriers to 45–6
   channels 46
   definition 43
   downward 46
   good practice in 46
   horizontal 46
   improvement 53
   lines of 45, 47
   non-verbal 45
   oral 44
   physical conditions 46
   types 43–5
   upward 46
   visual 44–5
   written 43–4
Companies Acts 24, 36
company size 24, 33, 36
competition 9, 36
complaints, dealing with 89–91, 97–8
Confederation of British Industry 88
consultants 93, 109
Consumer Credit Act 1974 95
consumer durables 4
consumer goods 15
Consumer Protection Act 1987 95, 124
consumer protection legislation 94
consumer sovereignty 3, 9
Consumers' Association 89, 124
contract of employment 97
Cooperative Wholesale Society 25
cooperatives 25
coordination 27, 28
corporation tax 78
costs 63
council tax 80
coursework 127–37
   analysis of data 132–3
   choosing a title 129–30
   choosing a topic 128–9
   elements 132
   evaluation 133–4
   guidelines 131, 134–7
   marking criteria 127
   organisation 131–2

   presentation 130–4
   presentation of data 132
   sources 134–7
   starting 128
credit ratios 72–3
current assets 72
current liabilities 72
current ratio 72
customs duty 79

decision-making 28
delegation 29
demand 2, 8, 13, 32, 117
   unlimited 2
demotivation 49
Department of Trade and Industry (DTI) 21, 39
depreciation 71
depressed areas 20
development areas 20
direct mail 113
diseconomies of scale 40–1
distribution process 3–5, 114
diversification 32, 36
division of labour 122

economic problem 2, 8
economies of concentration 19
economies of scale 13, 19, 32, 36–8, 41
economy 3
   control 78
   market 8–9
   mixed 9–10, 12
   planned 8
   traditional 8
   types 8–12
education 4
Education Reform Act 1988 92
efficiency 13–14, 16, 33
efficiency gain 14
e-mail 45, 46
employee behaviour 55
employee cooperatives 25
employers' association 88
Employment Act 1990 87
employment protection 95
Employment Protection (Consolidation) Act 1978
   96, 97
enterprise 2, 13
enterprise zones 20
entrepreneurs 12, 13

environmental groups 32
equal opportunities 96
Equal Pay Act 1970 96
equality 4
European Commission 82
European Council of Ministers 83, 84
European Court of Justice 83
European Free Trade Association 82
European Parliament 83
European Union 11, 20, 84
   as trade group 83
   formation 82
   structure 82–3
examination paper 138–40
   sample exam paper with outline answers and advice 146–8
   sample specimen materials 140–5
excise duty 79
expansion 32
export opportunities 84–5
external economies of scale 19
external growth 38
external influences 77–99
external recruitment 58

factors of production 2, 4, 13, 15
fax 45, 46
feedback 43
films 45
finance see business finance
financial controls 71–6
financial economies 38
financial help 20
financial motivators 49, 50
financial records 67–8
financial soundness 72
firms
   growth of 36–42
   sources of information 135
fiscal policy 78
fixed assets 71
fixed cost curve 65
fixed costs 63, 66
flow production 123
fringe benefits 50

General National Vocational Qualification (GNVQ) 92
geographical location 18
government

forms of income 79
   grants to local government 80
government expenditure 78
government role 32, 77–9
   in business location 19–20
grapevine 46
graphs 45
gross profit ratio 73

health 4
Health and Safety at Work Act 1974 95
Health and Safety Commission 95
Health and Safety Executive 95–6
health and safety laws 32
Herzberg, Frederick 52
hierarchy 27, 28
high street banks 60
human resources 43–59
hypothesis 130

image 33, 34
income tax 78
induction training 57
inequalities 10
information overload 46
information services 19
information technology (IT) 45, 46
infrastructure 18
inheritance tax 78
interest rates 32
intermediate areas 20
internal growth 38
internal recruitment 57–8
Internet 45
interviews 135
invoice 68

jargon 46
job analysis 57, 58
job description 57, 58
job enlargement 51
job enrichment 5–3
job production 122
job rotation 51
job satisfaction 52, 53

kitemark 124

labour 2, 13, 14
labour intensive production 3

labour productivity 14
labour supply 19
land 2, 13
legislation 94–9
liabilities 71
library 135
limited company 23, 24, 33, 61, 69
liquidity ratio 72
Local Enterprise Companies (LECs) 92
local government
   expenditure 80
   forms of income 80
   revenue 80
   role of 79–80
location of business 17–22

Maastricht Treaty 83
McGregor, Douglas 52
maintenance department 27
maintenance factors 52
Management Charter Initiative 93
management economies 38
Management of Health and Safety at Work
   Regulations 1992 95
managing director 27
manufacturer 114
marginal cost 64
marginal revenue 64
market economy 8–9
market research 100–5, 107, 111
   benefits 103
   costs 102–3
   external information, primary and secondary
     101
   internal information 101
   sources of information 100
market segment 111
market share 36, 111
marketing 110–15, 120
   environment 111
   four Ps 111–14
   objectives 111
   process 111
   promotion process 113, 115
marketing department 27
marketing mix 114, 118
markets 9, 12–13
   in business location 19
marking criteria in coursework 127
Maslow, Abraham 52

maximum profit 64
Mayo, Elton 52
merchant banks 60–1
merchantable quality 124
mergers 38–41
metrification policy 11
mixed economy 9–10, 12
monetary policy 79
monopolies 10
Monopolies and Mergers Commission (MMC) 39
monopoly power 32
mortgage 61
motivation 28, 48–55
   non-financial 51
   theories 51–2

National Insurance contributions 78
National Vocational Qualification (NVQ) 92
nationalisation 23
nationalised industries 23
needs 1–2, 4, 13, 52
net current assets 72
newspapers 134
non-financial motivators 51
notes, use in coursework 134

off-the-job training 57, 58
Office of Fair Trading 95
on-the-job training 56–8
opinions, changing 55
opportunity cost 15
organic growth 38
organisation charts 27–8
organisational structures 29
outdoor media 113
overdrafts 60

partnerships 24, 25, 30
payment systems 49–50
people, interviewing 135
performance-related pay 32
periodicals 134
person specification 57, 58
personnel department 27
petty cash book 67
physical geography 18
piece rate system of payment 49
planned economy 8
planning process 8
power sources 17–18

forces of location of business 18
prejudice 46
pressure groups 88
price mechanism 9
pricing policy 112–13
primary sector 14
principle of multiples 37
printed media 113
private enterprise 12
private limited companies (Ltd.) 24
private ownership 9
private sector 9, 12, 24–5, 31
privatisation 23
product concept 112
product development 106–10
product launch 107–8
product life cycle 117–21
   decline stage 118
   extending 118
   growth stage 117
   introduction stage 117
   maturity stage 117
   reappraisal 120
product portfolio 112, 118–19
product research 111
production
   capital intensive 3
   choice of method 3, 15, 121–6
   labour intensive 3
   options 3, 15
production department 27
production possibility frontier 15
productivity deals 49
products
   nature of 18
   weight-gaining 18
   weight-losing 18
professional bodies 88
profit 13, 25, 63
profit and loss account 71
profit maximisation 31–3
profit per unit 63–4
profit-related pay (PRP) 32, 49
profit sharing scheme 55
profitability 73
progressive taxation 78
promotion
   prospects 52
   training for 57
promotion process in marketing 113, 115

promotional mix 113
proportional taxation 78
prototypes 107
public goods 10
Public Limited Companies (PLCs) 23, 24, 33, 61
public revenue 78
public sector 9, 23
public services 77
purchase account 68

quality assurance 124
quality chains 124
quality control 123–4
quality control circles 51
questionnaires 102, 104, 109
quota sampling 101

Race Relations Act 1976 96
random sampling 101
raw materials 14, 18
recession 32, 84
reconciliation 68
recruitment 57–8
   policy 58
recycling 34
redundancy 5–6, 56, 97
regressive taxation 78
research and development 19, 27, 38, 106
resources, efficient use of 14
responsibility 29
restrictive practices 10
retailer 114
return on capital 73
revenue 63
risk bearing economies 38
risk reduction 36

Sale of Goods Act 1893 95
Sale of Goods Act 1979 95, 124
sales account 68
sales ledger 67, 68, 75
sales maximisation 32
sales promotion 113
sales revenue 31, 32
sample 101
scarce resources 2, 3
scarcity 1–8
screening 106
secondary sector 14
self-employed 6, 34

self-interest 9
service sector 14, 19
service specialists 19
Sex Discrimination Acts 1975 and 1986 96
share ownerships 49
share prices 33, 61–2
shareholders 24
Single Europe Act 1992 83
Single European Market 38
small businesses
   courses 66
   survey 21
small firms 33
Smith, Adam 122
social costs and benefits 10
social fund 20
social policies 78
social responsibility 33
sole trader 24
span of control 28
specialisation 122
specialist publications 134
specialist tasks 26, 30
specialist terms 46
statements of account 68
Stock Exchange 33, 61–2
subsidies 10
success measures 33
supervision 28
supply 8, 13
   curve 13
   limited 2
Supply of Goods and Services Act 1982 95
support services 19
survey 101
survival 32, 36
systematic sampling 101

takeovers 38, 39, 41
tax laws 32
taxation 10, 78–9
   direct 78
   indirect 78
Taylor, Frederick 49, 51
teacher, help from 136
technical economies 36–8
telesales 113
tertiary based economy 19
tertiary sector 14

test marketing 107
time rate system of payment 49
total assets 72
total cost curve 65
Total Quality Management (TQM) 124
Trade Descriptions Acts of 1968 and 1972 95
trade union laws 32
Trade Union Reform and Employment Rights Act 1993 97
trade unions 86–7
   functions 87
   membership 87
Trades Union Congress (TUC) 87
trading account 71
trading standards officers 94
traditional economy 8
training 56–7, 92–3
   policy 58
   types 57
Training Agency (TEC) 57
Training and Enterprise Councils (TECs) 58, 92
transport facilities 18
Treaty of Maastricht 83
Treaty of Rome 82
turnover 33, 36

unemployment 20
Unfair Contract Terms Act 1977 95
unfair dismissal 96
uniform business rate 80
unlimited demand 2
Unsolicited Goods and Services Act 1971 95

Value Added Tax (VAT) 79, 84
variable cost curve 65
variable costs 63, 66
videos 45
visits 136

Wage Act 1986 97
wants 1–2, 13
wholesaler 114
worker participation 51
working capital 30

X theory 52

Y theory 52